PALESTINIAN MEMORIES

THE STORY OF A PALESTINIAN MOTHER AND HER PEOPLE

ALEX AWAD

Cover design by Karim Awad
General page design by Jeff Tebbutt
Printed by NOUR Co. | design & print
Images in Part I were provided from family albums and friends (Special thanks to
Hilda Awad for editing family photos)
Images of American Colony Part I, page 24 by Basem Awad
Maps 1-12 and map on page 137 Applied Research Institute - Jerusalem ARIJ.
Page 101, 232 and 312 by PalMap / Good Shepherd Engineering & Computing
Photos in Part II Nayef Hashlamoun
Photos on pages 44 &123 From UNRWA (From UN offices in Gaza City)

Scripture quotations are taken from the Holy Bible, New International Version.

Special gratitude to the Bible College of New Zealand and Tear Fund, New
Zealand for their aid in getting the manuscript ready for printing.

This book is dedicated to all individuals and groups who, against many odds and setbacks, continue to be committed to a vision of a just peace for Israel, Palestine, and all the countries of the Middle East.

—Alex

CONTENTS

For many years, Christian tourists to the Holy Land were content to visit the holy sites and then return home. They wanted to be in touch with the historical roots of their faith. Their dream was to "walk where Jesus walked." In most cases, rushed from one place to another, they actually *ran* where Jesus had walked! The highlights were the Sea of Galilee and its surrounding sites where Jesus had spent most of his ministry, and the Bethlehem-Jerusalem area where he was born, crucified and resurrected. This is what tourists generally did and many of them went back home spiritually revitalized.

All the while, Palestinian Christians have encouraged visitors to take time to meet the indigenous Christians of the Land and to familiarize themselves with their lives and concerns. Gradually, a growing number of these visitors have started to heed this call and include in their itineraries opportunities to meet the "living stones" of the land. Christian responsibility demands knowledge and relationship with brothers and sisters of the faith. It is important to be exposed to Eastern Christians whose faith dates to the early Christian centuries; to Islam, one of the major religions in the world today; to the interplay between politics and religion in the Middle East; and not least, to the Israeli/Palestinian conflict and the prospects for peace and reconciliation.

The Reverend Alex Awad has for many years been inviting, welcoming and encouraging Western Christian visitors to come to the land and to meet the living stones. He has been able to touch the lives and hearts of many people as he spoke to groups both in the Land as well as outside of it. This book is an extension of Alex's ministry that intends to reach out to an ever-larger audience. It is the fruit of experience and knowledge. This is evident in the questions which help readers to focus on the essential points of the conflict, and in the clear and concise answers he provides them with. The same can be said of the maps that assist in clarifying the background of the conflict between Palestinians and Israelis. Besides the maps and the questions and answers, Alex has added a new and important human dimension to the book. This is the personal story of his family as centered around the life of his mother, Huda. In many ways, the story of the Awad family becomes representative of many Palestinian families who suffered disaster in the 1948 war that drastically changed their lives. Huda becomes a paradigm of many Palestinian mothers: In spite of the loss of her husband, and while her seven children were very young, she was able to care for, support, and manage her large household in the midst of difficult times, through her personal resilience and her strong faith in God. The Awad story becomes the living historical evidence that substantiates the contents of the book. In other words, the maps and the questions and answers relate the historical background, but the personal story gives proof, by presenting the living testimony of a Palestinian Christian family.

It is unrealistic to expect most people in the West to be aware of the complexities of the Israeli/Palestinian conflict. After all, it is not the only major conflict in the world today. Yet it is one that is capable of igniting a regional and possibly a global conflagration. Unfortunately, the Palestinian story and the Palestinian experience of suffering have been set, historically, over against the Jewish story and the Jewish experience of suffering. Whereas the Jewish story is familiar in the West, the Palestinian story is not only less known, but has been marred by prejudice, stereotyping and myths. Thus, there is a desperate need to help Western Christians understand the background to the conflict, to combat the widespread political and historical ignorance about the founding of the State of Israel. There is also confusion about the interpretation of certain Biblical texts that some Christians believe are related to the conflict. Furthermore, the media in the West has generally been biased towards Israel. The Palestinians have been cast in the role of terrorists and initiators of violence out to destroy Israel, which is normally viewed as peace-loving as well as the only democracy in the Middle East. This slanted media coverage has contributed to an anti-Palestinian sentiment among many people, and has obstructed the work of peace.

It has been our experience time and again that when Western Christians come to Israel-Palestine with an open mind to see for themselves, to listen to our story, and to experience first hand the agony of the Palestinian predicament, many are turned around. They discover that Israel is not as innocent as they supposed nor are the Palestinians as bad as they had been led to believe. As Romans 3:23 says, All have sinned and come short of the glory of God.

At the base of the conflict is the issue of justice. The maps in this book show clearly the injustice inflicted against the Palestinians. In addition to the 1948 injustice, Israel's policies in the West Bank and the Gaza Strip since the 1967 war have over time become more and more oppressive.

They include: closures and sieges of Palestinian towns and villages, the restriction of Palestinian movement, the demolishing of their homes, the prevention of Palestinians from receiving medical care, the assassination of their leaders, the confiscation of their land, the building and expansion of illegal settlements, the detention and imprisonment of thousands of Palestinians, the total crippling and shattering of the Palestinian economy and infrastructure, and the building of the Separation Wall which stands as the epitome of discrimination and injustice. The oppression has been extensive. The injustice to the Palestinians can well be summarized in the words of the prophet Isaiah: *You are always planning something evil, and you hasten to murder innocent people. You leave ruin and destruction wherever you go, and no one is safe when you are around. Everything you do is unjust. You follow a crooked path, and no one who walks that path will ever be safe.* (Isaiah 59:7–8)

The Oslo Peace Process that started in 1993 was meant to address all these issues and to find a solution to the intractable conflict. Its collapse, however, was largely due to the fact that while the Palestinian and Israeli leadership were talking peace, Israel's repressive policies grew fiercer and were met in turn by intensified Palestinian resistance that included suicide bombings. No one was able to curb the injustice. Every aspect of Palestinian life suffered and deteriorated. When the second Palestinian Intifada started on September 28, 2000, the Palestinians had given up on the possibility of a just peace.

Following the war on Iraq to oust Saddam Hussein in March 2003, the United States, as part of a quartet of powers that included the United Nations, the European Union and Russia, presented the Road Map for peace in Palestine. Although the Road Map received much initial support, its success has been limited and hampered. It is very much dependent on the American administration being willing to exert sufficient pressure on Israel to implement the UN resolutions on Palestine. This has not happened.

As Christians, we continue to pray and work for peace. Yet genuine peace can only be built on justice. Specifically, this means the end of the Israeli occupation of the Palestinian territories of the Gaza Strip and the West Bank, including East Jerusalem, and the establishment of a sovereign, independent and viable Palestinian state alongside the State of Israel. Since the land ultimately belongs to God and all of us are "foreigners and tenants only" (Leviticus 25:23), both nations will have to share the land, under God, and be good stewards of it.

The establishment of peace will give us the opportunity to embark on the work of reconciliation. The ultimate goal must be reconciliation and healing between Israelis and Palestinians. Christians must be ready for such an involvement: *All this is from God, who reconciled us to himself through Christ, and has given us the ministry of reconciliation; that is, in Christ God was reconciling the world to himself, not counting their trespasses against them, and entrusting the message of reconciliation to us. So we are ambassadors for Christ...* (2 Corinthians 5:18–20).

We must become channels of peace, reconciliation, forgiveness and healing. We urge readers to pray for *all* the people of the Holy Land, Palestinians and Israelis, that both can find peace and security. The words of the prophet Isaiah are very apt in this regard: *The doing of justice will bring peace, and the work of justice will bring quietness and security forever* (Isaiah 32:17).

Reverend Naim Ateek
Director
Sabeel Ecumenical Liberation Theology Center
Jerusalem
www.sabeel.org

INTRODUCTION

There is no shortage of public information on the Arab-Israeli conflict. Volumes have been written, documenting in great detail that which has brought the Middle East to its current crisis. Furthermore, the conflict receives much media coverage around the world. In an age of global communication, those who wish to pay attention to the tragic events in Israel/Palestine will find information only a click away.

So why write another book on the conflict? First, though there is much coverage of the conflict, such coverage rarely focuses on its human dimension. The media focuses on facts, especially numbers of deaths and injuries, but not on stories of the real people enduring the day-to-day trials associated with the wars and occupation in this land. I believe that in order to fully understand this conflict, people must be able to understand not only the facts and numbers, not only words like 'terrorism' and 'civilian casualties', but also the human stories that give all these numbers, facts, and words meaning.

When I was in the final stages of writing this book, my mother, Huda Awad, died in 2006 at the age of 90. After her funeral, my brothers, sisters, and other relatives and loved ones who knew her recounted story after story from her rich life. It was while hearing these wonderful stories again that I was inspired to include them in this book, so that it could be a witness to my mother's and my family's remarkable history. Born in 1916, Mother experienced firsthand the turbulent modern history of Palestine. Her story, in its fullness, is one of love, faith, endurance and victory in the face of personal and national tragedy. In a larger sense, it reflects the life stories of several generations of Palestinian Christians in the Holy Land of her era. Through Mother's story, you will meet a person who will help you understand this country in a personal way. I hope and pray that you will be as blessed reading this story as I was in writing it.

The second part of this book turns to a political and historical overview of the Arab-Israeli conflict. Much of the content of this part is revised from the first book that I wrote, *Through the Eyes of the Victims*. Part II has been completely updated and expanded to include the latest current events as well as relevant articles, personal accounts, peace agreements, quotes, and pertinent international law. I received some criticism over the title of my previous book because it gave some readers the impression that I was appropriating "victimhood" exclusively for the Palestinian people. That was never my intention. I certainly do not think that Palestinians are the only victims of the Arab-Israeli conflict. Every Jew who has suffered death or injury as a result of the conflict, and every American, Brit, or other foreign national who has suffered as a result of the conflict, is a victim. Every non-Palestinian Arab, Muslim or non-Muslim, who has been slain or injured as a result of the conflict is also a victim. And Jews, historically, have been victims long before the current conflict, most appallingly during the Holocaust.

But none of this negates the tragedies suffered by the Palestinian people. When I survey the history of the Palestinians over the last 100 years, it is clear that we have faced many hardships and injustices. In 1948, my own family and I became victims when Zionist-Israeli forces invaded our neighborhood, causing the death of my father and forcing my family to become refugees. Prior to this event, we did not harbor animosity towards our Jewish neighbors, nor did we participate in political activities against them. Yet we, and millions of other Palestinians in similar situations, lost homes and livelihoods just because of our ethnicity. Perhaps the central question of this book can be summed up by asking: "Is this just?" – a question that remains relevant to this very day.

Despite the abundant information available about the conflict, Palestinians consistently feel that our story is, in the end, marginalized. We believe that the Israeli perspective virtually saturates public discourse, leaving us voiceless, misunderstood, and stereotyped. We do not have the political, military, or financial strength of our oppressors, who often use their power to sway world opinion and to conceal or alter the historical facts behind our suffering. Thus, by necessity, Palestinians must take every opportunity possible to share our story.

I regularly give lectures to groups of people who are only beginning to become acquainted with the Arab-Israeli conflict. Interested individuals often ask for a copy of the lecture and the powerpoint presentation, including the maps and charts I used to illustrate stages of the conflict. I have found that people benefit from having a tangible resource to take with them, something to help them process and internalize the information they have heard, and to make sense of the ongoing struggle. This book is not meant to be a comprehensive nor a completely unbiased analysis of history and current events. I don't think anyone can be completely unbiased when covering a situation as sensitive and emotionally charged as this one. This book is, rather, a summary of the conflict from a Palestinian perspective, and hopefully after reading it you will appreciate how most Palestinians understand not only their history but also their rightful place in this shared land.

The main target audience for this book is Western Christians, to whom I most often lecture and whose positive influence I wish were more strongly felt in the Holy Land. However, I believe that people from all religious persuasions (or no religious persuasion) will find the book equally beneficial. My hope is that by viewing the conflict from the perspective of a Palestinian Christian in the Holy Land, the reader will gain a more complete and nuanced understanding of the situation, from its historical origins right down to present-day realities.

The main body of Part II is followed by questions I am frequently asked, and of course my answers, along with postscript, bibliography and several appendices. I suggest that readers look first at Appendix I, a glossary of words important in understanding and defining the conflict, as it will familiarize you with how certain terms are used in this text. Appendix II highlights biographies of some key political figures. Appendix III documents sections from international law relevant to the Arab-Israeli conflict, and Appendix IV provides the full texts of key peace proposals. Finally, Appendix V presents resources for further information and involvement, with a list of organizations working for justice and peace in Palestine and Israel.

I want to express appreciation to all who heard my lectures or read this manuscript and offered advice in assuring its usefulness and accuracy. My deep gratitude goes to Sara Bailey-Makari, Luke Carey, Peter Davies, Ruth Haines, Nathan Musselman, Ben White, Dr. Debra Ricci, Judy Sarriot, Vanessa De Bruyn, Tom Powers, Vivian Colson, Jennifer Sebring, Ruth Sayers, my wife Brenda and our children, Christy, Basem and Randy, and many others whose help in completing the manuscript has been invaluable. I would also like to thank Meredith Alexander, Emily Lawrence, Ryan Rodrick Beiler, and my daughter Christy Waltz for editing and updating the second edition of this book. To my siblings – Nicola, Bishara, Elizabeth, Ellen, Mubarak and Diana – my thanks for sharing the anecdotes and reminiscences that allowed me to relate with greater fidelity and richness our Mother's story.

PART ONE

HUDA ELIAS AWAD: THE STORY OF A PALESTINIAN MOTHER

"I was broke many times in my life, but I was never poor."
—Huda

Huda was born on January 14, 1916 in Jerusalem to Palestinian Arab Greek Orthodox parents, Nazirah and Musa Kuttab. She was born during the last years of Ottoman rule over the Holy Land. Huda's parents, and most Palestinian Arabs, who comprised over 75% of the population, called their homeland *Filastin*, the Arabic word for Palestine.

When Huda was only two years old, British troops conquered Palestine under the leadership of General Allenby and shortly thereafter, in 1922, Britain became the new occupier of Palestine under a regime called the British Mandate, which ended 400 years of Ottoman rule over Palestine. During that period, the Christian population of Palestine was slightly smaller in number than the Jewish population, while Muslims accounted for more than two-thirds of the total population. At the time, there was a good measure of peaceful coexistence between the three religious groups. Both Christians and Muslims shared a common Arabic culture and history while many Jews living in Palestine also considered themselves Palestinians, spoke Arabic and identified in numerous ways with their Christian and Muslim neighbors.

Neither young Huda, nor her parents could have predicted the incredible political and social upheavals that were in store for Palestine. Reverend John Walker, who was Huda's pastor for the last 10 years of her life, wrote of her birth:

Huda's birth in some ways paralleled another birth. When Jesus was eight days old he was brought to the temple in Jerusalem, "to present him to the Lord." Scripture says at that time an old man in the temple by the name of Simon said of Jesus: "Behold this child is set for the fall and rising of many in Israel." Although neither history nor scriptures took any noticeable account of the birth of Huda in Jerusalem almost two thousand years later, the same thing might have been said of the history of Palestine since her birth.

Huda was born into a loving family which had been Christian for generations. Indeed, from the birth of the church on the Day of Pentecost, there have been Christians in the Holy Land. Today's Palestinian Christians are remnants of the earliest Christians; they have kept the Christian presence alive in Palestine since the days of the apostles. But if life prior to the pre-British Mandate was difficult for the average Palestinian, it was particularly difficult for Palestinian Christians. As a shrinking minority, Christians felt the loss of every member of the community. They were also mistrustful of their Muslim Turkish rulers, and many fled to foreign countries to escape being drafted into the Turkish army. It was a well known fact that most young men who entered the Turkish army never returned home. What Huda wrote about her family illustrates the challenges of living as a Palestinian during the Ottoman Period:

19

> *My father, Musa Kuttab, was a strong, handsome man of high character. He worked hard and made good money, and he was the only one who could provide for his mother, whose husband had died at an early age. When the Turkish authorities came to enlist him to fight with the Ottoman army in 1913, my grandmother knew well that many of the young people who left for the army never returned. Moreover, she was getting very old and her son was the sole breadwinner in the family. She implored the Ottomans to release him from duty, but they dismissed her pleas, refusing to accept a 'no' from anyone. All the young men of Jerusalem had to join the army, no exceptions. So my grandmother appealed to the extended family to redeem her son. The family sacrificed and raised enough money to satisfy the demands of Sultan Abed Al-Hameed in order to insure Musa's release. To their surprise it worked; he was released, but then, painfully, the following year, the Ottoman forces enlisted him again and the family was once more driven to amass a new sum of money for his ransom. In spite of the financial hardship, the family was jubilant both times the Sultan accepted the ransom money.*

After his release from the Ottoman army, Musa met Nazirah, an elegant Christian lady from one of Jerusalem's aristocratic families. Musa fell in love with this lively and attractive woman. They were married and eventually had four children. Huda was their first child. The second child was weak from birth and died before he was a year old. Two more boys followed; Costandi in 1918 and George in 1922.

Clockwise from top left:

Huda in 1916

Nazirah, her brother Awad Fattaleh and Musa's sister, Miriam (left to right)

General Allenby takes over Jerusalem

Domian, Aunt Miriam, Musa and Nazirah Kuttab (left to right)

As the First World War dragged on, the Palestinian population grew increasingly impoverished. Musa lost his job. To survive, Nazirah would knead dough for baking bread and Musa would sell it in the market. He did this until Jerusalem's wheat supply was cut off, putting the family in an even more desperate situation.

The challenges of foreign domination, poverty, and war did not hinder Palestinian Christians from finding hope and comfort in their faith. Huda was always delighted to tell her children and grandchildren the story of her great grandmother, Rihaneh. Rihaneh was 105 years old when she died, and the graceful way in which she died had a profound influence on Huda's spiritual development.

Rihaneh loved children. She always showed them kindness and never hesitated to play or communicate with them. In turn, children loved her. On her last day on this side of eternity, Rihaneh gathered together many children in her neighborhood's central courtyard. In Jerusalem's Old City, the houses were built around a courtyard which was a meeting and gathering place for the entire extended family. Huda, along with eleven other children, responded to her great grandmother's invitation. Rihaneh had tea and cookies prepared for all her little guests. After she served the refreshments, Rihaneh listened to the children as they sang the choruses that they had learned to sing in church. Then Rihaneh asked the children to fetch their mothers. When Rihaneh asked Nazirah to dress her in a long white gown, another woman, understanding what was about to happen, rushed to call the priest. The priest arrived with the sacred elements of bread and wine in his hands. Rihaneh, lying on her mattress looking more like an angel than a dying person, received communion, said her prayers, kissed the children good-bye, gave final instructions, and bade farewell to the women. Then she closed her eyes and died.

There was much love and happiness in Huda's family. One tragic incident, however, affected Musa deeply. His mother, Huda's paternal grandmother, began to lose her vision. One day, as she was going down the stone stairs of her Jerusalem home, she fell and broke her hip and died shortly thereafter. Musa was absolutely devastated by the death of his gracious mother who had sacrificed so much to shield him from being drafted into the Ottoman army. The loss of his mother sent him into depression which led to a dependence on alcohol.

Musa struggled with his alcoholism for a period, but he was eventually able to stop drinking and resume work at his carpentry shop and he returned to his family broken and repentant. Unfortunately, his alcoholism had already taken a toll on his immune system and on July 5, 1923 he died after contracting pneumonia. Huda was only seven years old. She reminisced with Reverend Walker about her childhood with her mother and father, and how she discovered her beloved parent had died.

I felt much loved as a child. I remember my mother singing a lot as she ironed linen. I would sit in my father's lap as he played backgammon with his friends. He always seemed to have something to share with me or with my brothers. He loved the outdoors. I remember him making barbecues, not only for his immediate family, but also for aunts, uncles, members of the extended family and friends.

When Father died, they took me and my brothers to Abu Abdullah Sahar's house for three days. Everyone was extremely kind to us, but no one told me that my father had died. When we were taken back home, the first thing I wanted to do was see my father. But he was not at home. I looked for him at the carpentry shop, but he was not there.

"Where's my father?" I asked Abu Abdullah. "He's with Jesus," he said. "Fine," I replied. "When will he be back?" "I don't know," he answered. "Did you take him there?" I asked. With tears pouring down his face, he put his arms around me and said, "My dear, your dad is in heaven." I protested, "Last year he came back after a long journey." (I was thinking of his sudden appearance after returning from a trip he had made to North America). "No, my dear Huda. This time he will not come back." I was utterly crushed when I realized that my father had gone to his final home.

Because my father died when I was seven years old, my mother supported the family by ironing for the American Colony Hotel in Jerusalem. Though we did not possess much in the way of material goods, at an early age, we were taught stories from the Bible. We memorized the Ten Commandments and were always reminded to love one another and love our enemies.

Reverend Walker concluded that Huda's enormous love for friend and foe alike was her most remarkable characteristic. Surely this love was the source of power that enabled her to push through the seemingly insurmountable obstacles she faced throughout her life.

Uncle George, in his auto-biography, revealed the poor conditions of the Kuttabs after the death of Musa when he wrote:

After a forty-day mourning period, we faced an even worse problem than we could have imagined. As before, mother sent seven-year old Huda and four-year old Costandi to Abu Ali, our grocer, for food like rice and sugar. But Abu Ali said that our grocery debt was due at the end of the month, or we would not get more food from him.

On hearing the gloomy news, mother knelt down to ask the Mother Virgin for help. She then went to the cupboard for her seegha (bride's jewelry dowry) for money to pay her debt to Abu Ali, but she could not find it. When mother asked Um Iskander, her sister-in-law, if she had taken the jewels, she replied, "Of course, I did… They belonged to my brother. I am the legitimate heir of all his house and property; I took them." A heated quarrel ended painfully, with my aunt shoving my mother down the stairs.

Mother broke her arm in that fall. A government hospital set her broken arm in a gypsum cast. When the grocer Abu Ali, heard it, he continued to give our family groceries. Later, when mother and Uncle Awad Fattaleh sold father's grocery shop, its bench, tools, and wood, and so forth, the money received was still not enough to pay baker, butcher and grocery bills. Soon after, Uncle Awad got a government job in Gaza with the Department of Customs, (a job removing him from us, far beyond walking distance of Jerusalem) – leaving mother without a husband or a brother to help support her family. Eventually she had to place us in orphanage schools.[1]

Musa's sister, Miriam, lived in a neighborhood of Jerusalem called Musrara. After Musa's death, she embraced the children even more closely and showed them much love while Nazirah searched for a job. One of Miriam's neighbors was an American woman named Mrs. Bertha Spafford who was connected with the American Colony Hotel, which was then a Christian establishment. Her Father wrote the song, *It is Well with My Soul*, a hymn that has warmed the hearts of millions of worshipers for many generations. Mrs. Spafford conducted a Bible study for adults and a Sunday school for the neighborhood children. Huda started attending the Sunday school and loved it. Her passion for singing the songs, listening to Bible stories and memorizing Bible verses captured Mrs. Spafford's attention.

Clockwise from top:
American Colony Hotel today
American Colony Hotel today
Jerusalem from Mount Olives today

Huda's winning a competition for reciting Bible verses led Mrs. Spafford to visit Huda's home. Mrs. Spafford was greatly moved by the poor condition of the Kuttab's quarters. As a widow, with no income, struggling to raise three children, Nazirah spent much of her spare time making beautiful pieces of needlepoint to sell. Despite their beauty, they did not generate enough income to put food on the table. Mrs. Spafford recommended that Nazirah place Huda in a Pentecostal (Assemblies of God) mission boarding school located on Mamila Street near the Old City's Jaffa Gate. The school was run by a young American missionary named Miss Elizabeth Brown. Mrs. Spafford also offered Nazirah a job ironing linen at the American Colony.

As delighted as Nazirah was to be employed, it was a grueling job for a delicate woman and often made her sick. Not even the Americans had electric irons or steam-ironing machines in Jerusalem during the 1930's. Nazirah's job consisted of heating charcoal and filling the heavy, old-fashioned, cast iron hand iron with red-hot embers. Then she quickly pressed as many of the pure white linen sheets from the Colony's beds as possible before the iron cooled and she had to empty the sooty coals and begin the process all over again. It was hot, strenuous work. As she worked, the fumes rose into her face and she frequently became ill from smoke inhalation.

Huda and her siblings learned volumes from their mother's resilience. Nazirah taught them the values and skills she practiced throughout her own life. Nazirah lived the early years of her life in the dark ages of Ottoman rule. At that time in Palestine, as in other parts of the world, educating women was considered a waste of time. Thus Nazirah never had the opportunity to attend school and she was illiterate. For years, Nazirah yearned to be able to read and often voiced the wish to read the Bible and the words to her favorite Christian songs. When her children went to school and started learning to read, she could stand it no more. She would take one of them – Huda, Costandi or George – aside and say, "What did you learn today at school?" She then proceeded to have them take out their reading books and notebooks and recite the day's lessons to her. This was valuable practice for the children, even if it also served Nazirah's ulterior motive of enhancing her own education. It worked; over time, Nazirah had taught herself to read with the help of her young teachers.

From then on, she always had two books to read from and never a single other. The first book was the Bible and the second was the church hymnal. Nazirah was so pleased at having learned to read that she made it her habit always to read the Bible and sing hymns in a loud voice. Unfortunately for all in her company on such occasions, Nazirah's singing had a kind of crystal-breaking high-pitched quality about it that made singing along nearly impossible. This was the butt of many jokes, but as it turned out, Nazirah's singing was much more tolerable than that of her son, Uncle George, who also had the knack for singing at glass-shattering decibels. Regardless, no one ever dared try to prevent either of the two from praising God with a "joyful noise."

Like her own mother, Huda was clever and industrious. She loved school and her teachers, and had many friends. Huda excelled in whatever she set her mind to. She told of a childhood memory which illustrates her resourcefulness at a young age:

> *Mother taught me how to cross-stitch and do needlepoint. Even as a young girl, I used to make children's hats which I sold. I did not make enough money to turn a profit, but just enough to buy more material and make more hats.*

In her last years of high school Huda attended Talitha Kumi, a Lutheran school for girls. Reverend Walker described a visit with Huda in which he discovered what an outstanding student she was:

> *Almost with an attitude of embarrassment she went to a drawer and pulled out a number of certificates substantiating her excellence in almost everything she did. She still had her graduation diploma, yellow with age, which included her grades, all of which were 90% and above. In 1935, when she was only 15 years old, she received a certificate of excellence in sewing. While still in high school she took some courses in nursing, never dreaming how important that knowledge would be during the turbulent days of her tomorrow.*

Her brother, Costandi, was enrolled at the Schneller School, a Lutheran school for boys, while George attended St. George's School, a Church of England establishment in Jerusalem.

As Huda grew, so did her faith. In the spring, she could hardly wait for the annual revival meetings at the Church of Missionary Alliance in Jerusalem. Her hunger for God was satisfied in one of those meetings. She described that experience by recalling:

Clockwise from top:
Sample of Grandma's needle work
Grandma Nazirah (Huda's Mom) doing needle work
Church of the Nativity in Bethlehem
Huda studies nursing

On April 5, 1932, I went with my friend, Sofi, to the revival meeting. There our hearts soared to heaven as the faithful sang the songs of salvation and the Word of God was preached to the poor and the brokenhearted. In one of those meetings, I made a personal decision to accept Jesus Christ as my Savior and my Lord, confessing my sins and accepting God's grace upon my life. The joy of salvation filled my soul. What a wonderful feeling to realize that I had become a child of God.

Huda and her family belonged to the Greek Orthodox Church. Throughout her life Huda had great respect for her mother church. Her children never heard her say anything negative about it, and she never discouraged them to attend services at the Orthodox Church. At the same time, Huda found something special in the message of the Evangelical missionaries that touched her heart in a profound and personal way. While she respected the rich liturgy and long history of endurance of her former church, that liturgy did not address the great challenges of life that she and her family faced.

In the Pentecostal mission school run by Miss Brown and in the Protestant Sunday School and Bible study associated with the American Colony, people spoke about Jesus in an intimate way, a Jesus who was exceedingly near and cared personally for each individual. They also spoke of God's Spirit dwelling in humble people and giving them the power to face life's harsh circumstances. Huda's passion for the new mission societies in Mandate Jerusalem was not a rejection of her former Orthodox heritage but rather a transformation to a different level of her relationship with God. Besides that, the genuine love and personal attention and concern that she, her mother, and her siblings received from Miss Brown and Mrs. Spafford had a great impact on all dimensions of her life.

In spite of her top high school grades and certificates, not to mention many other skills, Huda was unable to find a job upon graduating in 1934. So she decided to advance her nursing studies at the Nazareth Hospital located in the historic town it was named after. Along with studying, Huda's time was divided between church activities and old-fashioned courtship.

Reverend Walker, looking through Huda's photo collection, noted that at this time Huda was very pretty, with light skin and long black hair. Her outgoing nature and beauty proved a combination that kept many young men interested. There were several requests for her hand.

Clockwise from top left:

Maronite Church in Jaffa – Built from donations by Alexander Awad

Plaque commemorates benevolence of Alexander Awad to Maronite Church

Elizabeth Brown, founder of Mission School in Mamila, Jerusalem

Bishara standing next to bust of Great Grandfather, Alexander Awad

In that conservative society young people were strictly observed, and this was especially true in Huda's family. Parents were very careful about what kind of friends their young children made, and young girls were always carefully chaperoned. They were not allowed to date at all until parents gave their approval of a particular individual, and even then they were never permitted to be together without a chaperone.

Huda's first engagement turned out to be a horrible disappointment. A young man named Michael Beita, a wealthy landowner considered a prominent and noble figure in Jerusalem, asked for her hand and immediately received the acceptance of Huda's mother and uncle. Once Huda also agreed to the marriage, it was socially acceptable for her and her family to visit Michael and his family. Her prospective bridegroom must not have been aware that Huda believed in abstaining from alcohol. At the gathering, Huda was put off when her fiancé offered her liquor. But she was incredulous when she saw her fiancé's father offering liquor to a three-year old boy! She was even more passionate about this than other young ladies as alcoholism had contributed to her father's untimely death. As soon as the party was over and Huda and her family were at home, she took off her ring, gave it to her mother and ended the engagement.

After the failed engagement, Huda attended sewing courses in Ramallah conducted by a famous designer seamstress named Madam Ruffleh. After the six-month course, she passed the exam and was employed at the school herself as a sewing instructor.

One day, Huda and Nazirah went to visit Nazirah's brother. At the same time, an exceptionally handsome young man named Elias Awad and his mother, Nyfeh, were visiting Huda's uncle's home. Elias hailed from a prominent family in Jaffa. One of his great grandparents, Alexander Awad, was once the mayor of the city. Today, a visitor to the Maronite Church in Jaffa will see two marble-engraved stones plastered across from each other on the church's wall that give witness to the fact that Alexander Awad and his wife, Helen, contributed generously to build the church. A stone bust of Alexander Awad stands in the churchyard.

When Elias saw Huda he immediately fell in love with her. Huda, on the other hand, was not so easily swept away by his good looks. Her greatest priority was her spiritual life, and she was drawn to be with those who shared her passion for God's word. The week she met Elias, she was focused on church activities. Elias's thoughts, however, were focused on Huda. When she went to pay a visit to a local family, he intentionally visited the same family; when she went to church, he went to church. At the church's entrance, he asked if he could talk to her.

"If you wish to speak with me, come to church," she replied. When the services are over, maybe we can talk."

From that day onward every time Huda went to church, she had company. Before long, Elias went to Miss Brown and asked for Huda's hand in marriage.

"I'm not her mother," Miss Brown said. "If you wish to marry her, ask Nazirah."

Huda soon fell in love with Elias and accepted his proposal with her mother's blessing.

One day during her engagement to Elias, an incident occurred at the sewing school that caused quite a tumultuous row between Huda and her mother. Huda's colleague, Farha, also a student at the sewing school, was jealous of Huda's beauty, skills, and perhaps most of all, of Huda's new fiancé. It was an era in Palestine when it was considered very unseemly for a woman not to have long hair, and respectable young Palestinian women usually wore their hair in braided pigtails. One day in sewing class Farha, who might have been hoping to sabotage Huda's engagement, took her sewing scissors and chopped off one of Huda's braids before Huda had a chance to process what was happening. Huda was naturally both shocked and angry when she realized what had happened, but she was more concerned about the reaction of her mother, her fiancé and society in general. Regardless, she knew she could not be seen in public with a single braid on one side of her head, so she was left with one choice. She took the scissors and cut off the remaining braid. It happened that one of Huda's friends was a hairdresser, and Huda immediately went to her friend for damage control. Huda's efforts however, were to no avail. Her mother exploded in anger as soon as Huda arrived home, giving her no chance to explain what had happened. Clearly, Nazirah believed that Huda had intentionally gotten her hair cut. After the screaming and scolding died down, the two did not speak for several days. Eventually they reconciled, a process aided by Huda's hair growing back again!

Elias had a much more favorable reaction to Huda's new hairdo. "You look even more beautiful than before," he said.

Huda and Elias were married just two months after meeting, on February 24th 1937. They made their nest in a little rented house on a hill just outside the New Gate of Jerusalem's Old City, behind Notre Dame

Cathedral, in a neighborhood called Musrara. They were happy there and lived as good neighbors to Jews, Muslims and fellow Christians. Elias was employed overseeing the laundry services at a hospital in West Jerusalem. Huda's occupation was to care for their children. In the first eleven years of marriage, Huda gave birth to eight children. Seven of them survived but one baby girl, Teresa, was weak when born and died within a few months.

One spring day, while our family was temporarily residing in Beit Safafa, a village near Jerusalem, my sister Ellen approached mother as she was working in the kitchen and began nagging and pulling her skirt. Ellen was not yet two years old and in baby talk kept saying: "Mommy – Mommy – Baby – Baby." Mother tried to get her to play outside but little Ellen kept crying, "Mommy – Mommy – Baby – Baby" and pulling on Mother's skirt. Finally Mother yielded to Ellen's cries and let her direct her outside to the well. Mother was surprised to see that the lid covering the well was opened. As she peered into the well, she saw her daughter, Elizabeth, in the water, struggling for life. Elizabeth was four years old at the time and could barely swim. Though the water in the well was high in springtime, it was not high enough to be reachable at arm's length. Huda hurried to the house, found a cord which she quickly tied to a large empty butter can and rushed back to the well. Lowering the can into the well, she called Elizabeth to sit on the can and hold onto the cord. Elizabeth did so and Huda pulled her to safety.

When Elizabeth emerged from the well, she was blue, swollen and totally unconscious. Mother took her by the feet and spanked her on the buttocks until she began crying. Fortunately Elizabeth was saved. Mother, however, was puzzled about how Elizabeth had held onto the string when she was so weak and breathless. Later, when Elizabeth was able to talk, mother asked her, "Habibti (dear), how were you able to keep holding the cord and stay on the can when you were so weak?"

"A man with a white beard held my hands and body until you were able to get me," Elizabeth said.

Elizabeth later believed it to be Saint Elias himself who held her. Beit Safafa, where we then lived, is close to the monastery of Saint Elias on the main road from Jerusalem to Bethlehem. As she grew older, Elizabeth vowed to light a candle, the exact length of her height once a year and place it in the monastery in memory of what she believed to be the divine intervention that saved her life.

Clockwise from top left:

Huda as a young woman with braids (1936)

Young Elias

Huda & Elias on their honeymoon (3-1-1937)

Huda & Elias on their wedding day (2-24-1937)

My older siblings remember only a few stories from the life of Mom and Dad during the first twelve years of their marriage. Nicola, who is the oldest, remembers his father Elias as an exceedingly loving and generous man, first toward his family and then to all neighbors and friends. Hospitality was his specialty. Our home was always open to relatives, friends, and strangers. Nicola recalled an incident that highlighted Elias's hospitality to strangers:

Once while we were living in Beit Safafa, an unexpected knock fell on our door. When Father answered, he saw an agitated young man, panting heavily, and looking with fearful, pleading eyes at him. Father urged the man to enter his home. After being given time to rest and compose himself, the young man recounted his story. He came from Beit Ummar, a Muslim village near Hebron. He had gotten into a quarrel with another young man from his village. One bad move led to another. Words turned into fists, and then by accident, the young man killed his fellow villager. Now the relatives of the dead man were furious and looking for him. The young man was afraid that if they found him, they would kill him.

He pleaded that Father hide and protect him. While it was not completely strange for a family to receive an asylum seeker, it was unusual for a Muslim to seek asylum from a Christian family. This man must have been directed to our home by acquaintances who, knowing Father's welcoming nature, felt confident that he would protect the young man. My father calmed the young man and agreed to protect him until the reconciliation process between the two families was completed.

In Palestine and much of the Middle East, it is traditional to settle conflicts, especially those involving death and injury, through a process called "sulha" which literally means reconciliation. Sulha is a time-tested process that has proven itself countless times. As soon as possible after an injury, the family of the perpetrator begins negotiations with the family of the victim. During the negotiations, the family of the perpetrator makes conciliatory offers to appease and satisfy the family of the victim. The ransom offered can be in funds, land, or other material benefits. If the family of the victim rejects the ransom, a feud could erupt between the families lasting many years and claiming lives on both sides of the feud. So while negotiations between the families can be arduous, participants in the sulha understand that the alternative to reaching a settlement can be disastrous.

By hiding the young man, Father was able to buy some time for him and his family. This allowed for simmering heads to cool and for the young man's family to approach the dead man's family and initiate the sulha process with them. After two weeks of negotiation, a settlement was agreed upon by both families.

Since father and our family had protected the young man, his family asked him to take part in the sulha process. I remember my father taking a rope with a noose at one end and tying it around the neck of the young man as if he were preparing him to be hung. Then, father led him along with his family to the home of the bereaved family. At the home, Father handed the rope with the noose still around the young man's neck to the father of the victim. This was a symbolic act signifying that the perpetrator's family was putting the young man's fate in the hands of the bereaved family. The victim's father then untied the rope from around the assailant's neck, signifying that he had accepted the terms of the settlement and that he and his family were now granting full pardon to the young man. The meeting concluded by both families drinking coffee together, signifying their reconciliation. The young man's family became

From left to right:
Spire Adorning St. Elias' Monastery
Nicola (baby) and Elias (1938)

friends with our family for years to come. I was impressed by my father's welcoming heart and how his natural hospitality had helped save these two families from a bitter feud.

36   Bishara recalls:

My father was very loving, but also very protective of his children. I remember him carrying me upon his shoulders and walking and hopping around to make me happy. Once when I was confronted with a neighborhood bully, Father immediately came to my rescue chasing the bully away.

By the time the British gave up their mandate over Palestine in 1948, my parents, Elias and Huda had seven children. But their seemingly idyllic life would not last, as large and dark clouds lay waiting just over the horizon.

Mubarak & Bishara (1950)

"My first hobby is to see my children grow and my second is to learn from them as they grow."
    —Huda

It is said that more people betray their humanity in war than at any other time. In 1948, my family found itself at the center of one of the hundreds of battles that were being waged throughout Palestine, where many war crimes and injustices were taking place. The Jewish Zionist army was determined to take over Musrara, our neighborhood, because of its strategic location overlooking New Gate, Damascus Gate and much of the Old City. At the same time, the Jordanian army was determined to protect Musrara from the advancing Zionist army. My family was trapped between the two clashing armies outside the walls of the Old City of Jerusalem. In 1948 the Jordanian army was made up mainly of Bedouin troops who were unfamiliar with the life and culture of Jerusalem. Most of these soldiers were not able to distinguish between Jews and the Palestinian Christians who lived in Musrara.

The Zionists, on the other hand, were engaged in massacres throughout Palestine, among which was on the village of Deir Yasin to the northwest of Jerusalem. Determined to realize their dream of a Jewish homeland, they demolished and/or depopulated over four hundred Palestinian towns and villages in 1948 alone.

The day after Israel declared its independence on May 17, 1948, heavy fighting broke out in Musrara for several days. Many families had managed to escape before the war broke out but as a family with seven young children, we had no means to flee. We were scared. Ours and several other Christian families, some forty men, women and children, were trapped in the war zone. For several days the shooting was so heavy that no one dared leave home. The families who were left were encouraged by Elias and Huda to remain together in the shelters of the stone houses near the Awads' residence.

Top: Musrara in 1900
Bottom: Musrara today (2006)

The great challenge was how to feed so many mouths when no one could leave home without risking his or her life. Huda's oldest boy, Nicola, who was eleven years old, remembers how, without instructions from adults, he and his friends, most of whom were not yet fifteen years old, decided to fight their hunger by raiding the vacated homes of Musrara looking for food items. The boys knew their neighborhood well and knew the homes that would have the biggest amounts of food. Creeping like field rodents, in the middle of the night, they would silently gather whatever food they could find and carry it back to Huda and Nyfeh, Elias's mother, to cook during the day. This lasted for more than two weeks.

One day our family had no food left on the main floor of the house and we could not enter the second level because an Israeli army post was stationed on the side of the house where a stairway led up to the pantry. Anyone who tried to traverse the stairway risked being killed. But a family of seven children needs food. Mother, like a cunning tigress, took to the task of feeding her kittens.

As Huda began climbing the steps, the army saw her and immediately started shooting. She wasted no time in her ascent to the top floor while the steps below her crumbled, the result of unrelenting artillery bombardment. No doubt frightened, Huda, a survivor at heart, lit a fire in another section of the house in order to distract the soldiers. She then resumed her original mission, packing what food she could find into a basket and lowering it through the window to the children below. To this day, her children do not remember when or how she made it back down to them.

On May 24, 1948 my father, noticing that there had been much less shooting the previous two days, decided to step outside the shelter to see if it was safe and if the war was over. Mother escorted him as he went out, but saw that he had forgotten to put on his Red Cross armband which identified him as a hospital worker and a non-combatant. Mother looked behind her and realized that Nicola was following behind them so she called Nicola to fetch Dad's armband. When Nicola returned with the armband he saw Dad on the ground and Mother screaming over him, placing her hand on his head where he was wounded. Mother yelled to Nicola to get help and he returned immediately with some men who carried the body inside the shelter. Mother desperately tried to perform first aid to revive Elias. But it was already too late, her husband was dead. Dad was hit in the head with a bullet and killed instantly.

Huda fell sobbing and screaming on her husband's lifeless body. Within moments Nyfeh too realized that her beloved son had been killed. She was so emotionally overwhelmed by the disturbing impact of the scene that she would never recover.

The women and the children of my family waited six days hoping to receive help from either Jews or Arabs. No outsider, however, dared enter or leave Musrara at that time. So Mother, Grandmother and my elder siblings, with the help of some near neighbors, dug a shallow grave at the back of the house. Since there was no pastor or priest around us, Mother read from her Bible, our family said prayers over his body, bid their last goodbyes and laid my father to rest. Elizabeth, my older sister, recalls collecting flowers from around the house for her and Bishara to place on our father's grave.

The Psalmist seemed to address the situation of my family at the time when he wrote:

> For look, the wicked bend their bows;
> they set their arrows against the strings
> to shoot from the shadows
> at the upright in heart.
>
> When the foundations are being destroyed,
> what can the righteous do?
>
> The LORD is in his holy temple;
> the LORD is on his heavenly throne.
> He observes the sons of men;
> his eyes examine them. Psalm 11:2–4 (NIV)

Now that our family's foundations were shaken, the questions that begged to be answered were: What will we do? How will we overcome this great loss and survive in the midst of war? My father had left seven children and two widows totally unprotected in the heart of a war zone. Of the seven children, Nicola, the oldest, was eleven years old and Diana, the youngest, was just six months old with Bishara, Elizabeth, Ellen, Mubarak and me ranging in ages between the two.

A few days after we buried my father, we heard loud shouting outside the house, then a strong bang at the front door. Nick, holding Diana in his arms, went to see what was happening. As soon as he opened the door,

Jordanian soldiers surrounded us. The mostly Bedouin soldiers wanted to ascertain our identity. We told them that we were Christians, but they could not understand or believe that we could be Arabs, probably because of the more Western style of clothing that we wore. Later, the troops who remained behind ordered the women to cook and wash laundry for the senior officers.

Strange and ironic incidents often happen during war. The very soldiers who were defending Musrara and bullying our family were frequently themselves starved for food. They would break into the abandoned homes of people who had fled in order to get rations such as rice, beans and oil. Then, they would take the items to the good cooks in the area, such as Huda and Nyfeh, to prepare savory meals for them. This extra food, stolen by the very soldiers who had threatened our lives, also helped us survive until our escape.

One day, Nyfeh noticed that the skirt Huda was wearing while busy working, had shifted and was not completely covering her knees. So in order that the soldiers would not understand what she was saying, she whispered to Huda in German that she might want to keep herself modest in front of the soldiers. Both Huda and Nyfeh had gone to a German Lutheran school, named Talitha Kumi, and could speak German. An officer who overheard them assumed that they were talking in Hebrew which eroded the officer's confidence in them. He instantly accused them of concealing their Jewish identity and ordered his soldiers to shoot all thirteen remaining women and children.

Nicola vividly remembers how they lined us up against a wall, a soldier with a machine gun poised to shoot upon orders from his officer's command. Just as the soldier crouched down to fire, Mother rushed up to him, with the gun pointing right into her chest, and said, "Hold it! You say we are Jewish, but even if that was true, your Holy Book, the Koran says that you must not kill widows and orphans." She recited an entire passage from the Koran which forbids Muslims from killing defenseless women, children or the elderly.[2] The officer, astounded at mother's fluency in Arabic and at the fact that she quoted the Koran from memory, suspended the shooting and decided to first have two Palestinian national guards from Jerusalem check our identity to verify that we were indeed Arab Christians. One of the national guards, a Muslim native of Jerusalem named Mustafa Abdullah Hassan, immediately pieced together, upon a brief observation of our family, that we were Palestinian Arab Christians. It was actually the first time Mustafa had met us, but he faked having known us for years to spare our lives. To our family's great relief the officers accepted his testimony and we were unscathed. Later Mustafa and his family became close friends of the Awad family.

After discovering that Huda had some nursing skills, the commander left an injured soldier with her. His injuries were not serious and Huda was able to attend his wounds and revive him. For a short time this incident restored the troops' confidence in us. The next day, however, the commander gave her a critically wounded soldier and again ordered her to nurse him back to health. Huda used all her medical skills to try to help the injured soldier. However, with no access to medicine or the proper medical equipment, she was unable to save his life and the soldier died. Later that day when the captain and his soldiers came to collect their now dead comrade the captain was furious and accused the family of killing him. He ordered his soldiers to take the body away and in a menacing voice swore to avenge the death of his comrade saying, "I will be back to deal with you killers." With that, he and the soldiers left and we were terrified what they would do upon their return. Once again, the threat of assassination was heavy on every heart. Huda feared that this time, quoting the Koran would not make any difference. All she could do was whisper a prayer to God.

At about 9:30 p.m. that same evening, a group of officers did indeed pay us another visit, but they had a totally different agenda. The commander ordered Mom and the rest of us to leave Musrara and to make our way

Mustafa Hasan; our family's friend and Good Samaritan. Taken in the U.S.

to East Jerusalem immediately, announcing that the Jewish Zionist army would be taking over the neighborhood within minutes.

Although shaken, we were encouraged by the fact that God had heard our prayers and at the right moment provided a way for us to escape certain assassination. These two incidents confirmed in Huda's heart and mind that, in spite of the death of her husband, God would not abandon her and her children. With that faith, she would find the courage to escape from Musrara with her family.

Mother's faith in God and peaceful spirit in the face of such hardship astounded everyone around her. Although she was trodden with sadness, she did not harbor a spirit of revenge or resignation. Instead, she was determined not to allow the past to ruin her future nor that of her children. One of Mother's favorite passages of scripture which repeatedly pulled her out from despair to hope was Paul's declaration of triumph in the book of Romans:

> Who shall separate us from the love of Christ? Shall trouble or hardship or persecution or famine or nakedness or danger or sword? As it is written:
> "For your sake we face death all day long; we are considered as sheep to be slaughtered." No, in all these things we are more than conquerors through him who loved us. For I am convinced that neither death nor life, neither angels nor demons, neither the present nor the future, nor any powers, neither height nor depth, nor anything else in all creation, will be able to separate us from the love of God that is in Christ Jesus our Lord. Romans 8:39(NIV)

Mother had no time to plan our family's night flight from Musrara to East Jerusalem. She begged an officer to let her just go upstairs to get her purse but he strongly objected, insisting that she only had time to wrap her children in blankets and run eastward. My sister, Ellen, who was five years old, remembers that she had a few pretty dresses she couldn't part with, and because there was no time to change she quickly began putting them all on – one on top of another. Though perhaps cumbersome, those dresses would prove handy in the coming few weeks not only for Ellen but also for her sister Elizabeth, who like her siblings, left the home in nothing but sleepwear.

Clockwise from top left:

Palestinian girl and her baby sister in Mieh Mieh Refugee Camp, Lebanon (UNRWA 1951)

UN provides cement block dwellings for Palestinian refugees

Caravan of Palestinian refugees in 1948 (UNRWA 1948)

We hurriedly locked the house and began moving towards East Jerusalem. As we began our short but dangerous trail of tears, none of us fathomed that we would never again return to live in the neighborhood we had grown up in and in which we had just buried our father. At the same time that we left Musrara the neighborhood fell to the Zionist army and all remaining Palestinian residents, both Muslims and Christians, were forcibly evicted. Nicola remembers seeing the Zionist army approach as our family fled. Our neighborhood was instantly declared a no man's zone.

That first night in East Jerusalem, Mother went to the Old City and at midnight knocked on the door of her Christian friend and relative, Georgette, to see if we could stay with her. Georgette welcomed us into her home where we stayed for three days. Afterwards a Muslim friend of the family, Bajat Abu Gharbiyeh, the founder and director of a private high school, came to our rescue and invited us to stay in his school. But once we arrived at the school, we found that all the classrooms and halls were crowded with other refugees who faced the same plight as our own. Abu Gharbiyeh then invited us to use a narrow storage space under a stairwell. Bishara has often said "I can never forget the terrible odor of kerosene that filled that tiny place." Mother, Grandmother, my siblings and I stayed for several days in that narrow space under the stairwell until Abu Gharbiyeh was able to give us a room in his school across the road. He was able to do so because many of the refugees accepted the Red Cross's offer to relocate to newly established refugee camps. We stayed in the school for twenty days while Mother did what she could to arrange for us to be placed in orphanages or boarding schools. Throughout this time Mother, Nyfeh and some 30,000 Palestinian refugees from west Jerusalem, who had run to east Jerusalem, or other places, wistfully hoped that in a few days the war would end, enabling them the opportunity to return home and resume life as before.

Our first days as refugees in East Jerusalem were extremely difficult. Mother had no job, we had no home, and food was very scarce. Mother, however, didn't miss a beat. First on her agenda was to find food and shelter for her children, then to find a job, and last, to find schools for us, preferably boarding schools. Huda was given the option of joining one of the refugee camps that had been established by the Red Cross to shelter some 750,000 displaced Palestinians. But she passionately refused to take us to a refugee camp. Instead, she placed most of her children in new boarding schools that had been opened to provide homes for children who had lost one or both parents during the war.

Top: Huda holds Registered Nursing Degree (1953)

Bottom: Our Family (Clockwise from top left) Mubarak, Bishara, Elizabeth, Ellen, Diana, Huda, Nicola and Alex (1953)

Forty days after the war, the United Nations, the Jordanians and the Israelis agreed to allow displaced inhabitants of the various no-man's-lands to return to their abandoned homes for the duration of three hours to collect left valuables. This enabled Mother to collect some precious family certificates, photos and other valuable items.

Meanwhile, my grandmother fled to Gaza to be with her daughter, Bertha. Her move to Gaza was a relief for Huda because although she helped with the children, the carnage that had taken the life of my father was too much for Nyfeh to bear. Elias had been her only living son following the death of her oldest son, uncle Bishara, before 1948. For six months after Elias's death she continued to weep and mourn. Finally, she lost the will to live and died in Gaza within a year of my father's death. Though not shot with a bullet, Nyfeh was hit in the heart and became another casualty of the horrific war.

There was no social security system after the war to care for displaced people like our family. But somehow, the Jordanian government, perhaps with help from the UN and the international community, managed to set up a fund to help refugees. Huda was encouraged to go to a Jordanian office for some assistance. When she arrived at the office she told her story.

The officer asked Huda, "Who killed your husband?" At that time Huda was uncertain. So she simply said, "I don't know." "Did the Jews kill him?" he asked. "I don't know," she said. "Did the Iraqi soldiers kill him?" "I don't know," she said again. Finally the officer asked, "Did the Jordanian troops kill him?" "I'm not sure," she said. The officer put his hand into his desk drawer and took out fifty Jordanian dinars. "Take this to compensate you your loss." Huda stared at the fifty dinars (at that time of equivalent to an employee salary for a year) but could not bring herself to take the money. She left the office and returned home empty handed. In all likelihood, she could not bear the idea of accepting money in exchange for such a great and tragic loss. Later, Mustafa, the family's new friend and hero, counseled Mother to return to the office and take the money so she would be able to care for the family until she could find a job. She took his advice.

Who killed Father remains a mystery to the family. Nicola believes that the direction from which the bullet was fired and the type of bullet that took his life were evidence that the Zionist troops had killed him. The bullet aimed at Elias was fired from a Hagana fighter who was stationed near the Notre Dame de France compound, the church which is directly across Jerusalem's New Gate. In her book, *Our Jerusalem*, Bertha Spafford Vester, describing those torturous days wrote:

Going to the hospital in the mornings I ran zigzag to avoid bullets. In spite of bombs and bullets, the work continued. The Infant Welfare Center was enlarged to serve all the sick people, regardless of age or creed. Our playground, where between five and six thousand children a month used to play, was occupied by Arab Legionnaires. They were repulsing attacks on the old city from Haganah troops in Notre Dame de France. The merry sound of children's voices was replaced by machine-gun and mortar shots."[3]

Mother was never ready or willing to discuss our father's death with us. She refused to point a finger of blame on anyone. She wanted to shield her children not only from hunger and poverty, but also from the spirit of hate and revenge.

Facing the realities of her forever changed life, Mother, with renewed courage, rose to meet the challenges, assuming responsibilities she had never before confronted. With what money she had, she rented an apartment in the Old City and almost immediately found work in a hospital, also in the Old City. But the Jordanian Ministry of Health considered her to be a trainee and a volunteer and did not pay her for her work for the first six months. Not despairing, she simultaneously enrolled at Augusta Victoria Hospital's Nursing School to become a registered nurse. She spent many nights studying at home under candlelight or a kerosene lamp and before long, achieved her goal.

As Mother poured herself into the nursing career, she soon excelled at it and eventually became proficient in a number of specialized skills such as vaccination and midwifery. In the fifties and into the early sixties, due to the lingering effects of the war, the Palestinian population became extremely poor. Mother often said,

"I must have delivered over one thousand babies; sometimes I was paid and sometimes I was not."

When Huda delivered a baby girl, her compensation would often be a box of chocolate, if she was paid at all. If, however, it was a boy (Palestinian society favored boys) she might receive one or two dinars. The falaheen (farmers) often gave her a basket of figs, some grapes or a bottle of olive oil in gratefulness for her services.

Pay was no indication of Mother's nursing skills. She was an exceptionally good nurse, and on July 20, 1951, she was told by the Jordanian Ministry of Health to report immediately to the Austrian Hospital in Jerusalem to treat an important patient. Mother rushed to the hospital to fulfill her duty.

To her surprise, the significant patient was King Abdullah, the first king of the Hashemite Kingdom of Jordan. While the King and his sixteen-year-old grandson Hussein had been worshipping at the Al Aqsa Mosque in Jerusalem during their usual Friday prayers, a lone gunman shot at them. King Abdullah was hit directly. But the bullet intended for Hussein was deflected by a medal he was wearing. Since the Austrian Hospice was the closest medical center to Al-Aqsa Mosque, the injured king was taken there. Mother was assigned to his bedside and she, along with the doctors, did their best to save his life. Despite their efforts, he died.

Mother told of another unusual experience which continues to intrigue our family. One day while on duty in the hospital, a young girl named Elaine appeared looking for mother. When Elaine saw Huda she greeted her warmly and invited her, on behalf of her mother, for dinner that night. Huda looked at the girl. "Do I know you? Do I know your Mom?" The girl looked astonished. "You were just with us last night and you treated my sick mother. Now she is well. Please come, my mother wishes to honor you."

Unable to dodge the invitation, Mother took directions to the house. Then in the evening, she went to visit the family. As Huda entered the house there was nothing to remind her that she had been there before. Confused, she apologized and was about to return home. Before she could go however, the lady of the house insisted Huda stay. As they sat to eat, the woman explained to Huda that she had been in great pain in the early morning hours of the previous day. She was screaming for help when Huda opened the door, gave the woman the proper medicine, prayed with her and left.

Huda kept insisting, "I don't remember any of this."

After the meal, as Huda was about to leave, the woman said, "Please pray for me like you prayed for me last night."

Huda prayed without remembering how – or even if – she had prayed for her before.

Mother's burden following the tragic death of her husband and sole family breadwinner was, unfortunately, not limited to her own survival. She had seven children ranging in age from six months to eleven years old and it was impossible to work as a nurse and simultaneously care for her young ones. Under the circumstances, her only real choice was to place us children in scattered boarding schools and orphanages which accepted us on charity.

Mother secured a place for Bishara and Mubarak at Dar Al Awlad (The Boys' Home), a boarding school that had been established by a Russian Orthodox woman, Madam Katy Antonious, the wife of George Antonious, the author of *The Arab Awakening: the Story of the Arab National Movement.* She registered Ellen and me (I was a little more than two years old and thus too young to board at Dar Al Awlad) at Dar Al-Tifel Al A'rabi (the Arab Children's Home). This home was established by Miss Hind El Husseini, a benevolent Palestinian Muslim philanthropist who was a relative of the famous Palestinian national leader and hero Abd Al Qader Al-Husseini who was slain in 1948 while defending Jerusalem. Sitt Hind, as people in Jerusalem called her, was touched by the misfortunes of Palestinian children after the war. She started collecting orphaned and displaced children and bringing them to her office in the Old City. This began one day as she was on her way to a meeting of the Women's Social Action Committee, a society that she herself had established. On the way to the meeting she noticed several huddles of little boys and girls sitting helplessly by the walls of the Church of the Holy Sepulcher with fear and anxiety in their eyes. She asked them, "What are you doing here and why don't you go to your homes?" One of the oldest, a nine year old boy, told her that they had just escaped the Deir Yasin massacre[4] and that they did not have any place to go to. Hind kept walking to the meeting but could not remove the images of those helpless children from her mind. Immediately she returned to the children, took them all to her two-room apartment, and began to provide care for them.

My mother had no choice but to place Ellen and me under Miss Husseini's care with the other children, now numbering approximately 60. Ellen remembers a rectangular room full of cots from wall to wall with hardly any walking space. That room, a small office and the adjoining bathroom comprised the entire campus. Before long, the ever-burgeoning number of orphans presented great challenges for Hind.

A few years later, I joined my brothers at Dar Al Awlad. The three of us, although boarding at Dar Al Awlad, actually studied at St. George's School, a topnotch school run by the Church of England. In no way could mother have afforded to enroll us at the prestigious St. George's School on her own. Fortunately, the Church of England provided scholarships for students who lost one or both parents during the 1948 Arab-Israeli War. My brothers and I have always been grateful for that great privilege and for the fine education we received at St. George's. One disadvantage of being poor students in one of the best schools in Jerusalem, in which children from the

Clockwise from top left:
Madam Antonius
Dar al Awlad
Mrs. Hind al Husseini
St George's Cathedral - Jerusalem
Dar it Tifl al Arabi

wealthiest families were enrolled, was that we could never keep up with our peers. We were penniless most of the time but never wanted our affluent peers to feel sorry for us.

Diana, my youngest sister, who was by then nine months old, was taken to The Babies' Home, an orphanage for babies in a neighborhood of Jerusalem called El-Sa'adyeh that was established by the Spafford family. Later, Church of the Nazarene missionary pastor Russell Ford and his wife opened their home as a temporary haven for Diana. Elizabeth was taken to a Greek Orthodox Church school in Bethany.

For us kids, life at boarding schools had many challenges. At times we did not see our mother for weeks or even months. The youngest of us were starved for our mother's love and attention. Often the food and accommodations at the boarding schools were unpleasant and inadequate, as was the treatment from the supervisors. Consequently, Huda had to move Elizabeth and Diana from one boarding school to another in search of an acceptable home. The search for a home for Diana extended even beyond the borders of Jordan.

An Armenian Christian Boarding School in Lebanon was highly recommended and Huda enrolled Diana there. One year later, when Huda visited Diana at the boarding school, she found that Diana was speaking fluent Armenian and had practically forgotten her Arabic. Huda quickly decided she must bring Diana back to Jerusalem. Diana wrote about that visit:

One day while at Bird's Nest School in Lebanon, Mom came to visit me with Frosina, my uncle's wife and her son, my cousin Jonathan. When Mom saw me she began crying and all of us cried much. I could not speak with her a word of Arabic, English or German. For a whole year the only language I'd heard and spoken was Armenian. But I understood my mother when, while tears still poured down her face, hugged me and said in Arabic, "I will never leave you here again. My heart has always been with you. I will soon arrange to bring you back home to be close to me and to your brothers and sisters." True to her word, within weeks mom arranged my travel back to Jerusalem.

Another story Ellen recalls tells again of mother's deep compassion for her children:

One Sunday night after having spent the weekend at home, it was time for me to return to the boarding school. Mother had to wait late until she was off duty to walk me back to school. It was after seven in the evening and very dark. As we walked I could not stop crying. Mother was very patient and tried to comfort me. Finally she asked, "Why are you crying so? You're not usually afraid to go back to school." "But who is going to walk you home in the dark?" I replied. Mother, now realizing the cause of my tears, hugged me with tears in her eyes and said, "Let's go home together and I'll take you to school in the early morning." My tears instantly vanished.

Even boarding schools and orphanages were not secure during the turbulent period that followed the 1948 Arab-Israeli War. My sister, Ellen, recalls how she, I and some fifty children from Dar Al-Tifel Al-Arabi escaped certain death a few weeks after the war. It was on a day when Miss Husseini, by chance, was invited by German Lutheran Church leaders to the Lutheran guesthouse in the Old City to discuss a plan for supporting her efforts. Not wanting to leave the children alone, Hind called on all the children to follow her to the Lutheran guesthouse. It must have been quite a sight to see a young lady herding a flock of over fifty poor children, – many of them newly orphaned – through the narrow streets of the Old City, passing the Via Dolorosa (Way of the Cross) and walking through Jerusalem's markets, souvenir shops and bazaars until they reached the Lutheran guesthouse near Jaffa Gate. After arriving all of us children were treated to lemonade and cookies and waited a long time for the meeting to conclude.

Ellen remembers it was getting dark when the meeting finished and we began walking back through the same streets to Hind's office. We were carrying many supplies that the Lutherans had donated to the newly formed boarding school and orphanage. Upon returning to Hind's office, to our utter shock and disbelief, we discovered that during our absence the rooms of the boarding house had been hit by two bombs and were completely destroyed. Miss Husseini, certainly horrified and shaken at the sight of the leveled structures, was perhaps even more relieved and awed by the fact that all of us children in her trust had escaped certain death due to the fact that she had, by nothing less than a miracle, taken us away that very afternoon. Her distress over the loss of her office was compensated by the survival of children who had already experienced so many traumas. Most of the children under her care had now escaped death twice during a few weeks' period. Hind took us children to the nearby Rosary Sisters Convent and we stayed there a few days until a first truce was signed. Taking advantage of the truce, Hind moved the entire cluster to the Husseini family estate north of the Old City beside the American Colony. The entire estate gradually became the new campus of the school and orphanage.

During the early 1950s, Mother rented an apartment in the Jewish Quarter of the Old City (at that time, under Jordanian control, no Jews remained in the "Jewish" Quarter). On Good Friday, 1951, Ellen and I walked home to spend the Easter holidays with Mom. We always welcomed holidays, which were times when we could leave the orphanage to spend time with Mother and the rest of the family. After arriving home, we would eat a delicious, home-cooked meal such as was never provided at the boarding school. Reunited, we talked and shared, catching up on each others' news and stories. But on this Good Friday, after dinner, we suddenly began to hear the sounds of an attack on our neighborhood (even then, more than two years after the end of the fighting of 1948, there were periodic skirmishes across the armistice lines). Mother instantly opened the front door (actually the only door in our apartment), most likely a civil defense technique she had learned to counter the concussion of bombs or shells. She then blew out the kerosene lamp and ordered us to quickly run and each hug a different corner of the room, with our faces to the wall and our bodies as low as possible. Mother made the right decision, because while we were huddled in the corners (I myself have no memory of this, being too young at the time) the *whizz* of a projectile was heard, followed by an explosion outside. The projectile entered through the window, traversed our one-room home, and passed out through the open door – without doing a bit of harm to any of us! Regretfully, we discovered the next morning that Abu Ziad, the grocer who lived and had his business across the road from us, was hit and killed, presumably by the same explosive that had passed harmlessly through our room.

Ellen seemed to have nine lives. One evening, as she and the other children were eating supper at Dar Al-Tifel Al A'rabi, fighting broke out and bombs began falling. Wasting no time, Sitt Hind took all the children to the safety of the basement. After making a head count, she realized Ellen was not among them. The bombing was so heavy that night that she gave up on seeing Ellen alive again. When the bombing was over, Sitt Hind rushed upstairs expecting to see a dead body among the debris and broken glass.

Ellen was not found in the dining hall or in the kitchen. Finally she looked in the bathroom and there was tiny Ellen hiding under the bathroom sink looking like a frightened chick. Her eyes were puffed from crying and her hands and feet were trembling. From that day on, Sitt Hind called her *Susa,* meaning tiny chick.

Elizabeth couldn't adjust to life and study in boarding schools. In her teens, therefore, she moved in with Mother and commuted to school. Being at home, Elizabeth learned numerous homemaking skills. Often when we returned home from boarding school for visits, we hardly saw Mother because she worked long hours at the hospital. But Elizabeth was always there for us. It was she who did all the important household chores: the cooking, the laundry, and the cleaning. Elizabeth, compassionate by nature, filled much of the emotional vacuum that mother couldn't provide because of her busy schedule. This was especially important for Diana and me, as we were the youngest of the children.

Nicola, my eldest brother, also could not take the confines of a boarding school. He insisted on staying to help Mom while going to a day school, so Mother enrolled him at St. George's School in East Jerusalem. Money was short and there was little that a young boy could do to earn money. Nick, however, an entrepreneur at age eleven, used to pick up old bullet shell casings and sell them to make a few piasters. If that did not bring him enough piasters, he would immediately think of something that would.

Mother was not a tough disciplinarian. She was very gentle and easy going with her children. We learned more from her powerful example than from her preaching or teaching. From her example we learned to love God and to love people. From her determination we learned to value education. From her attitude we learned the power of forgiveness and from her resiliency we learned the value of facing life's challenges with gratitude and integrity.

Ellen recalls a story which illustrates Mom's character:

One day when I was just a child in boarding school with my brother Alex, an incident took place that showed me why my mother earned so much respect from others. A woman arrived from a Palestinian village with her two very young daughters to ask Miss Hind to enroll them in the boarding school. Miss Hind, as was customary, asked her a few questions. "Are they orphans?"

"No," said the woman. "I am divorced and am married to another man. My new husband does not want the children."

Miss Hind took compassion on the children and their mother. The woman herself looked poor and ragged. Miss Hind accepted the children and told the mother not to worry about paying tuition.

Shortly afterwards on a Friday, the day on which parents or guardians would visit their children, the same woman arrived for a visit, this time dressed in a beautiful, clean, expensive dress, a shawl over her shoulders and brand new shoes. Her children came to meet her and she in turn greeted them with snacks and toys. While Miss Hind was watching this mother, her eyes fell upon Mom coming from work, with her iodine spotted nursing outfit to visit Alex and me. Mom asked me to take her to see Miss Hind and I led the way to my headmistress.

After exchanging formal greetings with Miss Hind, Mom said, "I have been promoted and now I can pay some money on my children's tuition."

Miss Hind was very touched by Mother's forthcoming generosity. "From now on, when you come to visit your children, come visit with them right here in my living room. Every time you come I want to talk with you and have tea with you. As for your children's tuition, I don't want you to pay a penny, because you are brave and diligent in your work and any promotion money deserves to be yours to keep."

The following day during the school assembly period, when we lined up to say the Muslim prayers (Alfatiha), Miss Hind stood and addressed all the children and teachers. Without mentioning any names she told the story of the two women, praising the nurse who came in her work clothes to visit her children rather than the lady who masqueraded as poor to obtain free tuition for her children. Miss Hind used Huda as a model to give a practical lesson to all the children in her care.

She concluded by saying, "Honesty, truth, and good conduct are much more important than education, certificates, and class." She then dismissed the assembly with, "This is our lesson for today and we will skip the prayers."

Ellen writes more about Mother's way of responding to people's needs:

Perhaps most outstanding about mother was her hospitality to strangers. Late one evening, I was at home in Bethlehem when Mom called from the hospital.

"Ellen, a family from a village around Bethlehem missed their bus and I invited them to stay the night with us. Please be good to them and treat them well. Serve them whatever food you have and give them clean sheets for the beds."

I asked her the family's name, but she said she did not recall. My first reaction was to resent my mom's hospitality, but I respected her and always wanted to do what she asked. The family walked all the way from the hospital to our house. By the way they were dressed, I could see that they were poor country people. Having no choice, I welcomed them and did exactly as Mom suggested. To my surprise, they were wonderful folks and kept praising Mom for her hospitality. For many months and years later they remained friends of the family. Not all of the strangers whom Mom invited in as guests turned out to be as nice as this family. I once commented to Mom that the last strangers in our home had stolen quite a few items from the house.

She said smiling, "They must have needed those things more than we needed them."

While serving at King Hussein Hospital in Beit Jala, Mother showed her compassionate nature by taking care of unclaimed corpses. It happened on more than one occasion, that after a person died in the hospital, no one would come to claim the corpse. This was either because their family was utterly poor and could not afford to transport the body to their town, or that the deceased had no living relatives.

On such occasions, Abu Ali, the hospital's gate keeper, would go to Huda, knowing exactly how she was going to respond.

"Sitt Huda, what shall I do with the body of so and so?" he would ask. "No one in his or her family is willing to take them away."

Huda characteristically responded by taking some dinars from her purse and instructing Abu Ali to hire a poor man to take the body and bury it in an honorable way. Her memory of the frustration that she experienced after the death of her husband made her kindhearted toward the folks who could not afford to bury their own dead.

Though Mother had been forced to quickly learn how to juggle many roles, certainly not least on her heart was her spiritual search. It was a very significant part of her life that helped her mature in her relationship with God and face the challenging life before her. Soon after the dust of the 1948 volcano settled, Huda resumed her church activities. At church, she was never satisfied to be merely a recipient of God's blessings and graces. She always looked for an opportunity to serve. She would open her home for Bible studies for women or she would collect the neighborhood children and begin Sunday school classes for them. When she met with the women, she always seemed to have another miracle in her life that she wished to share with them. Ellen wrote:

> *My mother prayed a lot and she depended on God for 'our daily bread.' One Easter holiday Mom wanted to prepare a special roast beef dinner for us kids, knowing that we'd all be home for the occasion. She knew she couldn't afford it, so that day in her prayers she asked the Lord for thirty piasters.*
> *"Why did you ask God for just thirty piasters?" I asked. "That's the price of the roast beef," she said. Hardly finished with her prayer, Mom heard a knock at the door. She got up to answer the door and there stood a neighbor of ours with thirty piasters in her hand. "Forgive me for returning your money so late," she said, handing the money to Mother.*
> *Mom had forgotten that she had previously lent this woman some money. As one might imagine, my prayer life experienced something of a revival. For Mom, God's promises were as good as bank notes.*
> *One of her favorites: And my God will meet all your needs according to his glorious riches in Christ Jesus. Philippians 4:19(NIV)*

My uncle George was touched by his sister Huda's testimony and although he initially resisted the path that she took, he later followed her in fully dedicating his life to God and His service. George became a school teacher in the Church of the Nazarene in Jordan. Later he was ordained in the Church of God. George was very close to Mother and was utterly devastated by Father's death and the loss of our home in Musrara. He would seize every opportunity to offer financial or spiritual help to Huda and her children. Reflecting on George's generosity, Mother wrote:

Throughout my calamity, my brother George was very close to me. Whatever was available to him he was always ready to share with me and with my children. After he married Frosina, their home was always open to us. Frosina was no less generous than her husband. Occasionally, we moved to live with the Kuttabs in the same house along with Nazirah and we were a big happy family.

HUDA'S STORY: 1967–2006

"My greatest joy in life is to give regardless of who receives my gifts."
—Huda

As a registered nurse with the Jordanian Ministry of Health, Mother was transferred from one hospital to another according to the Ministry's needs and policies. Consequently, our family moved frequently, residing in various cities of what was at the time considered the Hashemite Kingdom of Jordan. We moved from Jerusalem to Ramallah, from Ramallah to Irbed, in Jordan, from Irbed to Hebron, and from Hebron to Bethlehem. This was only the beginning of the distant travels our family would later embark upon.

In 1963, the Jordanian Ministry of Health promoted Mother to the level of a hospital matron. With the privilege of promotion came the disadvantage of moving. She was ordered to move to Irbed, a city on the northeastern plains of Jordan. That move was difficult for us children since we were still in boarding schools. Now, we could only visit Mom on long vacations since the journey there took most of the day.

Once when she was living in Irbed, Mother wrote a letter to Mubarak describing her success in raising pigeons. She was fascinated by them. She admired their grace as they flew and was intrigued by how they always knew how to return home. The letter she wrote never arrived at its destination in Jerusalem. Instead, it was intercepted by the Jordanian Bureau of Investigations (the *mukhabarat*). In those days they opened and read most letters as a security measure. Evidently they found Mom's letter suspicious, because as soon after the letter was sent, two *mukhabarat* officers paid a visit to Mom's house in Irbed. They asked Mom who lived at her house. "Just me, and the children when they can visit," she said, rather mystified. The agents asked Mom to show them around the house. She showed them around her

Top: Huda (front row, one in from the right) and colleagues with Jordanian Minister of Health

Bottom: Huda Head Nurse at Hospital in Hebron

small place. Then she showed them the back yard and introduced them to her new pigeons.

The men looked at each other and laughed. They explained that they had come to this address because they suspected that the letter was more than just a friendly hello. The language used made them think the words "pigeon" and "pigeon coop" were code names for something secretive and sinister. No humans or birds were arrested that day and the pigeons kept fascinating Mom until the day the Jordanian Ministry of Health agreed to transfer her from Irbed to Hebron.

After being appointed as the head nurse at the government hospital in Hebron, Mother lived in Bethlehem. At that time, Uncle George was pastor of the Church of God, in Wadi um Ali, near the Church of the Nativity in Bethlehem; a distance of about two miles. He and his wife Frosina, with their six children, welcomed us to live with them at the parsonage. This was a blessing for Mother since her meager income then prevented her from acquiring independent housing. She also felt more at home in Bethlehem, where there was still a strong Christian presence. Not surprisingly, with two large families living in the same house, tensions often surfaced, especially on the long weekends and vacations when we were all there. Tensions eased when after a couple of years in Hebron, Mother was transferred back to the King Hussein Hospital, which was in Bethlehem. Around the same time, Uncle George and his family moved outside the Old City of Bethlehem into a house near Rachel's Tomb while mother stayed on at the Church of God parsonage.

Years later, Salwa, Bishara's wife, traveled with Mother to Amman, Jordan to check on Mom's retirement settlement with the Jordanian government. By then Mom had worked many years as a nurse in Jordanian owned hospitals. Salwa was deeply saddened when, as they looked at the records of Mom's salary, she found out how little Mom earned in her early years. Mom's first income was about twelve dollars a month, which would be approximately $97 today. With that, she had to keep a family of eight people going.

Not one to be deterred, by 1967 Huda was a staff nurse at King Hussein Hospital in Bethlehem. Nicola was working in Kuwait, and Bishara was studying at Dakota Wesleyan University in South Dakota. Mubarak was working in Amman, Jordan but in the same year and just at the outbreak of the Six Day War, he returned to Jerusalem and Bethlehem. Elizabeth was in Kuwait with her husband Ibrahim and four children. Ellen and Diana were still at home in Bethlehem, while I was studying in Switzerland. When the war began Uncle George and his family along with grandmother Nazirah returned, for security reasons, to live with Mother at the Church of God parsonage. At that time Hilda and Elias, my brother Nicola's children, whose mother had just passed away, were also staying there.

Mother worked more or less around-the-clock for the duration of the war. She treated untold numbers of injured men, women, and children. One day as she was receiving the bodies and limbs of the dead, the body of a particular young man caught her attention. The decapitated head was not with the body. After a careful examination, Mother abruptly fled from the hospital, sprinting the two miles as fast as she could to our home. When Mother got to the house, panting from both fear and exertion, she pounded on the door, yelling for someone to open up. Her nephew, Jonathan, opened the door, astonished to see his aunt in such a frenzied state. Without saying a word, mother took Jonathan firmly in her arms and began hugging him and kissing him as he had never been hugged and kissed before; with tears of joy running down her face she went inside the house and kissed the others. Then she immediately turned around and, with the same speed that had brought her home, ran back to the hospital to resume her duties. Everyone at home was thoroughly puzzled by Mother's behavior. It was only after the war that they learned the reason for her unusual behavior. When Mother had seen the headless body, it looked to her exactly like that of Jonathan. What a relief it had been for her when her beloved nephew answered the door, alive and well and in one piece! It was worth the marathon.

On June 4, 1967, our family along with all the Palestinian people were caught up in the throes of another war. Over the course of six days, Bethlehem, was snatched, along with the rest of the West Bank, from Jordanian control and became an Israeli-occupied city. Having reached a certain age and maturity, my brothers and sisters who were still living in Bethlehem were able during this war to be of some assistance to our compatriots. This came about in a unique way when Margaret Gaines, a Church of God missionary from the United States—who, for many years, had been serving in the village of Aboud—decided at the outbreak of the war to leave the country. Miss Gaines visited us briefly to ask the Kuttabs if they would look after her dog and her Volkswagen. That visit was a tremendous blessing as Margaret's VW was used intensively by the Awads and the Kuttabs to save lives during the war. The first thing the family did was to repaint the blue VW a brownish-khaki color in order to camouflage

Top: Kuttab Family (Clockwise from top left) Daoud, Phoebe,
Danny, Lydia, Jonathan, Samuel, Grace, Frosina and George (2001)
Middle: Ellen
Bottom: Jerusalem from Mount Olives (2007)

it. Then they took the back seats out, hung a Red Cross flag on it and turned it into a mini ambulance. They also made a makeshift emergency center in the front hall of the house. Beds and mattresses were prepared and all the windows were painted dark so the dim lights from the kerosene lamps in the hall would not attract the attention of bombers. Since Mom was on duty in the hospital, Aunt Frosina took charge of attending to the wounded and sick at the temporary emergency clinic. Mubarak became the official mini ambulance driver. His ears were tuned to the radio and whenever he heard of a bombing anywhere in Bethlehem, he rushed to save the injured. If the case was critical, he took the wounded to King Hussein Hospital; otherwise he took them to the makeshift clinic. During the war the Israeli Air Force bombed the traditional open air market in the heart of Bethlehem, killing and injuring several citizens. At the makeshift clinic, as with all of Bethlehem, there was no electricity for the duration of the war. The family used kerosene burners to sterilize needles and to cook food for the patients and themselves.

Just as they had done elsewhere in 1948, during the 1967 war, the Israelis drove their vehicles through the streets and alleys of Bethlehem, using loudspeakers to threaten people in order to scare them into leaving the city.. The Israelis spread rumors that they were about to destroy the city. Frosina recalls that one day, as she was meditating on God's Word, she received a conviction from the Lord that the family would be safe staying in Bethlehem. Trusting that affirmation, she encouraged Huda and the rest of the family to stay.

During the war, hundreds of Bethlehemites fled, making the same mistake that many had made during the 1948 war, namely, abandoning their homes and places of birth from fear. It was then that Mubarak made it his duty to encourage people to stay. Many people listened to him and remained in Bethlehem. However, others left and lost their homeland for good. Mubarak remembers one doctor who actually used the hospital ambulance to take his family to Amman. Many native Jordanians were living in Bethlehem and other cities of the West Bank before 1967. When it was clear that the war was turning badly for Jordan, they felt the need to return with their families to safety east of the Jordan River. When Palestinians saw Jordanian friends and neighbors fleeing for Jordan, they thought it was prudent to accompany them.

I was quite shaken when the director of the Bible College I was attending in Switzerland informed me by phone that there was a letter for me from the Red Cross that had arrived from a hospital in Bethlehem. In wartime, those types of letters usually carry bad news. I warily went to see the director, expecting the worst, but when I opened the letter I found a message from Mother thoughtfully assuring me that the family was safe and that none of them were hurt.

Upon finishing school in Switzerland that same year, I intended to return home to pastor a church in Bethlehem; I discovered, however, that the Israeli occupation forces had enforced new laws that prevented me, along with thousands of other Palestinian students and workers who were abroad, from returning home. It was then, for the first time, that I realized I had suddenly become a person without a country.

Switzerland did not want me, and Israel had made the West Bank a closed territory to Palestinians who were abroad. Unable to reunite with my church and family, I applied to study in the United States. God was gracious and, within a few months, I received a scholarship to Lee College (now Lee University) in Cleveland, Tennessee, where I continued to work towards a degree in Biblical Studies.

The day after the war was over, Mubarak and Ellen decided to go to Jerusalem to check on their former boarding schools, Dar Al Awlad and Dar Al-Tifel Al A'rabi. They had heard that East Jerusalem was bombed more heavily than Bethlehem. Out of concern and curiosity, they decided to walk a new shortcut road from Bethlehem to Jerusalem that passed by Talpiot. In order to not alarm mother or any relatives, they kept their venture a secret. The walk went well until they passed the St. Elias Church on the main road connecting Jerusalem to Hebron. An Israeli army vehicle spotted them and steered the Jeep towards them. With their guns pointed at Mubarak and Ellen, the Israeli soldiers ordered them to stop and immediately enter the Jeep. Mubarak and Ellen, although shaken and frightened of what might happen next, were nevertheless, also very curious. This was their first face-to-face meeting with the new occupiers of their cities and towns. The soldiers were equally curious. This was also their first encounter with members of the civilian population of what came to be known as the West Bank.

Soon after they sat down in the Jeep, they were showered with questions. The interrogations took place while the Jeep was traveling through the streets of West Jerusalem. Mubarak and Ellen listened to and answered the soldiers, all the while with their eyes fixed on the streets, buildings, and gardens of West Jerusalem. They were astonished at how modern and western looking West Jerusalem was. After the soldiers ran out of questions and felt secure with the Awads, they offered them food and drink.

"What do you want to see in Jerusalem?" they asked. Mubarak and Ellen were astonished at the soldiers' change of attitude. They politely asked for a tour of West Jerusalem and then of East Jerusalem. The soldiers obliged and thus the Awads became perhaps the first of the conquered Palestinians to tour West Jerusalem after the war. The soldiers even took them by Dar Al-Tifel Al A'rabi and Dar Al Awlad. Both schools had survived unscathed. Late that afternoon, the soldiers kindly dropped the Awads at the entrance to Bethlehem. Meanwhile, Mother and the rest of the family were growing sick with worry over Ellen and Mubarak's disappearance. The family was greatly relieved when they saw them walking towards the house and equally astonished when they were told of their first visit to Israel.

Mubarak became an activist against the Israeli military occupation while teaching at the Mennonite school in Beit Jala just days after the Six-Day War. The expatriate who had been heading the school in 1967 left by order of the American Consulate in Jerusalem. Mubarak then assumed the burden of keeping the orphanage open and operating. During the day he taught at the school but his evenings were spent with friends in Jerusalem who were willing to resist the occupation with him. Mother protested Mubarak's political activities, in spite of the fact that he was committed to non-violence. The suffering our family encountered in 1948 and afterward caused Mother to be understandably concerned about Mubarak's political activities.

On one occasion Mubarak printed thousands of leaflets encouraging Palestinians to strike. An informer told the Israeli authorities of Mubarak's plan and the details of the car he was using. One day when Mubarak's friend was driving Mubarak's car the Israeli's stopped him, found the leaflets in the trunk and then tortured him for additional information. Later, the Israelis imprisoned Mubarak and tortured him cruelly, but he refused to volunteer any information which might jeopardize any of his friends. He remained in prison for 40 days on charges of printing and distributing leaflets.

Soon, representatives of the Mennonite Central Committee intervened on Mubarak's behalf. To Mother's great relief, the Israelis agreed that Mubarak could be released but only if he left Israel. Mubarak left in 1969 and was given the opportunity to attend any Mennonite College in the States. He chose Bluffton College in Ohio. In the coming years, Bishara and I became involved in the ministry of the Mennonite school (Hope Secondary School) in Beit Jala.

Huda always remained an active participant in the Christian community regardless of how busy she was or what the political situation brought. She often invited friends and family along to worship with her. I learned of a bizarrely funny incident that occurred at one religious service Huda attended during her time in Ramallah. Mother invited her neighbor, Im Kamal, to the meeting that night. (Im is a title of respect which literally means "mother of.") It was Im Kamal's first time at a Protestant church service, and the style of worship was vastly different than the traditional Greek Orthodox style to which she was accustomed.

Reverend Maurice Gerges was a fiery Lebanese evangelist who preached that night. His sermon highlighted the story of Mary and Martha in which Martha complained to Jesus that she was so busy serving him while Mary squandered her time idly by Jesus' side. Attempting to engage the crowd, Reverend Gerges held the Bible in his left hand and began waving his right hand and repeating charismatically, "Martha, Martha, you worry about too many things but the need is for one!"

Suddenly, Im Kamal stood up and in an explosion of raw emotion, yelled, "It must be Huda! It must be Huda! It must be Huda who told you!"

Mom was utterly mystified and embarrassed, especially as every face in the meeting room instantly turned toward her and Im Kamal with rebuking eyes that seemed to say, "Shut up you two, so we can hear the evangelist!"

Mother had no clue why Im Kamal was so upset with her or why she was making such a commotion and shouting at the preacher while accusing her before all the assembly of gossiping against her. What had slipped Mother's mind at that awkward moment was that Im Kamal's first name was Martha. Im Kamal did not know that the preacher was referring to a woman named Martha who had lived about two thousand years ago. She thought the preacher was rebuking her personally and that Huda, her next door neighbor, must have told the preacher everything about her. It took a lot of persuasion on the part of Mother to convince Im Kamal that the preacher did not single her out personally.

A Miracle at Birth

In 2011, I was a guest speaker for a group of Palestinian women who gathered for a regular meeting at the Christmas Lutheran Church in Bethlehem. After the meeting, a 65-year old woman named Im Khader introduced herself to me and said, "You may not know me, but I knew your mother, Huda." She shared some about her family and then said, "I can never forget your mother because every time I look at my daughter's face, I thank God for your mother." Curious, I asked, "Why?" Im Khader said, "Your mother was the midwife when, at the age of 18, I gave birth to my daughter. Immediately after the birth, even before I'd had a chance to see the baby, my close relatives and friends of the family who had gathered for the momentous occasion began gasping and weeping as they caught sight of the baby. This frightened me. 'What's going on?' I asked Huda. 'Why are the women crying?' She forced the women out of the room, saying nothing to me. After locking the door she returned to my bedside, picked up my daughter, anointed her with oil, and prayed for her while making the sign of the cross over her. She then placed the baby in my arms and before my eyes the baby's face gradually shifted from deformed to normal. Huda then opened the door and allowed the women back into the room. The previous shock of seeing the deformed face and head of my daughter was replaced with gasps of awe, congratulations, and praise to God! Today this little miracle is 48 years old, married and has four children of her own."

HUDA'S STORY: THE EXODUS

The following is an account of the exodus of my uncles, mother and brothers and sisters from our native homeland. I am including these accounts, not because I think that the Awads or the Kuttabs had the most interesting or the most dramatic stories, but rather because what happened to the Awads and the Kuttabs is so typical of what thousands of Palestinian Muslims and Christians faced and are still facing as a result of the Zionist assault on our homeland.

The exodus of Christians from Palestine and other countries of the Middle East and North Africa began during the Ottoman period, but it drastically increased in numbers after the Israeli occupation of the Palestinian territories in 1948 and in 1967. Life under the Israeli occupation brought new constraints and hardships on the Palestinian people. As the Israelis solidified their grip on the territories, normal life became a nightmare for many Palestinians. Gradually, one member after another of the Awad and Kuttab families sought to emigrate. Some left because it became more difficult for them to sustain a family in the West Bank. Others left because their children had already gone ahead of them and they wanted to be re-united. Still others simply could not bear to live under military occupation with the psychological and emotional toll it exacted.

Uncle George was the first to leave for the United States. George took his wife, Frosina, his seven children and grandmother Nazirah and went to start life afresh in New Jersey. Nazirah lived with her son George until she died in 1978. Later, Huda's brother Costandi and his entire family found residence in Nashville, Tennessee. Huda was reluctant to leave her homeland. It was not economic factors that drove Huda out of Palestine. Rather it was her desire to be with her children. All of Huda's sons left, at different times, to the United States either for work or for study. Then, to their surprise, like many other Palestinian students and workers, they discovered that the new occupiers of their homeland did not want them back in their homeland. Each returning Palestinian was considered a threat to the security of the State of Israel and was not automatically granted the right of residency in his or her homeland. Huda's brother and his family, not to mention her own sons, were now residing in the United States and were often denied entry or residency in their homeland when they tried returning home. When it became apparent to Huda that there was no future for her family in Palestine, she decided to join her children in the States. In 1978, she chose to travel to Ohio to live with her son, Mubarak, his wife, Heidrun, and their two children, Tamara and Karim. This was a transitional period for Mother, who later applied for American citizenship, passed the exam, pledged allegiance before a judge, and became a citizen of the United States at the age of 69.

Elizabeth married Ibrahim Siryani from Bethlehem who pursued his career in Kuwait. They had three daughters, Sylvia, Nahlah, and Halah, and one son, Hani. Following Saddam Hussein's invasion of Kuwait and the ensuing U.S.-led invasion, most of the Palestinians living there were expelled. This was a catastrophe for the more than 200,000 Palestinians who had built their lives in Kuwait. The Siryani family eventually emigrated to the United States. They now live in Kansas.

Ellen married Hani Sorour from Bethlehem. For lack of job opportunities in Bethlehem, Hani sought a teaching post in Libya. During the Six Day War, Hani, who was already living in Libya while his wife and daughter, Heidi, were in Bethlehem, was banned from returning to Bethlehem. For many months, Ellen petitioned the Israelis to permit him to return under a system agreed upon with the United Nations called Family Reunification. During this period, Israeli intelligence agents exerted tremendous pressure on Ellen, hoping to capitalize on her desperate situation. They attempted to entice her into working as a spy in return for favorable treatment for her husband. Ellen was then teaching at Bethlehem High School for girls, and the Israeli officials wanted her to report to them whatever went on in the school. As Ellen refused to cooperate, it took even longer for her family to be reunited. Thousands of Palestinians have been coerced by the Israeli officials to betray their people, and thousands more were severely punished for not collaborating with the Israelis against their homeland and their compatriots. A few years after their family's reunification in Bethlehem, and the birth of a son, Taufik, the Sorours decided to emigrate to the U.S.

Diana went to study in Germany. There she married Werner Wittman and became a German citizen. She, Werner, and their children, Tobias and Bianca, continue to live in Germany. Before her retirement, Diana was the director of a kindergarten in Augsburg, Germany.

My eldest brother, Nicola, married Katy Nasser, a Palestinian from the town of Beir Zeit. They sought employment in Kuwait, but Katy's health failed her and she died in 1966, leaving Nicola with two children, Elias and Hilda. Shortly after Katy's death, Nicola moved to the United States. Nicola had worked in Jordan in the optical business, and had gained experience in cutting lenses and selling glasses. Soon after he came to the States, he began working at an optical business in Kansas City, Missouri. Nicola went to visit our brother, Bishara, who was studying at Dakota Wesleyan University. There, through Bishara, Nicola met Patti Miller, then a student at Wesleyan University. They were married in 1969. They made a home for themselves in Overland Park, Kansas with Hilda and Elias, and Nicola opened his own optical store in Olathe, Kansas. Their daughter Angela was born in 1973.

HUDA'S STORY: BETWEEN TWO CONTINENTS

The calling, desire, and passion to serve our people and our church compelled Mubarak, Bishara, and me to return to Palestine regardless of circumstances.

Mubarak had studied at Bluffton College, a Mennonite liberal arts college in Ohio. While there he was exposed to the pacifist and non-violent teachings that characterize the peace churches. Mubarak believed that these non-violent resistance methods were what Palestinians needed in their struggle against the occupation of their land. Upon graduation from Bluffton College, Mubarak taught at the Mennonite School in Beit Jala and began to share with Palestinians the methods of Mahatma Gandhi and

Martin Luther King, Jr.

In 1985, Mubarak, who by then was married to Nancy Nye and had two children, Tamara and Karim, established the Palestinian Center for Democracy and the Study of Non-Violence in Jerusalem. As his movement grew and began to impact many Palestinian youth, the Israeli authorities were alarmed at the possibility of having a Palestinian Gandhi on their hands. In 1988, they imprisoned Mubarak for forty days and then deported him to the United States, where he went on to found the organization Nonviolence International.

Mubarak wore two big hats. He became known both for his nonviolent activism and founding Nonviolence International, as well as for founding, and directing for many years, the National Youth Advocate Program, which assisted at-risk youth in several states in the U.S. He later founded a new youth advocacy program with similar aims called the International Youth Advocate Foundation.

Bishara successfully returned to Bethlehem and married Salwa Andrea from Gaza. They had three children, Sami, Samir, and Dina. He taught at St. George's School in Jerusalem and later became the first Palestinian director of Hope Secondary School in Beit Jala. The Mennonite Central Committee first established Hope Secondary School in 1961 as a boarding and vocational center for disadvantaged Palestinian students.

Bishara's experience at the Hope School revolutionized his life. He was so eager to show the love of Christ to his students, many of whom came from traumatized homes. The signs of suffering and the emotional scars that these students had reminded him of himself when he was their age. Besides serving their physical and educational needs, Bishara was eager to show them the love of God and bring healing to their hearts. Though he tried hard, nothing he said or did seemed to work. One day as he was praying and struggling with this challenge, the Spirit of God brought him conviction for his own hate toward the Israelis who caused the death of his father, forced his family to become refugees, and occupied his entire homeland. The message of the Spirit of God was clear to him in that moment of his brokenness: "If you keep harboring these feelings of hate, you will not be able to be a blessing to your students." At that moment, Bishara poured out his heart to God in confession and repentance. He earnestly sought God to clean his heart from all hatred toward his national enemies. Brother Andrew, founder of Open Doors Ministries, in his book, *Light Force: The only Hope for the Middle East*, described Bishara's experience in these words:

Right: Ellen and Family
(Clockwise from top left:
Taufik, Heidi, Ellen and
Hani (1995)

Above: Mubarak and Family
(from left to right) Karim,
Nancy, Mubarak and Tamara
(2004)

Right: Elizabeth and
Family Clockwise from
top left) Hani, Hala,
Nahlah, Sylvia, Elizabeth
and Ibrahim (2006)

Tears welled up in his eyes. How would he, a man who had given his life to Jesus Christ a dozen years before, who committed to be an instrument of God in the Holy Land, help these angry young boys? There was only one answer. His voice broke the silence of the night: 'Lord, I beg You. Forgive me for hating the Jews and allowing the hatred to control my life.'[5]

Bishara bears witness that at that moment a miracle of healing took place in his heart that transformed his ministry. "I felt like a burden fell off my shoulders and for the first time in my life I was able to live up to the directive of Christ to 'Love your enemies...'." The change in his heart also had a profound impact on the students he was serving and he saw many of them commit their lives to following Christ and serving him. Then in 1979, while still directing the Hope Secondary School, Bishara conceived and founded Bethlehem Bible College in neighboring Bethlehem.

While director of the Hope Secondary School, Bishara noticed that a number of the students who graduated from the school and desired to prepare themselves to serve the Church were leaving Palestine to enroll in Bible colleges or theological schools in Europe and in the United States. Bishara also noted that most of these students, due to political or economic obstacles, did not return to serve local churches in Palestine. He called for a meeting of church leaders from various Christian denominations, shared his concerns with them, and suggested that a Bible college be established in Bethlehem. The leaders responded favorably, saying that if God had placed such a commitment on his heart, then he should proceed with their blessing. Reverend Earl Morgan, pastor of the Church of the Nazarene in Jerusalem, approached Bishara with twenty dollars in his hand and said to Bishara, "Here! Take this and start your college." With a big smile on his face, Bishara snatched the twenty dollars from Reverend Morgan's hand and with it, started Bethlehem Bible College. People who visit Bethlehem Bible College today are amazed by how God has used those founding twenty dollars.

Bishara began enrolling the first Bible College students in evening classes that initially met at the Hope School, where he served as principal. As the number of students grew, Bishara kept looking for a new campus. One day as he was walking along Hebron Road in Bethlehem, he noticed that three buildings belonging to the Bible Lands Society were vacant. The buildings had once housed the Helen Keller School for the Blind.

The school had been moved to another building north of Jerusalem. The buildings in Bethlehem had become a nesting place for birds and were gradually deteriorating. Bishara approached officials from Bible Lands and asked if the buildings could be used to house Bethlehem Bible College. The response was discouraging. The officials told Bishara that Bible Lands abided by charity laws that prohibited them from giving him the buildings. Refusing to accept no for an answer, Bishara took his case to God in prayer. Every time he passed Hebron Road he would say: "Thank you Jesus for giving us these buildings." And a miracle happened! Bible Lands officials approached Bishara on September 1, 1990, his birthday, and offered him the following arrangement: Bethlehem Bible College could have the building for five years free of rent but at the end of those five years, Bethlehem Bible College had to make a decision, either come up with the funds to purchase the buildings or find another place to meet. Bishara was delighted, and students, faculty and staff moved to the new campus after much renovation.

At the end of the five years the Bible College did not have $1.8 million to pay Bible Lands but no one was ready to give up the college. Bishara asked Bible Lands for a grace period which would be a time to seek God's will and share the College's challenge with friends and supporters. He was granted another year. During that year another miracle occurred. Before the end of the year, Bethlehem Bible College had raised enough to pay Bible Lands the entire amount. The campus became the property of Bethlehem Bible College. Bishara likes to point out that the greatest miracle is that which takes place in the lives and in the ministries of the men and women that God has entrusted to the Bethlehem Bible College.

One day in 1981, Bishara and Ellen went to visit an outdoor fruit and vegetable market in Fresno, California. Bishara had taken a year's leave from Bethlehem Bible College to further his theological education at a Mennonite Seminary in Fresno. As they were enjoying their shopping, a lady overheard them speaking in Arabic. She came closer. "This language is familiar to me. Are you speaking Arabic?" she asked. "Yes," Ellen said. "We are Palestinians from Jerusalem." The lady was now really curious and began to ask more questions. "Years ago I use to be a missionary in Jerusalem but I left there very discouraged and disheartened just as the political situation worsened." She added, "I wonder if I made an impact on anyone while there… I wonder what happened to Huda." This ignited the curiosity of Ellen and Bishara. "Our mother's name is also Huda," Bishara said. As the conversation converged to details it was discovered that the lady was Miss

Top: Nicola and Family (left to right) Elias, Angela, Hilda, Patti & Nicola (2007)

Bottom: Diana and Family (Left to Right) Diana, Werner, Tobias and Bianca (2011)

Top: Bishara and Family (from left to right) Samir, Bishara, Dina, Salwa, and Sami (1989)
Bottom: Alex and Family- Christy, Brenda, Randy, Alex, and Basem

Black, who in the 1930's and early 1940's had been a young volunteer teacher and missionary at Miss Brown's Assemblies of God School in Jerusalem, the very school Mother had attended. What a joy for Miss Black to discover that Huda, her former student that she had thought of and prayed for over the years, had kept the faith, survived, and that her children were alive and serving the Lord. Bishara wasted no time; he bought a plane ticket for Mother to visit him in Fresno and soon after the teacher met her student after a forty year separation. Miss Black was fortunate enough to see, before her death, that her labor in God's field was not fruitless – at least not in Huda's life.

While I was completing my studies at Lee College, I met a beautiful young woman named Brenda Waddell. She was also studying at Lee. We went out on a few dates while I was studying Greek in preparation for seminary. Somehow, I forgot all about the Greek! Our courtship in Tennessee was short-lived because I enrolled at Midwestern Baptist Theological Seminary in Kansas City, Missouri. For the following year and a half we corresponded by mail. Then, after one semester in Missouri, I had the opportunity to return to Palestine under an Israeli family reunification program that would reinstate my residency rights in Palestine. Mother, who was still in Palestine, worked patiently and diligently with the stubborn Israeli bureaucracy, making sure that once I returned I would have all of my residency papers. I spent a year and a half in Palestine. During this time, Brenda and I continued our correspondence. We declared our love for each other and our intention to get married by mail.

I returned to America in 1972. Brenda and I were married that year in Neon, Kentucky, where she was born and raised. We lived in northern Georgia for a few years, where we taught school and completed our graduate education. We had our first child, Christy, there and greatly enjoyed our new family life.

But I felt that God had called me to minister in Palestine and I discussed this calling with Brenda. We both felt right about answering Bishara's request for us to leave the peaceful hills of northern Georgia to come and help him establish the Bible College in Bethlehem. Thus, in 1979, we both resigned our teaching positions, and I also resigned from the pastorate of a local church.

Upon returning home, I once again experienced the frustration of being a Palestinian under Israeli occupation. Although I was born and raised in

Jerusalem, the Israelis did not recognize my old residency papers that Mother had worked so hard to receive. They told me my residency had been revoked because I had spent too much time in America. I was branded a foreigner and told the only way I could enter Israel was as an American with a tourist visa. I contacted a lawyer to see if I could have my residency rights reinstated but to my dismay, I discovered that the lawyers were powerless. The only way I could acquire my papers would have been by bribing a Palestinian informer working for the Israelis, which I was unwilling to do. To this day, I have only American citizenship, even though I was born in Jerusalem and all of my blood relatives are Palestinian. Many of my siblings have similar stories of losing their residency papers due to arbitrary Israeli measures meant to keep Palestinians out of Palestine/Israel.

Brenda's and my stay in Palestine always hinged on the mercy of officials at the Israeli Ministry of Interior, as it still does to this day. In 1987, just before the start of the first Palestinian uprising (*Intifada*), the Israeli authorities ordered us to leave the country. At the time I was the director of Hope Secondary School, and was therefore summoned to appear at the Israeli military headquarters in Bethlehem, where an Israeli officer named Captain Doron told me that my visa had expired and that my family and I must leave the country within three days. While still trying to absorb the shock and hypocrisy of what was happening, I said, "For the last six months we have been trying very hard to renew our visas and every time you issue us the new visas they are already expired." The Captain raised his voice angrily. "I do not make the laws, I enforce them." In an attempt to appeal to his conscience I asked, "Where are you from?" "From Israel," the Captain said. "But where were you born?" I asked. "In Russia," he said, perhaps not realizing where I was leading him. "Here you are, an immigrant in this country, originally from Russia, ordering me, a native-born of Jerusalem, to leave the land!?" I said. I could hardly finish my sentence before he began shouting and threatening me at the top of his lungs in vulgar language. The more vulgar and loud he became, the more I realized his inability to face the truth of the issue. As I left his office, he threatened that if I did not leave the country in three days, the police would be after me. Now a family of five, we returned to the U.S. where I enrolled for further study at Asbury Theological Seminary. Between 1987 and 1994, we were banned from living in Palestine.

While at Asbury, I began to search for a mission agency that would commission Brenda and me to return to Palestine and serve the Christian community there. We needed a strong international mission board to advocate for us, particularly in acquiring visas to stay lawfully in Israel/ Palestine. We first tried the Southern Baptist Foreign Mission Board. Our applications, however, were refused on the grounds that the policy of the Baptist Foreign Mission Board does not encourage sending missionaries to their native homelands. The BFMB offered to send us to other Arabic-speaking countries but not Palestine. We were quite disheartened as we felt deeply that we were called to serve in Palestine. When I shared this challenge with one of my professors at Asbury Theological Seminary, Dr. Matthias Zahniser, he suggested that I contact the General Board of Global Ministries of the United Methodist Church. Meanwhile the former General Secretary of the World Methodist Council, Dr. Joe Hale, who was attending a board meeting at the seminary, paid my family and me a visit at our campus home. After I shared with him my passion to return to Palestine, he put me in touch with Dr. Sue Robinson, Area Secretary of Europe and the Middle East at the General Board of Global Ministries of the United Methodist Church. When I contacted her, we were mutually surprised to find out that she knew my brother, Mubarak, and the story of his recent deportation from Jerusalem by the Israeli authorities. My contact with Dr. Robinson paved the way for Brenda and I to initiate an application for overseas service with the General Board of Global Ministries. It felt like something of a miracle when in 1989, within six months of our first contact with GBGM, Brenda and I were commissioned as United Methodist missionaries to serve in Palestine. After being commissioned, we knew that the challenge now was to acquire visas to return to Palestine. In spite of the requests from our new sponsors, the mission board, the Israelis refused to issue us the needed visas. They still accused us, baselessly, of being a "threat" to the security of the State of Israel. For the next five years, the General Board of Global Ministries endorsed our cause and advocated on our behalf with Israeli and U.S. officials. Among the groups that worked diligently on our behalf were United Methodist Women chapters throughout the U.S. These groups of women launched a letter-writing campaign that resulted in thousands of letters being signed and sent to Israeli officials requesting our return. Another group, the Methodist Federation for Social Action (MFSA), began another letter writing campaign with the slogan; 'Let the Awads Go!' In 1991, a group from the MFSA organized a demonstration in front of the Israeli embassy in Washington, D.C., to draw attention to our cause. Church leaders from many denominations in the United States and

Top: Bethlehem Bible College
Middle: Bethlehem Bible College Choir
Bottom: East Jerusalem Baptist Church

Top: Huda and 7 children (Clockwise from top left) Nicola, Mubarak, Bishara, Alex, Elizabeth, Diana, Huda, and Ellen (1994)

Center: Huda and 19 grandchildren at granddaughter Hilda's wedding (1992)

Bottom: Huda displaying certificate of American citizenship in Ohio (1-25-1985)

around the world and several members of the U.S. Congress joined the campaign. In Israel, two members of the Israeli Knesset, Yossi Sarid and Dedi Zucker, along with a rabbinical human rights organization called Rabbis for Human Rights, began questioning the Israeli government's decision to refuse us the needed visas. As the campaign peaked, Israeli officials began a counter campaign, aiming at smearing our character by accusing us of violating Israeli laws and threatening the security of the State of Israel. For thousands of people in the United States, our case served as an eye opener to the great injustices that were going on in Israel against the Palestinian people.

In the years after our commissioning, we lived like modern nomads. Our suitcases were ready for the flight to Israel/Palestine but we had to wait for the visas. First, we went to live with Mother who was residing in Wapakoneta, Ohio. In spite of our challenges with the Israeli Ministry of Foreign Affairs, we and our children had a wonderful time enjoying Mother's great hospitality and encouragement. It was a splendid chance for our three children Christy, Basem, and Randy to bond with their grandmother. In Wapakoneta, Mother became active with the United Methodist Church. She enjoyed making beautiful quilts with her friends from the United Methodist Women's group who sold the quilts to raise funds for the church's humanitarian mission in the United States and around the world.

After one year in Wapakoneta, we moved to Syracuse, New York, and the following year to Dallas, Texas where we served with the Methodist Church as Peace with Justice Educators.

While in Syracuse in 1990, I decided to try and spend Christmas in Bethlehem. I knew that my prospects of getting there were very slim. Nevertheless, I wanted to test the ban. I booked my ticket with Lufthansa via Frankfurt to Tel Aviv. I flew out on December 22 with the hope of being in Bethlehem on Christmas Eve. The flight from New York to Frankfurt was eventless. I had arranged to have a free day in Germany so I could spend some time with my sister Diana and her husband Werner, who lived near Munich. Early the next morning, Werner and Diana drove me to the airport. As soon as I showed my passport, armed airport security personnel appeared and took me aside. Then, a high official informed me that the Israelis had banned my travel to Israel. So I returned with Werner and Diana and spent Christmas in Germany. After Christmas I returned to my family in Syracuse.

After the Oslo Accords were signed in September 1993, I decided to attempt another trip to Israel/Palestine. This time, I was not stopped in Europe, but was able to continue all the way to Tel Aviv. When I entered the airport, I was issued a standard three-month tourist visa. I got the impression that the earlier ban, which had kept me and my family out of the country for seven years, had been lifted. In August 1994, our family returned to Palestine to resume our ministries both in Bethlehem and Jerusalem under the sponsorship of the General Board of Global Ministries of the United Methodist Church.

Much of my motivation to return and minister in the land was connected to my mother, who always inspired me through her faith and courage. Mother was so grateful to God for her children. She considered each one of us a gift from God that helped compensate her for much of the pain and toil that she encountered early in her life. We were seven children with all the normal sicknesses, growing pains, discipline problems, common learning skills or disabilities and other challenges. Mother alone had to address all of our ups and downs, headaches, and needs. As children, we thought she was invincible. She was our problem solver, but as we were growing up, we hardly thought of her needs. Each of us seemed to have been born with his or her challenges and limitations. When I was a child, I was sick and in poor health most of the time. My allergies and other sicknesses kept me rotating between boarding school and home. When I went home, Mom had to take off from work to take care of me. As we grew up, our challenges grew up with us, but so also Mom's wisdom to advise and direct us. She was always there, be it a wedding, divorce, death of a spouse, confrontation with authorities, or celebration. Through the good and bad, joys and sorrows, we depended on her to be a bastion of strength, and she was, more often than not, available and ready to help us.

We brothers and sisters, and our children, loved and respected Mother very much. She was the bond that kept the family together in spite of the distances between us and all the troubles we encountered.

While living in the United States, Mother never lost sight of her homeland. She took every opportunity and family occasion as an excuse to purchase a ticket to visit her children and grandchildren who had returned to live in Jerusalem and Bethlehem. She kept hopping between the two continents until her health would no longer allow it.

Mother spent her last years in Overland Park, Kansas, close to Ellen, Elizabeth, and Nicola. These were happy and fulfilling years in her life. But as she approached her 90th year, she became weaker and weaker and completely dependent on others for her physical needs and well- being. During this period, Ellen and the surrounding family were a Godsend to her, providing tremendous love and care. Although Mother was not ambulatory, she still sang her favorite hymns and read the Bible as was her custom throughout her life. Ellen wrote these words about Mother on Valentine's Day 2003:

Huda and Ellen at home in Overland Park, Kansas (December 1999)

Valentine's Day was made for you
You shine on us when things are blue
You showed us how much we can do
To love God before the age of two!
And sing each day in spite of a melody
And live content without plenty
You know what love is all about
You loved in bounty and in drought
This day was made for you.

On March 31st, 2006, Mother passed away. All of the brothers and sisters attended Mother's funeral, except for Diana, who was prevented from coming due to extraordinary obstacles. Although it was a sad occasion and brought tears to many eyes, for the most part, her funeral was a celebration of her life. I was honored to share these thoughts during her funeral.

When I reflect back on my mother's life, I remember her smiling face. Those of you who remember her most likely remember the constant, radiant smile on her face. The fact that my father was killed in 1948 and left her with seven children and the fact that she and her children became poor refugees never wiped away that smile from her face. That smile was a reflection of the confidence that she had as a result of her faith in God. With that faith and with that smile she was able to overcome all of her difficult circumstances and keep smiling.

When I reflect on my mother's life, I remember her hands. Mother was always using her hands to minister to other people. At the various hospitals where she served most of her life, her hands cared for the sick or injured and when she returned from work and before resting, her hands got busy fixing a meal for her children. If she had a spare moment her fingers engaged in spinning colorful wool to create beautiful heart-warming crocheted gifts of quilts, gloves and slippers that brought joy, warmth and comfort to children, grandchildren and friends.

When I reflect on my mother's life, I remember her feet. I don't remember Mother ever wearing high heels. She always wore inexpensive but comfortable flat shoes to help her walk her daily marathons in hospital corridors. In her early years as a mid-wife she never had a car and so she walked back and forth from neighborhood to neighborhood in the streets of Jerusalem and Ramallah delivering babies and caring for mothers.

When I reflect on my mother's life, I remember her eyes. Mother had eyes full of compassion. She loved people. Her home was open not only to her children and grandchildren but also to all their friends and the friends of their friends. She went far beyond the normal Palestinian hospitality to make all people feel welcome.

When I reflect on my mother's life, I remember her faith. In her calamity at the early death of my father, my brothers and sisters never heard her say, "Why God?" She always said, "How God?" She never wanted us to look back and focus on the tragedy. Rather, she advised us to look forward and focus on the opportunities. She never wanted us to harbor hate or a spirit of revenge but she taught us to forgive and to forget. She was always consistent in her attitudes at home, at work or at church. When we were little, Mother taught us to sing hymns of praise to the Lord. She kept singing praises until the last days of her life. When I last visited her, we were not able to have a meaningful conversation but, together, we were able to sing one of her favorite songs of praise.

When I remember my mother, I bow my head and give thanks to God.
—*Alex*

In memory of Huda her children established the Huda Awad Nursing Scholarship Fund. This Fund provides grants for young Palestinian men and women who choose to study nursing in Palestinian Colleges.

*Smiles
of
Huda*

PART TWO

THE STORY OF THE PALESTINIAN PEOPLE

Jerusalem Old City-1900 by Zaki Baboun (2006)

CHAPTER ONE

THE MAKINGS OF A PALESTINIAN CATASTROPHE

There is something unnatural about a people without a territory, just as there is about a man without a shadow.
—Leo Pinsker, a founding father of Zionism

The Jewish villages were built in the place of Arab villages. You do not even know the names of these Arab villages, and I don't blame you because geography books no longer exist, not only do the books not exist, the Arab villages are not there either. Nahlal arose in the place of Mahlul; Kibbbutz Gvat in the place of Jibta; Kibbutz Sarid in the place of Huneifis; and Kefar Yehushu's in the place of Tal al-Shuman. There is not one single place built in this country that did not have a former Arab population.
-Moshe Dayan

Many Westerners view the Arab-Israeli conflict through distorted lenses, and not surprisingly, their understanding of the realities on the ground is influenced by blurred, false or partial information. Notably, numerous Christians in the United States and the West view the Arab-Israeli conflict from a perspective strongly influenced by popular sentiment relating to Biblical Israel and its place in the Promised Land and the way in which all of this relates to the political entity that is modern Israel. Pro-Israel groups such as the American Israel Public Affairs Committee (AIPAC), and the powerful Jewish-American lobby, have also had a significant effect on both Christian and secular perceptions. These organizations influence – not control, but *influence* – many American institutions, including branches of government and the media. In addition, Hollywood has contributed much towards shaping Westerners' distorted perceptions of the Middle East, with many popular films advancing the very worst stereotyped, comic-book portrayals of Arabs, be it the murderous terrorist, the "primitive" nomad, or the depraved oil sheik. The events of September 11, 2001 have also resulted, perhaps understandably, in even greater polarization between the Arab and Western worlds. All these factors, combined with the tragic history of the Jews in Europe over the centuries, culminating in the Holocaust, have molded the lenses through which Westerners usually view the Arab-Israeli conflict. The purpose of this book, then, is to offer an overview of the land, its history and its people, one that might challenge and alter the prevailing assumptions with which the conflict is commonly seen.

CHALLENGING COMMON MISCONCEPTIONS AND MYTHS ABOUT THE ARAB-ISRAELI CONFLICT

One prevalent myth concerning the Arab-Israeli conflict is that Arabs and Jews are eternal enemies. In fact, Arabs and Jews lived side by side in relative harmony for many hundreds of years prior to the birth of the Zionist movement in the late 19th century. Both in historic Palestine and in countries such as Morocco, Egypt, Algeria, Tunisia, Iraq and Yemen, Jews and Arabs co-existed in cultural, political and social harmony for centuries. To generalize that they have been fighting for thousands of years, or since "day one," is simply an inaccurate reading of history.

Some Christians base this assumption of perpetual Jewish-Arab conflict on the biblical story of Abraham's sons, Ishmael and Isaac, who fought when they were children (Gen 21:9–10). In a traditional interpretation, Arabs are cast as Ishmael's descendants, and Jews as those of Isaac. However, the notion that the brothers' squabble spelled permanent war for their descendants, is a stretch. Most siblings fight occasionally, a fact which does not translate into lifelong animosity. Moreover, the Bible relates the account of Ishmael and Isaac uniting to bury their father, leaving readers with the image that they were reconciled as adults (Gen 25:7–10).

Furthermore, the claim that Jews are direct descendants of Isaac and Arabs direct descendants of Ishmael is in itself historically inaccurate. Even if this assertion were valid in ancient times, it does not hold true today, as it assumes, incorrectly, that there is still a pure bloodline traceable from Isaac to present-day Jews and from Ishmael to today's Arabs.

To give an example of how tracing such a pure lineage is impossible, one need only look at the lineage of many Muslim and Christian Palestinians. Many of them no doubt have Jewish ancestors from the time of Christ and earlier, some of whom became Christians after Christ proclaimed his Gospel, and others later, in the 4th century, when the Roman Empire effectively adopted Christianity as the state religion. Then, after Muslim Arabs conquered the Holy Land in the 7th century AD, many of the inhabitants of Palestine converted to Islam, but many also kept their Christian or Jewish faith, which was allowed under Muslim rule. Thus, many Christian and Muslim Arabs in Palestine may well have just as much, if not more "Jewish blood" than the millions of Jews of European descent, who mixed and intermarried for centuries with Gentile Europeans.

In short, the peoples of the Mediterranean and Middle East have intermingled to such a great extent since the time of the Old Testament that it is simply scientifically and historically erroneous to claim that whole nations have continued a four thousand-year-old quarrel between two brothers down through a consistent, unbroken lineage!

Other Christians believe the ancient conflict between the Jews and Philistines has carried over to the present. It is true that throughout the Old Testament the Jews fought with many different tribes, including the Jebusites, the Canaanites, the Ammonites, the Hittites and the Philistines (one of the Caucasian "Sea Peoples" tribes from the Greek Islands). Yes, modern Palestinians are the descendants of the Philistines – but also of Jews, Samaritans, Greeks, Romans, Persians, the Crusaders and many other nations that have invaded Palestine and intermingled with her natives for millennia. So the claim that the ancient Philistines are equivalent to today's Palestinians (or, indeed, that the ancient Israelites are the same people as modern Israeli Jews) is, again, scientifically and historically untenable. The two have little in common aside from the similarity of their names.

None of the people with whom the ancient Israelites engaged in major wars were Arabs. Indeed, the word "Arab" rarely appears in the Bible, and the Muslim Arabs did not conquer Palestine until the 7th century AD. It was only then that the land began to take on the overlay of Arabic language and culture which remains to the present day. And when the Arabs did take over Palestine they did not fight the Jews, because at the time there were few Jews living in Palestine. The Romans had already dispersed many of the Jews, first in AD 70 and later in AD 135, at which time Jerusalem was renamed Ælia Capitolina and Jews were banned from living there, on penalty of death. Thus, when Muslim Arabs invaded Palestine in the 7th century they fought against the Byzantines (Christianized Romans) who by then had been ruling Palestine for three hundred years.

Jews lived in various parts of the Middle East under Islamic sovereignty and were protected, along with Christians, as a "people of the Book." Though Christians and Jews were required to pay a tax, they were by no means threatened or persecuted in their daily lives. The following is just one historical example. When the Muslims recaptured Jerusalem from the Crusaders in 1187 under the command of Saladin, they showed reverence and compassion for the city and all its Christian, Jewish, and Muslim inhabitants. Historian Stanley Lane-Poole said "If the taking of Jerusalem were the only fact known of Saladin, it were enough to prove him the most chivalrous and great-hearted conqueror of his, and perhaps any age."[6]

The land of Palestine remained under various Islamic rulers from the middle of the 7th century until the fall of the Ottoman Turks in 1917, with the exception of the Crusader period. The Crusaders, who hailed from Europe, sporadically ruled parts of the Holy Land from 1099 until their final expulsion in 1291. During their reign, these Christian warriors often controlled their subjects with an iron fist and, especially enroute to the Holy Land and in their initial conquest, carried out callous acts of violence against Jews, Muslims and Eastern Christians alike.

If the Arabs of the Middle East do not have a history of persecuting Jews, the question naturally arises: Where have Jews in fact suffered persecution? One does not have to look back far in history to see that it is Christian

Europe that has a shameful record with regard to its Jewish population. Though they were mistreated throughout Europe, Jews endured the most intense persecution (in different periods) in Spain, Russia, and Germany.

Before 1492, Muslim Moors ruled the southern half of Spain. Under their dominion, approximately one million Jews who lived in Spain experienced what is often referred to as the "Golden Era" of the Jewish Diaspora. Along with highly cultured Muslim and Christian Arabs, Jews flourished in the fields of science, business, medicine, music, art and literature. "The unconverted Christians, or Mozarabes (Arabic, mustarib), enjoyed a high degree of tolerance and, like the Jews, formed prosperous communities in the cities... From the end of the 8th century until about 1200, Muslim Spain – or al-Andalus, as it was called – was the most civilized and materially advanced area of Western Europe."[7] But after Christian Europeans drove the Moors out, Jews no longer experienced the benevolent conditions they had formerly enjoyed and, indeed, the Spanish Inquisition in the Middle Ages came to threaten their very existence. Under the Inquisition no person could profess that he or she was a Jew, and any Jew who did not willingly convert to Christianity was either baptized by force, banished or killed.

Pogroms, which included a number of harsh discriminatory measures against Jews, were periodically instigated in Russia and Eastern Europe, beginning in 1881 and continuing into the early 20th century. In the pogroms, many Jews were killed by hostile Christians in what often amounted to officially-sanctioned riots. Others, who were spared the massacres, were unjustly forced off their properties and had to leave their homes and possessions behind, never to return.

It is a well-known fact that the worst atrocities against Jews took place in Germany and the rest of Nazi-controlled Europe prior to and during World War Two, a regime of persecution and finally mass killing that has come to be known as the Holocaust. Attempting to create a world dominated by a "superior" Aryan race, Hitler and the Nazis devised a plan to systematically eliminate the Jews, as well as other "inferior" races. Jews were targeted specifically during the Holocaust, culminating in the slaughter of some six million of them, at least half in special extermination camps, as well as in the dispossession of the land and property of countless others.

Historically, Jews in the Middle East and North Africa, under Arab-Islamic regimes, always fared much better than their counterparts in Europe. Since Arabs and Jews coexisted in peace for some thirteen centuries, there is no reason on earth – no historical reason, at least – why they should not continue to live as good neighbors in the future.

The question that begs to be asked, therefore, is why have Arabs and Jews engaged in five bloody wars and hundreds of smaller but very lethal confrontations in the last one hundred years? To shed light on the beginnings of the conflict, it is helpful to bear in mind the suffering of Jews in Europe, because there is a strong relationship between their plight and the creation of Israel in 1948. Some European Jews of the late 19th century, among them Moses Hess, Leo Pinsker and Theodor Herzl, came to the conclusion that Jews could never achieve freedom from persecution, let alone achieve respect, living in Europe. At the same time, the new ideology of nationalism was spreading rapidly throughout the continent, and it was becoming the norm for people of particular regional, linguistic, and ethnic groups to desire a sovereign state. Spurred by the persecution of Jews in Europe and influenced by this rise of nationalism on the continent, Herzl and others conceived the Zionist movement, with the goal of establishing a nation-state for all Jews in some part of the world.

In 1896, Herzl published the foundational text of Zionism, *Der Judenstaat* (The Jewish State), in Vienna. He believed that, with the fulfillment of the ideas in his book, "we [Jews] shall at last live as free men on our own soil and die peacefully in our own homeland."[8] However, Herzl was an agnostic, German-speaking Jew, and his knowledge of the great diversity within Judaism was limited. Thus Herzl argued about the Jews: "We are a people – one people." In his mind, this idealized concept of unity overcame all of the very real differences among Jews: linguistic, cultural, and religious. Therefore, although Zionism identified at points with traditional religious Judaism, it was in reality a largely secular ideology embracing the prevalent Western values of the day. Herzl's aspirations were *not* based on the Biblical conception of a promised land, rather his Zionism strove to create a modern political state, one equal to the European states of that time. Indeed, though Herzl would have preferred to form a state in Palestine, he considered the notion of a homeland for the Jews elsewhere: in Uganda, Cyprus, Egypt and Argentina, among other places. For him, the most important aspect of the nation was not its location, but its purpose: to provide a national homeland for world Jewry.[9]

Though already well-know as a writer, after the publication of *Der Judenstaat* Herzl took on a passion and drive that transformed him into a statesman – but one without a state. He became a political salesman of sorts, speaking with any international leader who would listen to him about the idea of the creation of a Jewish nation-state.

Herzl received mixed results from his various audiences. At the time, European Jews living in Western Europe, especially France, Germany, Austria and England, were living fairly prosperous lives. They were comfortably assimilating into their societies. Furthermore, there were a large number of Jews who firmly believed that Judaism was a religion, not a nationality. Many European Jews opposed Zionism because they felt it gave ammunition to anti-Semites who were opposed to the granting of rights to Jews. One Austrian Jewish writer commented on Herzl:

> *What foolishness is this that he has thought up and writes about? Why should we go to Palestine? Our language is German and not Hebrew, and beautiful Austria is our homeland...Why does he, who speaks as a Jew and who wishes to help Judaism, place arguments in the hands of our worst enemies and attempt to separate us, when every day brings us more closely and intimately into the German world?[10]*

Herzl proposed to hold a Zionist Congress to gather all Zionists and establish a plan in order to implement his dream. But the idea of convening a Zionist Congress received broad criticism, especially from German Jewry. A letter issued by the Executive Committee of the Association of German Rabbis voiced the concerns of German Jews on this issue:

> *1) The efforts of so-called Zionists to found a Jewish national state in Palestine contradict the messianic promises of Judaism as contained in the Holy Writ and in later religious sources. 2) Judaism obligates its adherents to serve with all devotion the Fatherland to which they belong, and to further its national interests with all their heart and with their strength... Religion and patriotism both lay upon us the duty of asking all who are concerned with the welfare of Judaism to stay away from the above-mentioned Zionist endeavors and most particularly from the Congress which is still being planned, despite all warnings against it.[11]*

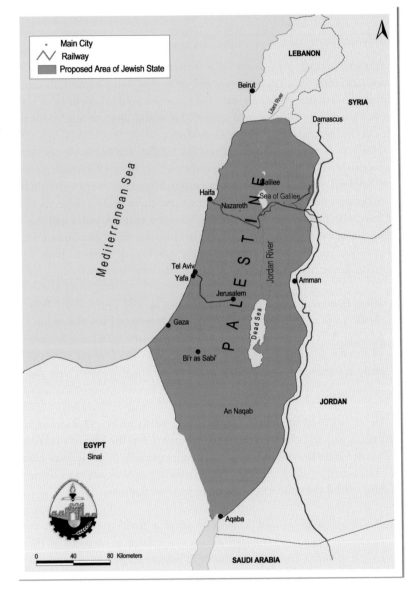

Map 1: Zionist Plan for Palestine – 1919

Despite such criticism, however, Herzl was also garnering significant support for his mission from other quarters. Herzl received much support from Eastern European Jewry, who were then suffering the brunt of anti-Semitism. In addition, many Christians supported Herzl. These Christians, who came to be known as Christian Zionists, dreamed of a return of the Jews to the Land of Israel, in accordance with their interpretation of the Bible. They believed that Biblical prophecies foretold a specific set of events that would culminate in Jesus' return to the Holy Land in the End Times, and one of these prerequisite events was the return of Jews to the Promised Land. Reverend William Hechler, a Christian Zionist who wrote the book *The Restoration of the Jews to Palestine According to the Prophets*, was convinced that Herzl was sent by God "to fulfill prophecy."[12] With the help of their supporters, the Zionists continued to plan the Congress and it eventually convened in August, 1897 in Basel, Switzerland. The First Zionist Congress adopted the following program:

1) The systematic promotion of the settlement of Palestine with Jewish agriculturalists, artisans, and craftsmen. 2) The organization and federation of all Jewry by means of local and general institutions in conformity with local laws. 3) The strengthening of Jewish sentiment and national consciousness. 4) Preparatory steps for the procuring of such government assets as are necessary for achieving the object of Zionism. [13]

Map 1 clearly shows the Zionists' intentions and aspirations for the land. They hoped to create a state throughout Palestine, as well as in the adjacent territories that today form part of Lebanon, Syria and Jordan, as indicated by area shaded in red on the map.

With all of the preparation and plans they had made, the Zionists somehow overlooked one troublesome fact: Palestine was *already* inhabited by other people, namely Christian and Muslim Arabs who were then subjects of the Ottoman Empire.

Palestinians are the descendants of the many cultures and civilizations which, down through history, have inhabited the small piece of land that has been called by several different names, including Canaan, Palestine, Israel and the Holy Land.

When Zionism was being formulated, the predominant language spoken in Palestine was Arabic, and the majority of its inhabitants were Muslim. There was also a sizeable Christian minority consisting of a number of traditional Christian communities, of which the majority were Greek Orthodox. In addition there was also a small minority of Jews, although they were not Zionists. Under the Ottoman Empire the land of Palestine was part of a larger region that included present-day Jordan, Syria, and Lebanon (all of which together were called _Al-Sham_), with Damascus functioning as the administrative capital of the area.

At the beginning of the 20th century, Palestinians, like most people throughout the world, did not possess a nationalistic ideology. Thus, during Ottoman-Turkish rule it was not unusual for the inhabitants of Palestine to possess multiple and divergent loyalties: toward the Ottoman Empire, toward their faith, toward their Arabic language and culture, toward their country (Palestine), their city or region, and their family. All of these loyalties were held simultaneously without seeming to be in conflict to Palestinians, and, taken together, they formed the foundation for Palestinian nationalism which reached a concrete formation between 1917–1923.[14]

The percentage of Jews in Palestine at the time was tiny – no more than 5% – most of whom were deeply religious and actually hostile to Zionism.[15] Herzl and other Zionists, who felt great compassion for the suffering of European Jewry, knew that Palestine was inhabited by Arabs, but they gave scarcely any realistic consideration to this fact, and even less showed any concern for the welfare of the indigenous people. Indeed, some Zionists propagated the now-infamous slogan which promoted Palestine for the Jews as "A land without a people, for a people without a land." Herzl revealed his shrewd intentions for the native population when he wrote in his diary:

Both the expropriation and the removal of the poor must be carried out discreetly and circumspectly... [by] spiriting the penniless population across the border, by procuring employment for it in the transit countries, while denying it any employment in our own country.[16]

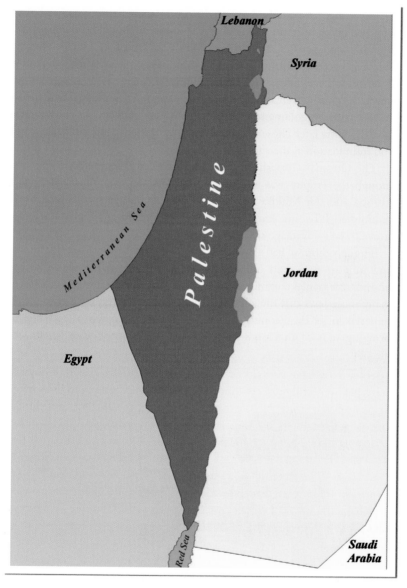

Map 2: Palestine under British Mandate – 1922-May 1948

Herzl died in 1904, and although some Zionist leaders who followed him had different notions of what the Jewish state should be, the prevailing opinions and powers always agreed with the spirit of Herzl's musings: Palestine native population had to be dispossessde in order for the goals of Zionism to be fulfilled. Coexistence with the Arabs based on equality has never, to this day, been attempted nor even seriously considered by Zionists. In fact, far from holding to Herzl's "circumspect" strategy for cleansing the land, Zionists later chose far more extreme tactics, using violence, terror, and intimidation as their tools of dispossession.

The Ottoman-Turkish Empire had controlled Palestine since 1517 and, though the empire was enormous and stretched over much of Eastern Europe and the Middle East, by the 19th century its power was much diminished. It became known as the "sick man of Europe," and the Zionists strove to take advantage of that weakness.

Though Zionism had a rough start, it eventually began to gain legitimacy and support from both the Jewish and international communities. The unthinkable crimes committed against Jews under Nazi Germany convinced many more Jews that the Zionist credo was correct. Intensive efforts were undertaken by the Zionists to change the demographics of Palestine by bringing tens of thousands of Jews into the country, both legally and illegally.

General Allenby dismounted and entered Jerusalem on foot out of respect for the Holy City, December 11, 1917

Zionist ideology was, to say the least, difficult for the native majority Arab Palestinian population to accept. Zionist Jews had completely different goals from Jews who had been previously living on the land. Whereas the established, non-Zionist Jews (who were almost exclusively religious) lived according to the centuries-old tradition of coexistence under Muslim rule, Zionist Jews sought a nation-state that was free and independent of all others. They wanted to take land that had been Arab for centuries, and turn it into their homeland.

From 1908 onwards, a concerted effort on the part of Palestinian Arabs against Zionism was initiated, with Palestinian Christians and Muslims opposing Zionist immigration, land purchases, and Jewish exclusiveness in general. Palestinians voiced their opposition to Zionism in the Ottoman parliament. Palestinian peasants frequently fought being dispossessed of their land and livelihood by Zionist settlers. Jewish land purchases were often made from absentee, even foreign landlords, without notice to the Palestinian tenants. This opposition to the Zionist impact on Palestine was documented in and supported by Palestinian Arabic newspapers such as *al-Karmil* and *Filastin*.[17]

BRITAIN OCCUPIES PALESTINE

The British took over rule of Palestine in 1919 following their victory in the First World War and the collapse of the Ottoman Empire. In 1922, Britain officially received a Mandate for Palestine from the League of Nations. However, even before Britain received the Mandate, many influential Zionists had worked to sway the British public to support their nationalistic aspirations and were highly successful. In their favor, a Christian Zionist theology of dispensationalism, which held that Jews should be restored to the land of Israel, was gaining popularity among public officials in England. This was seen most notably in the form of the Balfour Declaration of 1917 in which the British Foreign Secretary, Sir Arthur Balfour, wrote to Lord Rothschild, a British representative of the Zionist Organization's political committee:

I have much pleasure in conveying to you, on behalf of His Majesty's Government, the following declaration of sympathy with Jewish Zionist aspirations which has been submitted to, and approved by the Cabinet: 'His Majesty's Government view with favor the establishment in Palestine of a national home for the Jewish people, and will use their best endeavours to facilitate the achievement of the object, it being clearly understood that nothing shall be done which may prejudice the civil and religious rights of existing non-Jewish communities in Palestine, or the rights and political status enjoyed by Jews in any other country.'[18]

Balfour had been brought up in a Christian Zionist home and was strongly influenced by dispensationalist theology. He went so far as to have Jews write both the first and final drafts of the declaration.[19] This important declaration, outlining British policy in Palestine for the next twenty years, made no reference to Palestinian Arabs as a people, even though they comprised approximately 90% of the population. Like other Zionists before him, Balfour of course knew that Palestine was already inhabited. He commented in a letter to a colleague:

Zionism, be it right or wrong, good or bad, is rooted in age-long traditions, in present needs, in future hopes, of far profounder import than the desires or prejudices of the 700,000 Arabs who now inhabit that ancient land.[20]

From the outset of the British Mandate, therefore, the Arabs who called Palestine home were neglected and ignored by the ruling power that would decide much of their fate.

You cannot have humane Zionism; it is a contradiction in terms.
—The late Professor Israel Shahak, Hebrew University

Despite Britain's open support of Zionism, many Zionists in Palestine felt hostility toward the Mandatory government, and the British policies on Jewish immigration to Palestine particularly frustrated them. As occupiers, the British had the complex job of trying to pacify both the Arabs and the Jews while simultaneously advancing their own political agenda. British support for the Zionists clearly went against the wishes of the native Arabs, who themselves were developing national aspirations and yearned for the establishment of an independent Arab state in Palestine, free from British control.[21] They felt, rightly, that their demands were being ignored while those of the Jews were being advanced. Angry over the injustices perpetrated by their British occupiers and at seeing their land being overtaken by foreigners, the Palestinians revolted in 1936. This included a general strike by all Arab workers and government employees, a boycott of Jewish goods and sales to Jews, and attacks on Jews and Jewish settlements. This revolt virtually paralyzed Palestine for nearly three years.[22]

THE PEEL COMMISSION PLAN

In the midst of the Arab Revolt, Britain sent a commission of inquiry to Palestine under the supervision of Lord Peel to determine the causes of the rebellion. While the Peel Commission was meeting, the Palestinian leadership of the day decided to halt its six-month general strike. The Commission found the causes of the uprising to be a Palestinian desire for independence and their fear of the establishment of a Jewish national home in Palestine. The Commission's solution was to recommend the division of Mandatory Palestine into three zones, as shown on *Map 3*. Under Peel's plan, it was decided that the yellow zone would be allocated to the Jews for a state, the red zone was granted to the Palestinians, and the green zone was to remain under British Mandate control.

The British bias in favor of the Jews was evident in the recommendations of the plan. In 1937 the Arabs of Palestine (plus various other interests, such as church bodies) owned over 94% of the country, while Jews (native Palestinian Jews and recent immigrants together) owned less than 6% of the land. Of the 1,401,794 people living in Palestine at the time, 395,836 (or about 28%) were Jewish.[23] Almost half of the population in the yellow zone (proposed Jewish state) was Arab. It is important to bear in mind that *all* Palestine – the yellow, red and green areas combined – is approximately the size of the state of Maryland! Thus, a very small territory indeed lies at the heart of the Arab-Israeli conflict. The Peel Commission's suggestion meant that 250,000 Palestinians would be evacuated from the yellow zone to make room for a Jewish state.[24] Naturally, the Palestinians felt it was grossly unfair for the British to take a portion of their country and give it to foreigners. Not surprisingly, therefore, the Palestinian rebellion resumed in full force following the release of the commission's recommendations, for the large number of Palestinians living in the "yellow zone" understandably had no desire to leave their homes.

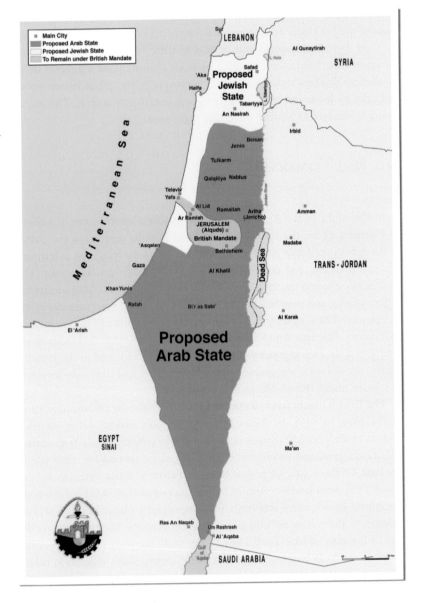

Map 3: Peel Commission Plan – 1937

The Zionist response to the Peel partition plan was mixed. Many did not approve because they believed the land granted to them was insufficient. Others, such as Zionist leaders David Ben-Gurion and Chaim Weizmann, accepted the partition in principle, although their long-term aspirations encompassed larger, unspecified borders. They did not feel that a Jewish state would ultimately be confined to the suggested borders, instead they hoped that once they *had* a sovereign state, territorial expansion would be possible. In a speech to the World Zionist Organization in August 1937, Ben-Gurion announced that although "there could be no question... of giving up any part of the Land of Israel,... it was arguable that the ultimate goal would be achieved most quickly by accepting the Peel proposals."[25]

Palestinians were well aware of the Zionists' tactics, and Palestinian leadership totally opposed the partition plan. Because of opposition to the Peel plan, the partition was never implemented, and subsequent negotiations always failed to bridge the rift. The Arab Revolt then resumed and became much more violent, and British forces were now also targeted. The British responded harshly to the revolt, killing and imprisoning thousands of Palestinian rebels.

THE MACDONALD WHITE PAPER

Attempting to provide a better solution, the British government issued what became known as the MacDonald White Paper in 1939. In a break from British policy since the beginning of the Mandate, the document rescinded the 1937 partition decision, stating that the Balfour Declaration "could not have intended that Palestine should be converted into a Jewish State against the will of the Arab population of the country." Instead, the White Paper declared that Palestine would become independent in 1949 as a unified state in which both Arabs and Jews would share in government. It also set limits on Jewish immigration into the country. The Zionists were outraged. A conference of American and international Zionist groups in New York City issued a statement rejecting it and, for the first time, insisting publicly on an independent Jewish state. Meanwhile, the Zionist leadership ignored the new immigration limits and encouraged illegal immigration to Palestine, to the extent that illegal immigrants accounted for approximately forty percent of immigration in 1939.[26] Palestinians, on the other hand, rejected the White Paper because it failed to end Jewish immigration or grant the Arabs immediate political independence.

By the beginning of the Second World War, while the Arab rebellion against the British Mandate had been suppressed, the Zionists, sensing that Western support for their plans was weakening, had developed their own methods of resistance to the British colonialists. Some efforts focused on increasing illegal immigration to Palestine, while other more extreme factions began a campaign of assassinations, bombings and terrorism.[27] The *Brihah* ("escape") organization illegally moved more than 150,000 Jews past British patrols into Palestine from 1945–1948.[28] At the same time, the Irgun, a militant Zionist group led by Menachem Begin, the future prime minister of Israel, began to attack British administrative buildings and police personnel and bomb Palestinian gathering places. Indeed, it was the Irgun that engineered the infamous 1946 bombing of the King David Hotel in Jerusalem, part of which housed British military headquarters, an attack which left 91 dead. Later, an underground extremist Jewish organization called LEHI (Fighters for the Freedom of Israel), whose leaders included another future Israeli prime minister, Yitzhak Shamir, waged a campaign of assassination against British officials.[29]

This tri-party conflict between Palestinian Arabs, Jews, and the British continued until 1947, when the British acknowledged their failure in trying to rule the area. Feeling the need to concentrate their energies and resources on rebuilding post-war Britain, they washed their hands of the entire Palestine problem and turned it over to the United Nations.

THE UNITED NATIONS PARTITION PLAN

In 1947, the newly established United Nations debated what should be done about Palestine. The central question was whether to propose a single country for both Arabs and Jews or attempt once again to partition the land into two states. In the end, on November 29, 1947, the UN voted 33 to 13, with 10 abstentions, in favor of a newly-conceived division of the country. The UN partition plan was based on a Zionist one which the American President Harry Truman had endorsed in August 1946. The partition

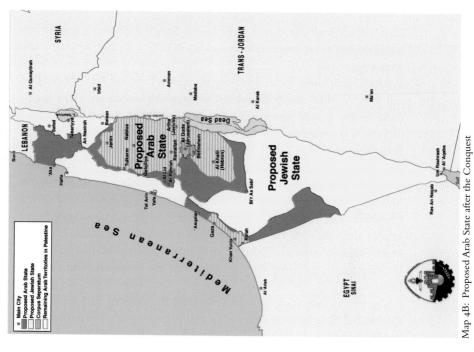

Map 4B: Proposed Arab State after the Conquest

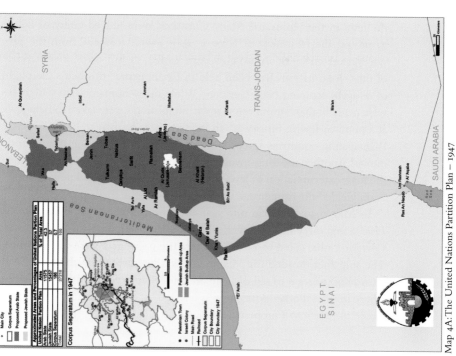

Map 4A: The United Nations Partition Plan – 1947

included a Palestinian state, a (now larger) Jewish state, and a smaller area which would be an internationally-governed zone including Jerusalem (*See Map 4A*).

Once again, there were objections from both Jews and Arabs. Some Jews still felt they had not been offered enough. Most, however, particularly those in the Jewish Agency (a group led by David Ben-Gurion whose purpose was to facilitate the immigration of Jews from around the world to Palestine) decided to accept the partition. At the time, Palestinians owned approximately 87.5% of Palestine, while Jews owned 6.6 % of the total land mass. The remaining 5.9% was "state land" as classified under the British Mandate.[30] The Palestinians, who still accounted for approximately 65% of the population, could not comprehend why the Jewish population, some 35% of the total, was being granted 54% of historic Palestine. Losing so much of their country to foreigners was unacceptable, and not surprisingly, the Palestinian leadership did not agree with the proposed division of the land.

One need only look at world events at the time to understand why the United Nations proposed such a generous division of Palestine to the Jews in 1947. Following the end of the Second World War, much of the Western world felt directly or indirectly responsible for what happened to the Jews in the Holocaust. Many Christians were indeed guilty of failing to protest the treatment of Jews or assist Jewish refugees, from the pre-war period onwards. Almost 10 years earlier, in July 1938, a conference of thirty-two nations had been held in Evian, France to discuss the plight of refugees escaping Nazi Germany. While many humanitarian statements were made in that famous resort town, no measures were taken to help Jews, at a point in Jewish history when millions were known to be endangered. Participating countries agreed only to uphold their existing immigration quotas! Another meeting involving Britain and the U.S. in 1943 — when the mass extermination of Jews was well underway *and* was known about — again yielded no assistance.

In May 1939, less than one year after the conference in Evian, the *St. Louis*, a ship carrying 937 Jews fleeing Germany with supposedly valid entry visas for Cuba, sailed to Havana, where the passengers were refused entry. The ship then headed for Miami, but was intercepted by the U.S. Coast Guard and warned to sail on. The *St. Louis* attempted to put its passengers ashore in several other ports but was rejected each time. Finally the ship was forced to return to Europe where most of the passengers were given refuge in places such as Holland, Belgium and England. Eventually, when most of Western Europe fell under Nazi occupation only a year later, most of the refugees perished in the Holocaust. The *St. Louis* affair was later exposed as a cynical Nazi propaganda ploy, but their point was made: Nobody else, it seemed, wanted the Jews either.

In an anti-Communist and isolationist era, many of the world's immigration laws were xenophobic. Restrictive immigration and unequal quotas had been in place in the U.S. since 1917 to limit the number of immigrants entering America. In 1917 Congress passed the first phase of what, in its final stages, became known as the National Origins Quota Act of 1924 (the Johnson-Reed Act). The basic provision of this federal law limited the number of immigrants who could be admitted annually from any given country to 2% of the number of people native to that country who were already living in the United States in 1890 (according to the 1890 Census); certain nationalities, however, were barred altogether. These quotas, which continued essentially unchanged until the 1960s, were particularly unfavorable toward southern and eastern Europeans.

In the wake of the Second World War, some members of the United Nations – Russia, France, England and the U.S. – wanted, rightly, to somehow compensate the Jews for their horrific suffering, even if only symbolically. However, in line with their isolationist tendencies, they wished to solve the Jewish problem without absorbing masses of Jewish refugee immigrants into their own countries.[31]

Unfortunately for the Palestinians, neither Germany, the U.S., nor any other nation welcomed the Jews. Rather, the Western powers took it upon themselves to divide Palestine and give a large portion of it to the Jews. If, instead of choosing the land of Palestine, the Zionists had decided to create an independent homeland in, say, Maryland, against the will of its residents, how would the American people have reacted? In the same way, one might ask: Was it right and just that the burden of solving the problem of the European Jewish Diaspora fell primarily on the shoulders of the Palestinian people, a people who were responsible neither for the historic suffering of Jews in Europe, which had given rise to Zionism, nor for the horrendous tragedy of the Holocaust?

By imposing the solution of partition, the Western powers, as the founders and most influential members of the UN, allowed for and legitimized the creation of the modern State of Israel. In effect, they attempted to solve the Jewish problem at the expense of the native inhabitants of Palestine and, in the process, they helped create a crisis that has threatened world peace for over half a century.

Artist's depiction of refugee family of 1948.
Tahani Skeik, Waiting for Peace, oil on Canvas, 1993

CHAPTER TWO

THE ARAB-ISRAELI WARS AND THE REFUGEE CRISIS

It would be an offense against the principles of elemental justice if these innocent victims of the conflict were denied the right to return to their homes, while Jewish immigrants flow into Palestine, and, indeed, at least offer the threat of permanent replacement of the Arab refugees who have been rooted in the land for centuries.
– Count Folke Bernadotte, in a report to the UN

We must expel Arabs and take their places.
- David Ben Gurion, 1937

We must use terror, assassination, intimidation, land confiscation, and the cutting of all social services to rid the Galilee of its Arab population.
- David Ben-Gurion, May 1948

Despite the fact that the Palestinian people and the Arab nations did not accept the UN's partition, the Zionists quickly embarked upon a plan not only to enforce their share of the partitioned land, but also to expand it.[32] Thus the Haganah, the pre-state Zionist army, launched offensives to capture, occupy, and destroy Palestinian villages that lay in the Tel Aviv–Jerusalem corridor, most of which had not been assigned to the Jewish state at all. Zionist forces also forcefully evicted Palestinians who lived in other areas within what is shown on *Map 4A* as the yellow zone. It may be concluded – and the evidence for this, drawn from declassified Israeli archives, is overwhelming – that to a large extent the ethnic cleansing of the areas under Zionist control was *not* incidental, but instead resulted from a clear strategy reflecting Zionist desires for a Jewish state with an overwhelming Jewish majority.

THE WAR OF 1948

One of the actions marking the beginning of the ethnic cleansing of Palestine occurred at Deir Yassin, a village on the western outskirts of Jerusalem, on April 9, 1948. This incident occurred before the outbreak of the broader war prompted by the invasion by the neighboring Arab countries in May. On that day, members of the Irgun and LEHI (sometimes called the Stern Gang), a more extreme branch of the former group, entered the village and proceeded to massacre its inhabitants. According to the best estimates, at least 100 Palestinian civilians were killed that day, though the wild rumors and panic the attack generated have always made the death toll hard to pin down. After raiding the village, the Zionist forces rounded up some of the survivors and paraded them through Jewish areas of Jerusalem, before taking them to a quarry and shooting them to death.[33]

A Survivor's Memory Of Deir Yassin

A survivor who was 12 years old during the massacre recounted that she was hiding with her family, when the door was blasted open and they were taken outside in time to witness a man being shot:

> "When one of his daughters screamed, they shot her too. They then
> called my brother Mahmoud and shot him in our presence, and when
> my mother screamed and bent over my brother (she was carrying
> my little sister Khadra who was still being breastfed), they shot my
> mother too."

News of Deir Yassin spread throughout the Arab world, implanting
terror in the hearts of hundreds of thousands of Palestinians and causing
the Arab states to consider intervention in the conflict. Thereafter many
other Palestinian areas, towns, and villages were overrun by Zionist forces
in attacks that were often brutal and involved psychological warfare. For
example, Zionist units went through Arab areas warning that they would
suffer the fate of Deir Yassin if they did not flee. The brute violence that the
Zionist forces used emanated from their belief that without the expulsion
of the Palestinians from their land, Zionist goals would be untenable. As
hundreds of thousands of Palestinians fled to safer areas of Palestine and
to neighboring Arab states, the Arab states ordered their armies into battle
with the emergent state of Israel. Thus began the Arab-Israeli War of 1948.

> *A Soldier Relates Israeli Scare Tactics*
>
> "As uncontrolled panic spread through all Arab quarters, the Israelis
> brought up jeeps with loudspeakers which broadcast recorded 'horror
> sounds.' These included shrieks, wails and anguished moans of Arab
> women, the wail of sirens and the clang of fire alarm bells, interrupted
> by a sepulchral voice calling out in Arabic: 'Save your souls all ye
> faithful: the Jews are using poison gas and atomic weapons. Run for
> your lives in the name of Allah.'"
> —Israeli Army reserve officer who fought in 1948
> *Published in Marine Corps Gazette, June 1964*

The War of 1948 is typically heralded as a miraculous, David-versus-
Goliath victory for Israel. As the legend goes, the weak, recently established
state of Israel immediately faced the prospect of annihilation by its Arab

neighbors, but by a seeming act of providence, the Israeli forces defeated their enemies and secured their independent state. However the historical facts, which have been documented by modern Israeli historians, prove this story to be false. During the British Mandate, Jews were not only permitted to form governing bodies under the Jewish Agency, they were also allowed to possess arms and were trained to use them in militias and police units organized by the British to quell the Palestinian uprising. Additionally, they were allowed to import the equipment necessary to form their own weapons industry.

116

The
Arab-Israeli
Wars and
the Refugee
Crisis

The political and military organization of the Jews allowed them to prepare effectively for the war to come. Meanwhile, Palestinian Arabs had no such decision-making privileges. nor were they permitted to have weapons. Furthermore, they had been thoroughly crushed during their 1936–39 revolt against the British Mandate. Thousands of Palestinians had been killed and injured during the revolt, a fact that heavily impeded their ability to defend themselves against the Zionists. The surrounding Arab countries were reluctant to enter into war, hoping instead for Western intervention. In the end, however, Jordan, Egypt and several other Arab countries went to war against Israel. But their efforts were too little, too late. The armies of these neighboring Arab countries were inferior and their leaders had little strength after being handicapped by colonial rule. They were unorganized and did not work together. One surprising but little-known fact is that King Abdullah of Jordan, who controlled the most powerful Arab army, colluded with the Zionists because he dreamed of annexing to his kingdom the land allocated under partition to an Arab-Palestinian state.[34]

Examining the comparative military capabilities of both sides, then, it is no surprise that Israel was victorious. By the time the war ended, the State of Israel had managed to conquer even more Arab land than was allocated to it in the Partition plan, again altering the map of Palestine; plus they had succeeded in ethnically cleansing most of the area under their control.

Several attempts were made by Arab countries during the war to establish a ceasefire and reassess the partition plan. As Israeli scholar Simha Flapan puts it, "The Arabs were strongly inclined to acquiesce to the existence of a Jewish state", as witnessed by "proposals for compromise tendered at secret meetings"[35]. But the Zionists stalled and impeded such efforts for as long as possible, at times resorting to extreme measures. On September 17, 1948, Swedish diplomat Count Folke Bernadotte, the chief UN representative in the country, was gunned down in Jerusalem in a carefully planned assassination by Jewish-Zionist terrorists. Why? Because the previous day Bernadotte had released an alternative to the UN partition plan that he thought might bring about peace. The Zionists, howerver, were not happy with Bernadotte's assessment, and so the extremist LEHI group intervened and took the diplomat's life in order to halt the plan. A day before his assassination Bernadotte wrote:

> *The right of the Arab refugees to return to their homes in Jewish-controlled territory at the earliest possible date should be affirmed by the United Nations, and their repatriation, resettlement and economic and social rehabilitation, and payment of adequate compensation for the property of those not choosing to return, should be supervised and assisted by the United Nations conciliation commission...'[36]*

THE 1949 ARMISTICE

The results of the 1949 armistice show the extent of the Zionists' victory. Everything in yellow (*Map 4B and Map5*) became the State of Israel. This area constituted 78% of Mandatory Palestine, 22% more of Palestine than had been allocated by the UN. Put another way, it was some 40% more land than had been assigned to a Jewish state. The remaining 22% was taken by Jordan and Egypt. Jordan took over the portion of land that is called the West Bank today, so named because of its position on the west bank of the Jordan River. The Egyptians retained a small strip of land on the Mediterranean coast known as the Gaza Strip. Additionally, Jerusalem was divided: East Jerusalem continued to be an Arab city under Jordanian control, while West Jerusalem became an Israeli city and their self-declared capital. Nothing, however, remained for the Palestinians.

THE AFTERMATH OF THE FIRST ARAB-ISRAELI WAR

The underlying human tragedy of 1948 can best be understood from *Map 6*. 418 Palestinian towns and villages that were destroyed or depopulated. and were either flattened by Israeli bulldozers or cleared of residents to

118

*The
Arab-Israeli
Wars and
the Refugee
Crisis*

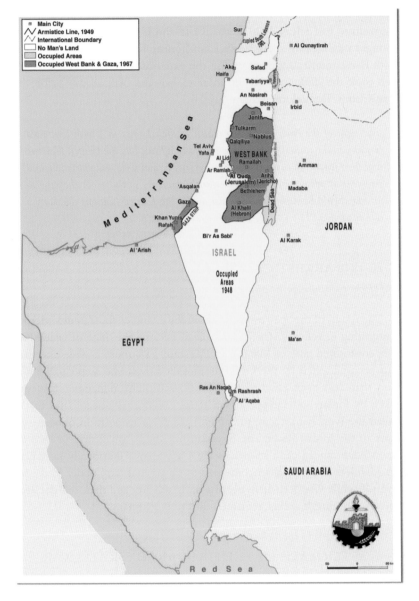

Map 5: Wars and Border changes

provide homes and farms for Jews. The myth that Palestinians left largely at the instigation of their own leaders has been thoroughly disproved by Israeli historians such as Ilan Pappe and Benny Morris.[37]

THE CATASTROPHE (AL-NAKBA)

Eighty percent of the Palestinians living in the yellow zone (*Map 5*) fled out of fear or were forcibly evicted by the Zionists. Most of those who were not pushed out lived on the periphery of the Zionist military action, particularly in the Galilee, and thus managed to stay put, primarily because a cease-fire was signed before they could be evicted. It was essential, however, for the Zionists to prohibit those who left from returning to their homes, despite international pressure and UN resolutions, and despite Israel's own promises, made in return for recognition by and membership in the United Nations.

UN Resolution 194

"Refugees wishing to return to their homes and live at peace with their neighbors should be permitted to do so at the earliest practicable date, and those wishing not to return should be compensated for their property."

The 750,000 Palestinians who fled lost all their land and possessions in 1948 and became refugees. Just as Jews in Europe were driven from their homes due to pogroms, Palestinians were forced to leave their homes and land because of Zionist ethnic cleansing. In what may be termed a Middle Eastern "trail of tears," refugees from all over the yellow zone trekked to Lebanon, Jordan, Syria, and other surrounding states. Their journey was terrible. Most of them went on foot, and many of those who were weak or ailing were lost as they traversed harsh wilderness areas trying to reach safety.

Although some Palestinians realized they would not return to their homes, many held onto the hope that they were only going away for days or weeks at most, until the turmoil in the land had settled. Thus, they left with the expectation of returning, taking only the clothes on their backs and carrying the house keys in their pockets. Unfortunately, return became impossible when the Israelis took control of the country and closed and fortified the borders.[38] No Palestinian, man, woman or child was allowed to return, and those caught trying were shot as infiltrators. Hence, the majority of Palestinians who left their country ended up in refugee camps, yet they always nurtured the dream of returning to their homes.

120

The
Arab-Israeli
Wars and
the Refugee
Crisis

The 'Dirty Work' of Zionism

"I don't mind if, after the job is done, you put me in front of a Nuremberg Trial and then jail me for life. Hang me if you want, as a war criminal. What you don't understand is that the dirty work of Zionism is not finished yet, far from it."

—Ariel Sharon
to the editor of Davar, December 17, 1982

The banishment of the Palestinians, referred to as *Al-Nakba* (Arabic for 'the catastrophe'), created a highly volatile situation, demographically and politically, both in Palestine and in the rest of the Arab world. Is it possible for a nation to forcibly evacuate three-quarters of a million people from their homes and still believe that living in peace and security is tenable? The simple but perhaps uncomfortable truth is that this profound tragedy, *Al-Nakba*, underlies much of the tension between the Arabs and the Jews over the last sixty years.

THE CHRISTIAN ZIONIST REACTION

While Zionist forces committed atrocities against Christian and Muslim Palestinians, Christian Zionists tacitly supported such ethnic cleansing. Dr. M. R. DeHaan, a well-known Christian Zionist who for years broadcast his Biblical interpretations on over 600 radio stations worldwide, described the failure of the British to set aside all of Palestine for the Jews as "the greatest mistake in all history." He called the creation of the state of Israel "the greatest piece of prophetic news that we have had in the 20th century."[39]

WHAT HAS HAPPENED TO THE PALESTINIAN REFUGEES?

Palestinian Refugees: Where Are They?

Table 1: Distribution of Palestinian Refugees, as of June 2000

	Jordan	West Bank	Gaza	Lebanon	Syria	Total
UN Registered Refugees	1,570,192	583,009	824,622	376,472	383,199	3,737,494
%	42	16	22	10	10	100
Camp Population	280,191	157,676	451,186	210,715	111,712	1,211,480
%	23	13	37	18	9	100

Source: United Nations Relief and Works Agency (UNRWA)

Today, after almost sixty years, refugee camps are still scattered throughout the West Bank, the Gaza Strip, Jordan, Lebanon and Syria. Approximately 1.2 million Palestinians live in these camps. In addition, over four million other Palestinian refugees do not live in the camps but are scattered throughout the countries of the Middle East and the rest of the world.[40] The plight of these millions of Palestinian refugees (the original refugees, plus their descendants) has yet to be resolved. They have never been compensated, and it is unlikely that they will be reunited with their homeland in the foreseeable future. The refusal of Israel to allow Palestinian refugees the right to return to their homes is one of the most difficult issues in any future Arab-Israeli peace negotiations. It also demonstrates the clear double standard Israel maintains regarding Jewish versus Arab-

122

The
Arab-Israeli
Wars and
the Refugee
Crisis

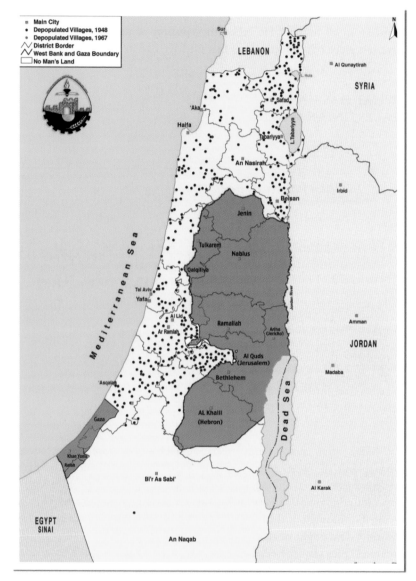

Map 6: Destroyed and Depopulated Palestinian Towns and Villages, 1948

Refugees of the 1948 Arab-Israeli War. UNRWA

Palestinian rights. While any Jew anywhere in the world can immigrate to Israel (known in Israel as 'making *aliya*') and is granted automatic Israeli citizenship, Palestinians who were born in the country do not have the option of returning to their homeland.

124

The
Arab-Israeli
Wars and
the Refugee
Crisis

The United Nations has passed many resolutions with overwhelming majorities, suported in the early years by the United States, stating that the Palestinians have a right to return to their homeland. The United States, however, has repeatedly used its veto power in the UN Security Council to block the implementation of any resolution that requires significant concessions by Israel, including the return of the refugees. In March 1976, June 1976, and April 1980, the U.S. was the *sole* vetoing country of UN Security Council resolutions specifically calling on the return and/or compensation of Palestinian refugees (see Appendix III for a full summary of these vetoed resolutions). So the Palestinians have had to remain where they are, and over fifty years of American policy in the Middle East has in effect prolonged the conflict. Thus, the policies of the U.S. and other Western governments have long been a fundamental part of the problems in the region.

A Nobel Laureate on the Plight of Refugees

"The tragedy of the people of Palestine is that their country was 'given' by a foreign power to another people for the creation of a new state. The result was that many hundreds of thousands of innocent people were made permanently homeless. With every new conflict their numbers increased. How much longer is the world willing to endure this spectacle of wanton cruelty? It is abundantly clear that the refugees have every right to the homeland from which they were driven, and the denial of this right is at the heart of the continuing conflict. No people anywhere in the world would accept being expelled en masse from their country; how can anyone require the people of Palestine to accept a punishment that nobody else would tolerate? A permanent, just settlement of the refugees in their homeland is an essential ingredient of any genuine settlement in the Middle East."
—Bertrand Russell
Philosopher and Nobel Laureate in Literature

The fact that many refugees live in miserable conditions in refugee camps remains a pressing issue (*see Table 1, p121*). The existence of refugees in Arab countries has been a source of conflict, not only within those host countries but also between Israel and the Arab world. In the Arab countries in which they found themselves, Palestinian refugees tried to enlist the help of their new governments toward the goal of returning to their land. At the same time, they also often carried out cross-border raids on Israel from the neighboring Arab states. Thus, the Arab nations have always had difficulty striking a balance between, on the one hand, supporting their Palestinian brethren, and on the other, diffusing the tensions this support caused, both with Israel and within their own autocratic states. Such friction, indeed, has been a contributing factor to almost every Arab-Israeli war.

THE SIX-DAY WAR

Apart from the War of 1948, no other event shaped the fate of the Palestinian people or framed the current conflict more than the War of 1967, also referred to as the Six-Day War. Israelis and Arabs point accusing fingers at each other as to who started this war. Israelis point to unilateral actions taken by Egypt, such as ordering United Nations peacekeeping forces to leave the Sinai and putting in their place Egyptian tanks and troops. Egypt also closed the Straits of Tiran and blockaded the Israeli port of Eilat at the northern end of the Gulf of Aqaba. Israelis further claim that their requests for peace were left unanswered, creating a feeling of grave concern for the future of their state. They argue that the closing of the Straits in itself met the international criteria for an act of war.

Arabs point out that their leaders tried every avenue to avoid a war but all their efforts through the UN and the U.S. administration failed. Although the Israelis officially blame the Arabs for starting the war, several Israeli leaders have acknowledged that in spite of their threats, Arab leaders had no intention of engaging in a war.

While popular wisdom claims that the pre-emptive strike by the Israelis was made because Egyptian President Nasser was ordering military movements that suggested he intended to destroy Israel, the fact is that Israel was not forced to lash out at Egypt and could have avoided war

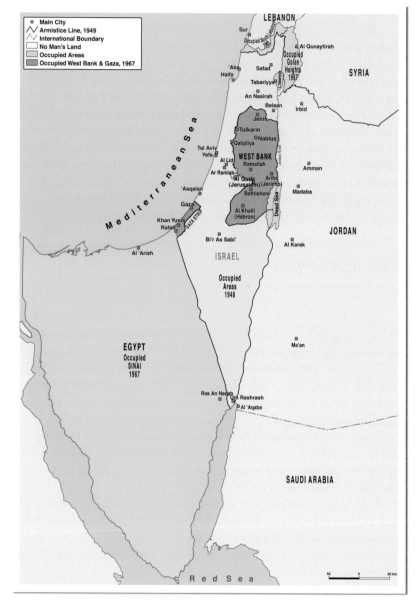

Map 7: Wars and Border Changes

altogether. This is revealed by the statements of three key Israeli generals and politicians. Ezer Weizmann, who was commander of the air force and responsible for much of the operational planning for the war, said in 1972 that there was no "threat of destruction" in 1967. Yitzhak Rabin, the Chief of Staff in the Israeli Defense Forces in 1967, echoed these sentiments when he stated, "I do not believe that Nasser wanted war. The two divisions he sent into Sinai on May 14 would not have been enough to unleash an offensive against Israel. He knew it and we knew it." And Menachem Begin, then a government minister, stated at the National Defense College, 8 August 1982:"The Egyptian army concentrations in the Sinai approaches do not prove that Nasser was really about to attack us. We must be honest with ourselves. We decided to attack him."[41]

Despite the military actions on both sides, it is difficult to dispute that a key factor igniting the 1967 Arab-Israeli war was the tension that had been created in the region by the 1948 war. The underlying injustice committed against the Palestinians had never been adequately addressed by Israel or the rest of the world, creating a situation ripe for violence.

Zionism's Expansionist Agenda

"After we become a strong force as the result of the creation of the state, we shall abolish partition and expand to the whole of Palestine."
—David Ben-Gurion

As a result of this war, all of historic Palestine and its Palestinian inhabitants came under Israeli control, in an occupation which continues to the present day (Map 7). Israel took the Golan Heights from Syria, the West Bank and East Jerusalem from Jordan, and the Gaza Strip and the entire Sinai Peninsula from Egypt. The result, predictably, was many more refugees, making a big problem even bigger. Israel initially claimed it was only holding these areas temporarily that "came into its control in a war it did not want," yet it immediately started to take over and use this property as its own. First, it formally annexed East Jerusalem, and then started planting exclusively Jewish settlements in the Occupied Territories.

128

The
Arab-Israeli
Wars and
the Refugee
Crisis

In annexing East Jerusalem, Israel once again defied the UN partition Resolution 181 of November 1947, which held that all of Jerusalem should be under international control. The war also left Israel in control of all sources of water extending from the Jordan River to the Mediterranean Sea. In the years that followed, Zionism was revealed to be an expansionist ideology (if there was any doubt), as Israelis systematically colonized the Gaza Strip and West Bank, including East Jerusalem. Every month Palestinians saw, and to this day continue to see, more and more of their land in the West Bank and Gaza Strip confiscated by the Israeli military and settlers.

Under the rule of a military regime, the reality of daily life for the Palestinians of the West Bank and Gaza Strip was and continues to be poverty, humiliation, detention without fair trial, torture, curfews, and violent suppression of dissent.

THE YOM KIPPUR WAR AND CAMP DAVID

Some Israeli leaders were always well aware of the implications of their actions against the Palestinian and Arab peoples. Some time after the War of 1967, Moshe Dayan, then Minister of Defense, made a statement that seemed to reflect the skepticism among many Israelis about the likelihood of success in negotiating a peace settlement with the Arab world. He said: "It is not true that the Arabs detest the Jews for personal, religious, or racial reasons. They consider us, reasonably from their point of view, as Westerners, foreigners, invaders who have seized an Arab country to make a Jewish state… [S]eeing that we are forced to realize our objectives expressly against the will of the Arab people, we have to live in a state of permanent war."[42] Dayan's statement was prophetic. Syria and Egypt in particular wanted to reclaim the properties lost in 1967 and started the Yom Kippur War specifically to regain these lands.

On October 6, 1973, on the Jewish holy day of Yom Kippur and during the Muslim month-long fast of Ramadan, Egypt and Syria resumed hostilities in a surprise attack against Israel. In the beginning, the Arabs pressed their advantage, and Syria re-captured part of the Golan Heights, while Egypt was able to regain some of the Sinai Peninsula. But the United States, under the leadership of President Nixon, sided with Israel and provided it with aid and weapons.

The massive American airlift of equipment to Israel during the 1973 war was the largest in history until the even larger 1990 Persian Gulf buildup. By the end of the war, Israel had recaptured the Golan Heights and most of the Sinai Peninsula. Nevertheless, the impact of the airlift on the fighting itself was minimal. Very little of the heavy equipment actually reached the battlefield before the shooting stopped on October 24. One Pentagon official said: "Israel didn't need the airlift of arms – it was a psychological and morale booster." Israel had no need of an emergency shipment of weapons because, as in the past, the country's military was well-equipped and well-funded due to longstanding policies of massive arms trading, a strong military-industrial complex, and support from abroad.[43]

U.S. President Jimmy Carter facilitated the meeting of Israeli Prime Minister Menachem Begin and Egyptian President Anwar Sadat at Camp David in 1979, where they signed the first ever Arab-Israeli peace accord. Under this agreement, all of the Sinai Peninsula was returned to Egypt and, in turn, Egypt became the first Arab nation to recognize Israel as a legitimate state in the Middle East. There was no peace accord forged between Israel and Syria, however. Syria at this time was suspicious of Sadat's eagerness to form a separate agreement with Israel, and Syrian President Hafez al-Assad did not want to negotiate with Israel unless the Arab nations formed a united front. In addition, Begin's defense minister, Ariel Sharon, wanted to drive Syria out of Lebanon, where their troops had been stationed since 1976.[44]

LEBANON: A NO-WIN WAR

For the next decade and a half, Israel was forced to defend its northern border with Lebanon. Palestinians in southern Lebanon kept up their struggle to infiltrate Israel by attacking settlers in northern Israel. Palestinians in Lebanon were living in deplorable conditions in refugee camps. These refugees were not assimilated into the general Lebanese population, as the predominantly Christian-led government feared a tilt in the balance of political power if it incorporated vast numbers of Muslim refugees as citizens. Because the United Nations could not enforce resolutions to have the refugees repatriated to Israel, the refugees have remained stuck in these camps (as well as camps in other Arab countries) in intolerable conditions since 1948. Moreover, the PLO, which had been expelled from Jordan, used this situation in Lebanon to continue its fight against Israel from there.

In 1982, Israel launched an enormous military offensive into Lebanon, the purpose being, in part, to destroy the PLO. But Israel also had larger plans. It had long been a dream of many Israeli leaders to install a Christian-dominated government in Lebanon, one that would be more compliant to Israeli wishes. Ariel Sharon, who commanded the assault, and others in the Israeli government, intended to eradicate the Palestinian Liberation Organization, then headquartered in Beirut, and oust its leader, Yasser Arafat.

During the invasion and occupation of Lebanon, Israel unleashed a barrage of unrestrained military force against the Lebanese, causing the death of thousands of innocent civilians. Israel invaded northward all the way to Beirut, leaving a trail of destruction marked by the shelling and bombing of civilian areas.

On September 14, 1982, Lebanese President Bashir Gemayel, the centerpiece of Israeli political control over Lebanon, was assassinated. With their hopes for an Israel-friendly regime thus dashed, the Israelis decided to complete the job of obliterating the Palestinian Liberation Organization from Lebanon themselves. Two days later, the Israeli army general staff issued Order Number 6 to Israeli soldiers in Beirut, which declared that "Searching and mopping up the camps [Sabra and Shatilla] will be done by the Phalangists and the Lebanese army." The Israeli-backed Christian Phalangists were already eager to avenge the killing of their leader Gemayel when then-Defense Minister Ariel Sharon met with the Phalangist leadership and granted them the perfect opportunity to exact their revenge.

From September 16 to 18 the Phalangist militia combed the refugee camps, brutally killing all who came across their path. Throughout the massacre, Israeli troops surrounded the camps, turning back any refugees who tried to escape. From their positions, the Israeli troops could observe the slaughter going on inside the camps, but they did nothing to stop it. Indeed, Israeli soldiers even lit the camps with flares at night, in order for the Phalangists to continue their killing spree. It is estimated that the Phalangists killed between 800 and 2,000 people in Sabra and Shatilla.

Shortly after the war in Lebanon, an Israeli investigation of the massacre, the Kahan Commission, found that Ariel Sharon bore "personal responsibility," eventually forcing him to step down as Defense Minister. Though significant, the Kahan Commission both exonerated the Israeli army and its commanders from direct responsibility for the massacre and

130

The
Arab-Israeli
Wars and
the Refugee
Crisis

also failed to investigate the political motives that lay behind the atrocity. Ariel Sharon himself was soon installed as Minister of Industry and Trade in the next Israeli government, and less than twenty years after the Kahan Commission, Sharon – who was indicted for war crimes and held accountable – became the Prime Minister of Israel.[45]

Despite all Israel's efforts, its plans in Lebanon backfired. Lebanon's puppet Christian government fell, Syria's hold on the country grew much stronger, and the war destabilized Lebanon for many years to come. Israel continued to occupy southern Lebanon for eighteen years, stationing a large military force there. At the same time, under the leadership of Hezbollah, a Lebanese national Islamic organization, the Lebanese in turn tried to push the Israeli army out of southern Lebanon and regain their homeland by force. Throughout this period, Israel was never free from conflict at the Israeli–Lebanese border, and both sides suffered losses, though Lebanese Palestinians, by comparison, suffered ten-fold. The Israelis and the Lebanese fought in this area until May 24, 2000 when Israeli troops, under the leadership of Prime Minister Ehud Barak, pulled out of Lebanon. Another war took place between Lebanon (mainly Hezbollah) and Israel during the month of August 2006.

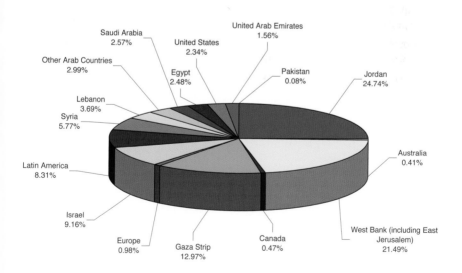

Palestinian Population Worldwide in 2006-2008

Above: Palestinian youth non-violently resist the occupation. N. Hashlamoun

CHAPTER THREE

THE OCCUPATION AND THE FIRST PALESTINIAN UPRISING

With straight posture, I walk.
With my forehead high, I walk.
In my hand is an olive branch
and on my shoulder is my coffin
And I walk, and I walk, and I walk, and I walk.

-"I Walk" (Ana amshi), by singer Marcel Khalife

The territories occupied by Israel in 1967, namely the Gaza Strip, the West Bank (including East Jerusalem), and the Golan Heights, remain a hotly contested issue to this day. For 40 years, Palestinians in the West Bank and Gaza Strip have lived under Israeli military occupation. According to international law, upon becoming an occupying power in 1967, it became the responsibility of Israel to develop and finance the necessary infrastructure for the occupied Palestinian population, from tax revenues collected from Palestinians in the Occupied Territories. Instead, Israel has neglected and hindered the development of Palestinian infrastructure, including roads, water and wastewater networks, solid waste management, industrial zones and telecommunications. Israel has also neglected and even restricted social infrastructure such as education, health and social welfare. C.D. Smith reported:

> *"Most Arab villages still do not have basic amenities because they must pay for their purchase out of taxes they must levy on their inhabitants. Because most are farmers and poor, little money is available for such services, whereas the Jewish settlements received nearly free electricity, paved roads, sewage systems, and the like. The same policy has been carried out on the West Bank."*[46]

From the outset of the occupation, Israel has taken actions that have, in effect, strangled the Palestinian economy, a policy that has forced Palestinians to depend upon Israel for the majority of their economic needs. For example, early in the occupation, one of Israel's first military orders was to confiscate almost all of the wells in the West Bank, forcing Palestinians to buy their water from the Israeli national water company, Mekorot. Palestinian water companies were thus rendered mere subsidiary distributors for the Israeli company.[47] Israel also closed Palestinian banks and denied Palestinians participation in electric power, communications, banking, agricultural and many other investments.

An analysis of the region's resource distribution, particularly of water aquifers, reveals what may have been Israel's chief motivation for waging the war of 1967 and maintaining its subsequent occupation of the West Bank and Gaza Strip, in defiance of unanimous international condemnation. Since 1967 about 30% of Israel's water has come from the Occupied Territories, translating into 80% of the Palestinians' total water supply, thus leaving only 20% of the Palestinians' water for their own consumption.[48] And, while the Palestinian population and its demand for water has increased significantly since 1967, Israel has capped the amount of water allocated to Palestinians at the 1967 levels. To enforce this, Israel forbids Palestinians from drilling any new wells without permission from the military authorities, and since 1967 a mere twenty-three drilling permits have been issued.[49]

Moreover, Israel places severe restrictions on Palestinian use of water from existing wells, and this restricted supply often leaves Palestinian communities without water for lengthy periods. For comparison, while Israelis consume an average of 350 liters of water per person per day, the average Palestinian in the Occupied Territories consumes only 60 liters per day. This falls well below the 100 liters of water per person per day recommended by the World Health Organization (WHO) and the United States Agency for International Development (USAID) as the minimum quantity for basic consumption.[50]

The Implications of Zionism

"It is the duty of Israeli leaders to explain to public opinion, clearly and courageously, a certain number of facts that are forgotten with time. The first of these is that there is no Zionism, colonialization or Jewish State without the eviction of the Arabs and the expropriation of their lands."
—Yoram Bar Porath, Israeli commentator
(in Yediot Aahronot, July 14, 1972)

The Palestinians have repeatedly asked Israel to return the areas occupied since 1967 – the West Bank and the Gaza Strip – in a peace agreement based on "land for peace." In other words, what Palestinians are asking for is control over two relatively small portions of the country, which together total only 22% of the original landmass of Palestine. The Syrians are likewise asking for the return of the Golan Heights through a similar deal.

Many Israelis feel that the only way to make peace with the Arabs is to allow the Palestinians to have the West Bank and Gaza Strip as their own independent state and to return the Golan Heights to Syria, in accordance with the "land for peace" concept.[51] Indeed, at various times in the course of peace negotiations, Israel has theoretically, albeit with stipulations, agreed to this idea of Palestinian autonomy over the West Bank.

136

The
Occupation
and the First
Palestinian
Uprising

One of the most difficult obstacles to peace between Israelis and Palestinians has always been Israel's policy of building illegal Jewish settlements, or housing colonies, in the West Bank (and, until the 2005 evacuation, in Gaza). Israel continues to construct and expand these settlements even though numerous negotiated agreements have been signed committing Israel to their restriction and removal. Israeli settlement building began with Israel's occupation of the West Bank and the Gaza Strip in 1967. Since then, the Israeli government and Israeli settlers (who are encouraged by the government and protected by Israeli troops) have snatched vast areas of Palestinian land, all of which is clearly designated as off-limits to Israelis under several UN resolutions. The UN has repeatedly affirmed that the Geneva Convention of 1948, which forbids an occupying power from transferring parts of its own civilian population into the territory it occupies, is applicable to the West Bank and Gaza Strip (See Appendix III for applicable articles of the Geneva Convention).

Nevertheless, over the years Jewish settlements have come to occupy numerous West Bank hilltops, erected in the midst of, or very near to, Palestinian lands and Palestinian population centers. Hundreds of thousands of settlers now live in the Occupied Territories, almost half of them residing in settlements in and around East Jerusalem,[52] and these settlements continue to expand at the expense of the Palestinian population and are at the heart of much of the ongoing violence.

Map 8 shows the pattern of settlement construction carried out since the Six-Day War of 1967. It is not difficult to see the gradual takeover of Palestinian land designated by the green, purple, orange, red and white areas. It is important to understand, too, that American tax money helps support the building of these Jewish settlements on Palestinian land.

Although much has been reported by the international media on the subject of Jewish settlements in the Occupied Territories, very few Westerners understand the depth of frustration felt by the Palestinian population of the West Bank and the Gaza Strip. The seizing of Palestinian land by Israeli settlers, although particularly painful to the landowners, takes a heavy toll on all Palestinians. Palestinians view these settlements as a cancer growing in their beloved homeland. With each acre of Palestinian land appropriated by Israelis, the hope of Palestinians for an independent state on a reasonable,

Distribution of Israeli Colonies in the West Bank by Date

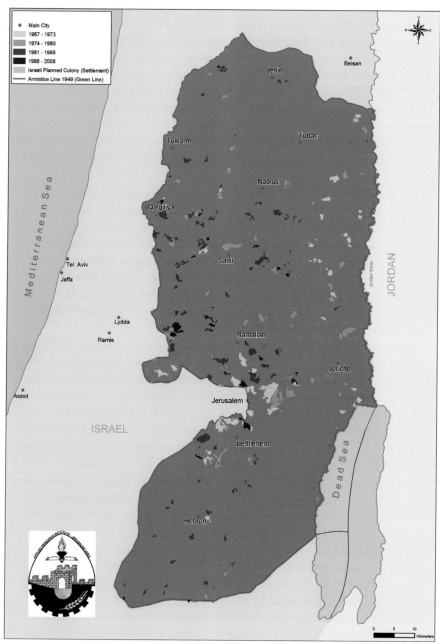

Map 8: Jewish Colonies in the West Bank from 1967 to 2010

contiguous area of their ancestral lands erodes. Moreover, thousands of Israel Defense Forces (IDF) soldiers are deployed in order to protect the settlements, and their presence on the outskirts of Palestinian villages and cities further discourages the Palestinians, many of whom still cling to the dream of an independent state. Consequently, many Palestinians regard each new settlement that is built as a nail hammered into the coffin of their national aspirations of independence and statehood, and of any would-be peaceful resolution of the dispute.

Palestinian land has been and is still being confiscated, both with and without court rulings, under the following pretexts:

1. Palestinians do not possess the required documents to prove land ownership. Even if the land in question might have been in the possession of a Palestinian family for generations, as is often the case, and even if the family does possess some type of document proving ownership, Israeli courts are usually unwilling to recognize it. The only document recognized by Israeli courts is the *Tabu* (Turkish) deed to the land, and only one-third of West Bank landowners are in possession of *Tabu* deeds. By this criterion, 72% of the West Bank is viewed by Israel as "state land."[54] A landowner without a *Tabu* has no recourse but to apply for the land deed through the Israeli bureaucratic system, but such court processes are expensive and, not surprisingly, weighted against Palestinians. Thus, requests for permits and documents made by Palestinian landowners are denied more often than not, if they produce a response at all.[54] Again, all lands not proven private are deemed "state land," which is reserved exclusively for Jewish use, and in this way the Israeli settlement enterprise has forcibly stolen hundreds of thousands of acres of Palestinian land, simply because the Palestinian owners did not have this litmus-test proof of land ownership. The fact that Israeli settlers staking claim to the same land almost never have the necessary documents is not questioned.

2. Palestinians have not been farming or tending the land. Again, it makes no difference that the Jewish settlers do not farm either. In addition, not all land is farmed all of the time, since Palestinian farmers traditionally depend on rain, not irrigation.

3. The land in question becomes designated as government land, and therefore the Israeli government claims it has the right to use and

develop it even if the land is being used/tended by Palestinians. The fact that Israel is an occupying government and that international law clearly prohibits an occupying force from developing the land it occupies makes no difference to Israeli authorities.

In August 2003, for example, the Israeli government offered a four-month financial incentive aimed at drawing young couples into the illegal Israeli settlement of Givat Ze'ev built in occupied East Jerusalem. Couples who moved into the settlement received an $11,400 grant matched by an additional $11,400 loan from Israel. This is only one of numerous examples of incentives used by Israel to lure Jews into internationally condemned settlements.[55]

According to a September 26, 2003 report published by the major Israeli newspaper *Ha'aretz*, the Israeli government's expenditure on settlements is $560 million per year *more* than the average amount it spends on the same number of citizens not living in settlements. The newspaper considered this to be a conservative estimate, since the report failed to include the costs of land acquisition and military expenditures directly attributable to the settler enterprise.

Israeli troops provide protection to settlers who have forcefully taken residence in the heart of Hebron. - *N. Hashlamoun*

140

*The
Occupation
and the First
Palestinian
Uprising*

Along with the continued construction of settlements, Israeli authorities have often confiscated Palestinian land for the construction of bypass roads that connect the settlements to each other and to Israel proper. Now totaling some three hundred miles in length, this network serves to strengthen Israel's grip on the Occupied Territories.

These roads, often called "bypass roads" because they bypass Palestinian localities, are not built for Palestinian use. Instead, the IDF controls traffic by means of checkpoints and roadblocks, closing these roads to Palestinian vehicles. Palestinian vehicles are recognized by their white license plates; Israeli license plates are yellow. In a report issued in August 2004, the Israeli human rights group B'tselem condemned what it called the "roads regime" in the West Bank as bearing "clear similarities to the racist apartheid regime that existed in South Africa until 1994."[56]

Little children face up to big guns.
—*N. Hashlamoun*

Home demolition in progress.
—*N. Hashlamoun*

The movement of Palestinians has been severely restricted by the introduction of a system of travel permits. These travel permits are required of anyone wishing to leave their town of residence, and they consequently have had a dramatic impact on the freedom of movement of Palestinians and on their ability to carry out the normal activities of life. (See Chapter 7 for a detailed explanation)

HOME DEMOLITIONS

During the same time period that Israel has built tens of thousands of houses for Jews in the West Bank (and, until 2005, the Gaza Strip), it has applied a calculated program of demolishing the homes of Palestinians. Since 1967 Israel's military government has destroyed almost 11,000 Palestinian houses in the West Bank and Gaza, 4,000 of which have been demolished since the start of the first Intifada in 1987.[57]

Israel's policy of home demolitions encompasses two different categories: demolition as punishment and administrative demolition. Punitive demolition, which is destroying the homes of Palestinians suspected of involvement in or collaboration with violent attacks, is a form of collective punishment forbidden by the Geneva Conventions, and thus constitutes a war crime.[58]

Administrative demolition is the Israeli government policy of destroying Palestinian homes, both in the Occupied Territories and inside Israel proper, built without the correct permit. As B'tselem explains, the legal justification for this practice is simply a façade: "Israel has created a situation in which thousands of Palestinians are unable to obtain permits to build on their land, and are compelled to build without a permit because they have no other way to provide shelter for their families."[59] About 500 so-called "illegal" Palestinian homes have been destroyed in this fashion since the start of the first intifada.[60]

When Home is No More

142

*The
Occupation
and the First
Palestinian
Uprising*

In some cases, Israel demolishes the homes of relatives of Palestinian activists, as a form of collective punishment. This policy is supposedly aimed at deterring Palestinians from sympathizing with resistance groups but in reality constitutes a grave breach of the Fourth Geneva Convention, which forbids all forms of collective punishment. Nevertheless, since unwarranted home demolitions, considering the large number of destroyed homes, are already part of an occupation policy regardless of Palestinian resistance activities, the issue of home demolition on the basis of absent building permits provides more insight into what really motivates Israel to conduct this policy.

These Israeli-issued building permits, required for building on Palestinian land, can only be given legal significance if the occupation itself is considered legal, which is a view strongly opposed by a vast number of UN resolutions. Palestinians in the West Bank and Gaza have had to endure military oppression for well over 35 years, and have had to apply for building permits from the occupying military forces, whose aim is obviously not to promote their well-being in any way. As a result, people rarely get a building permit if they apply for one, and therefore, the homes that become necessary due to the natural growth of the population are often simply built without them.

One can safely assume that many Palestinian houses built after 1967 have no building permits and can therefore be removed whenever the Israeli government decides to do so. According to a report by Amnesty International (1999), in East Jerusalem alone, 10,000 homes – housing one-third of the Palestinian population in the city – are threatened by demolition orders. Israel's handling of the issue demonstrates that only total control over Palestine and the Palestinians satisfies Israel's aspirations. According to the report, "the number of houses now threatened is three and a half times greater than the number that have been given permits since 1967."

In other words, the unspoken reason for large-scale house demolitions seems to be ethnically and demographically motivated. By placing practically no building restrictions upon Zionist colonists settling in the Occupied Territories, and conducting a suffocating policy towards Palestinian construction, Israel is clearly aiming to render large groups of Palestinians homeless, while increasing the number of settled Jewish colonists in the West Bank.

"Grab the hilltops," said Ariel Sharon during the first months of the second Intifada, calling upon Israeli colonists to seize control over Palestinian-owned land and start building settlements there. Many heeded the call, and the issue of building permits was never mentioned.

The fact that many Palestinians live in homes that are considered illegal by Israeli occupation legislation, which consists of self-made laws designed to fit the exact needs of the occupying forces, casts a shadow over any prospects of equality. It is a tangible example of the Israeli version of Apartheid, demonstrating that Zionism indeed deserves its place among other similar ethnocentric supremacist ideologies.

Israel's policy of house demolitions embodies Zionism's total and uncompromising claim over all of historical Palestine, and it contradicts Israel's repeated assertions of having peaceful intentions towards the Palestinians, and towards the restitution of their sovereignty.

Perhaps next time, when Israel razes yet another home and the media explain this war crime away as a simple matter of enforcing 'civil law', since it was a house without a 'building permit', you may realize that yet another Palestinian family will have been rendered homeless, and that Israel will have advanced yet a little more toward the dismantling of Palestinian society and the illegal confiscation of Palestinian land.

It is time that the international community demands from Israel that it show its own building permits for building on lands it has illegally confiscated. It does not suffice that a large number of international agreements have declared Israeli settlement policy illegal. Without a reinforcement of these rulings, injustices will continue to be perpetrated, and peace will become an ever more distant dream.

Published in *Palestine Chronicle* December 30 2002

144

_____

The
Occupation
and the First
Palestinian
Uprising

Because the Palestinians were a people under occupation with no government to speak for them, they had few resources at their disposal with which to curb Israeli aggression and the abuse of their fundamental human rights. Whatever resistance they attempted was quickly quelled by the Israeli military. Consequently, on December 8, 1987, in an incident that ignited much popular tension, four Palestinians were killed in a traffic accident in the Gaza Strip and in the already tense atmosphere many suspected the accident to be a deliberate attempt by Israelis to kill Palestinians. In light of growing unemployment and increased violence from the heavily-armed settler population, the incident unleashed Palestinian fury and had far-reaching implications.

Young Palestinians took to the streets confronting Israeli soldiers with nothing more than stones. Responding to the rocks with live gunfire, the soldiers shot and killed a 15-year old boy who became the first casualty of the Intifada. (Intifada literally means "shaking off" and is the Arabic term used for the Palestinian uprising). The next day a number of Palestinians were killed, including an infant. The rage felt by Palestinians intensified, and the Intifada soon spread to every town and village in the West Bank and Gaza Strip. Still more unarmed Palestinians were killed, and by the end of the first week a general strike was in effect. The following week, Bernard Mills of the United Nations Relief and Works Agency (UNRWA) said, "We're in a situation of either total lawlessness or a popular uprising".[61] Dayan's prophecy that the Jews of Israel must live in a permanent state of war with the Arabs was being played out once again, but this time it was a war between an unarmed Palestinian population and one of the most powerful military forces in the world.

THE ROLE OF PALESTINIAN YOUTH IN THE INTIFADA

All sectors of Palestinian society took part in the Intifada, but since 60% of the population was under the age of 15, youth became the most visible as a symbol of the movement. What would provoke unarmed youths to take

Making a living is suspended by IDF soldier in Hebron's Market place.
N. Hashlamoun

A woman from Hebron seeks shelter as Israeli tanks indiscriminately fire live bullets and teargas. *N. Hashlamoun*

Residents of Hebron negotiate with a soldier the possibility of allowing them to open their shops for normal business.
N. Hashlamoun.

to the streets in protest against such a powerful army? The answer is really quite simple: They had spent their entire lives under Israeli occupation, deprived of the inalienable right to freedom. Throughout their childhoods, these youths had been living in towns and villages whose streets were patrolled daily by the soldiers of the foreign Israeli army. Periodically, their schools were arbitrarily closed. They had seen family and friends thrown into prison and tortured. Their homes were often destroyed in response to defiance of the Israeli authorities, or for no reason at all, and they could be severely punished merely for displaying the colors of the Palestinian flag in public places or for writing slogans on walls. In addition, many had grown up witnessing their parents being humiliated at checkpoints and in house-to-house searches. Palestinian youth took to the streets to fight for their people's freedom and for basic human rights. American professor Charles Black, Jr. had the following to say about the role of the Palestinian youth during the first Intifada:

> *When we really look at them face to face, what do we see?*
>
> *Let's think about that. They count themselves part of a people; they believe this people to be grievously wronged. Their oppressors, as they see the matter, need fear nothing, being armed and protected beyond the possibility of fear by a great power across the ocean – whose hostility to themselves they cannot understand. They are spoken of by their oppressors with contempt and arrogance. They can expect nothing but cruelty. So what do they do, these young Palestinians?*
>
> *Against huge odds, quite without real weapons or any other resources, they at last decline to submit, and instead go out on the streets and pick up stones. They are beaten without letup or mercy. They are imprisoned under obscene conditions, after kangaroo trials or no trials at all. They are regularly shot at; enough of them are killed to make death as ever present and realistic a possibility as it was in our Korean and Vietnam Wars. Many are maimed; many are disfigured for life. Yet they come out in the streets again and again, these young people, some not much more than children, and they pick up stones.*
>
> *What name shall we give to the trait of character that produces conduct like that?... The word is "courage."*[62]

146

The
Occupation
and the First
Palestinian
Uprising

Though the importance of youth participation in the Intifada should not be underestimated, this movement was embraced by Palestinians of all ages. And while the best known image of the Intifada in the outside world is that of a stone-throwing Palestinian, the struggle of the Palestinians at that time was primarily *non*-violent. The nonviolent strategies used by the Palestinians included:

- Peaceful demonstrations and marches
- Obstruction (placing bodies in front of bulldozers, blocking roads)
- Non-cooperation with the occupation forces (refusal to work in Israeli factories, pay taxes, and carry identification cards; setting their own store hours and prices, etc.)
- Boycotts of Israeli goods
- Observance of general strikes.

Perhaps the most important nonviolent resistance to Israeli occupation was the establishment of a functioning Palestinian society, which involved creating an infrastructure *independent* of Israel, through institutions such as schools, hospitals, factories and other services. In addition, the Palestinians organized themselves into committees that provided for the needs of their population and united them in a common struggle.

As John R. Gee describes in *Unequal Conflict: The Palestinians and Israel*, "The Intifada was the greatest struggle mounted within their homeland by the Palestinians since the 1936–39 revolt. It brought into action women and young people on a scale unknown before in Palestine... [It] showed the world that the Palestinian people as a whole absolutely rejected Israel's occupation of the West Bank and the Gaza Strip."[63] However, the uprising and the worldwide recognition it brought to the Palestinian cause came with a heavy price. In reaction to the uprising, three times more soldiers were deployed to the West Bank than the number used to conquer it during the Six-Day War. By the end of 1993, over 1,000 Palestinians had been killed and many thousands more injured. Over 16,000 Palestinians were jailed, while on an average day 25,000 Palestinians were under curfew. Property also took a heavy toll, with almost 2,500 houses demolished or sealed.[64] During the same period, 481 Palestinians were deported.[65] Amnesty International and many others criticized Israel for using brutal methods to suppress the uprising. UNRWA official Angela Williams said, "We are deeply shocked by the evidence of the brutality with which people are evidently being beaten. We are especially shocked by the beatings of old men and women."[66]

By Dr. Mubarak Awad

148

*The
Occupation
and the First
Palestinian
Uprising*

It is unfortunate that within our Palestinian culture we do not always keep our stories, facts and history in written form. We have now lost record of a significant amount of the unique qualities inherent within the Palestinian nonviolent struggle. I base my own Palestinian nonviolent struggle on two fundamental criteria: 1) Religion/Spirituality. That as a human being, I, like all others am a child of God. So, for any person to kill the spirit of God found in every person is not right, no matter the circumstance. 2) Psychology. That despite our physical weaknesses, each human being has a right to resist occupation and the right to be free.

In 1983, I returned to Palestine as a psychologist who was interested in counseling Palestinians. This was to be my contribution to the Palestinian cause, to commit myself for one to two years of training, where I would promote the need for child and school counseling programs. I also wanted to bring to the attention of Palestinians a clear picture of what happens to a community under foreign occupation and to relay an understanding of the concept of being colonized by a group that has appeared to suffer more than most throughout history. It was also a way to make known to Palestinians that justice would not merely be handed to them, that despite their lack of power, they had the right to resist occupation and the right to be free like any other group in the world. I wanted Palestinians to understand that changes must be made in order to avoid having to depend on the goodwill and charity of Arabs and Muslims, the UN, the United States or Europe.

It is with this intention that I opened the Palestinian Center for the Study of Nonviolence, to bring actual facts, concerns and alternative solutions to the Palestinians. My emphasis was on drawing examples from nonviolence in the Islamic and Arabic cultures and from lessons learned by Gandhi in India and Martin Luther King, Jr. in the United States. The Palestinian idea of nonviolence, which I prefer to call "steadfastness" or "sabber" (meaning both patient and cactus in Arabic), reflects the Palestinian ingrained belief that through patient endurance we will ultimately triumph over occupation and aggression, as is reflected time and again throughout our history. This embedded cultural outlook saw the Palestinians through scores of invaders who occupied Palestine, only to give up over time and eventually withdraw. Thus even during the worst days of violence in the Arab-Israeli conflict, the majority of Palestinians, until today, have steered clear of violence.

I found it important to help my compatriots understand that unlike all previous occupiers of our homeland, Israelis were a different kind of adversary. Many Jews around the world have been at the forefront of civil, human, student and women's rights movements. In using our nonviolent approach in opposition to this particular opponent, I felt we ought to speak their language. It was an opportunity to use voices and moral concepts rather than bullets.

Consequently, during the Intifada some of the staunchest supporters of our cause were in fact Israeli and non-Israeli Jews. Unfortunately, as the second Intifada became bloody and lost many of its nonviolent deposits, many of these Jewish supporters dropped out.

During the first several years of the center's existence, beginning in 1982, we initiated educational programs as well as the organization of small campaigns designed to involve more people in the nonviolent movement on a daily basis. An example of this was our protest against the eating and drinking of anything other than local products. Both the Israeli Government and the PLO rejected this method of nonviolent action, each for different reasons. The Israelis felt threatened by the Palestinian movement and took it seriously enough to bring in experts from around the world to determine a course of action should it take hold. On the other hand, the PLO took this movement as a challenge to their authority. They had not been consulted about ways in which resistance could take place without an arms struggle. Despite the opposition, the campaigns proved successful, as they increased the use of the term "nonviolence." The concept began to seem less imported and Western.

Over time, we became more successful in relaying our message to rural villages, camps and universities, while the urban cities remained

150

*The
Occupation
and the First
Palestinian
Uprising*

skeptical. Our intent was to mobilize the Palestinian population and to confront occupation as a duty and responsibility, which belonged to every Palestinian, not only to the political factions or the PLO. In doing this, we needed to extract the fear factor from both sides and show Palestinians that the Israeli soldiers were indeed human and could also feel pain and be influenced by a conscience. We visited villages and refugee camps on a regular basis and spoke to whoever would listen to our cause. It was our goal to assess the needs of the Palestinian people and to help them achieve their needs through practical methods of nonviolent resistance. This included acts like the planting of trees in order to deter the confiscation of land and cutting off water to the Israeli settlements whose pipes ran through Arab villages. Most notably, we requested that those who had lost or fled from their homes return and place a single rose where they used to live. Those who passed by and saw the roses were given a picture into the lives and spirits of the refugees.

Eventually, it was the small-scale spread of nonviolent activities in both Palestine and Israel that became a threat to the Israelis. And it was a deliberate strategy involving Israeli peace groups in our campaign so that we could split the mindset of the Israeli government. It gave us a chance to have partners on both sides working for the same goal of redeeming Palestinian aspirations without threatening the security of Israelis. Due to the success of the campaign, the Israelis felt it would be in their own interest to put a stop to my actions by imprisoning and later deporting me.

In the meantime, we energetically sent youth to different universities to study first-hand the ways of peace, conflict resolution and nonviolence. The study of these practices positively led to the creation of more than 30 NGOs that committed themselves fully to nonviolence and democracy. They have since continued to apply these ideals in a more determined way in order to meet all of the challenges of both the Israeli occupation and higher ups in the PLO who opposed the nonviolent movement.

When traveling back to Palestine, despite the poor economy, lack of freedom of movement and deprivation of human rights by Israelis, I still find a favorable commitment to the nonviolent struggle.

I now find that there is more of an acceptance for those who have tried to find their own sense of self by questioning authority and for those who desire inclusion in the political process. And most of all, I find myself steadfast in my patience for a positive outcome.

Dr. Mubarak Awad is Director of Non-Violence International

Palestinian children, members of Al Watan Center, light candles in memory of all victims of 9/11.
N. Hashlamoun

Palestinians use non violence in an attempt to confront and stop an Israeli demolition vehicle.
N. Hashlamoun

Palestinian youth non-violently resist the occupation.
N. Hashlamoun

Looking forward to a peaceful future. Zaki Baboun's 2003

CHAPTER FOUR

TREACHEROUS PATH TO AN ELUSIVE PEACE

What sort of leaders accept such an arrangement on behalf of their people from a state and a mentality that has waged unremitting war against that people for at least half a century? What sort of leaders describe their failures as a triumph of politics and diplomacy even as they and their people are forced to endure continued enslavement and humiliation? Who is worse, more dishonest and cruel: the bloody-minded Israeli "peacemaker" or the complicit Palestinian? When will the two peoples at last wake up to what their leaders have wrought?

– Edward Said, 1994

The first Intifada proved to be a powerful force in gaining recognition for the rights of the Palestinians and giving legitimacy to the Palestine Liberation Organization (PLO). In November 1988, the Palestine National Council (PNC) convened in Algiers, where it acknowledged Israel's right to exist, renounced terrorism, and announced the constitution of the Arab state of Palestine, which was soon recognized by ninety countries. As a result of these actions the PLO began talks with the American government. Diplomatic stagnation set in almost immediately. However, with the advent of the Gulf War and the PLO's ill-conceived decision to give unqualified support to Saddam Hussein, the PLO were excluded from the Madrid Conference on the Middle East and were denied further financial aid by its cheif backers, the Gulf States. Thus, the decision to support Saddam Hussein came at a heavy price for the PLO. Meanwhile, the involvement of the Islamic resistance movement, Hamas, in the Intifada, both in the West Bank and Gaza, and the involvement of Zionist extremists in Israel, posed a serious threat to what little public security existed for both Israelis and Palestinians. Early in 1992, the political arena changed when Israeli Prime Minister, Yitzhak Shamir, leader of the right-wing Likud Party, called an election for June of that year. In that election two former prime ministers, Shimon Perez and Yitzhak Rabin, the leaders of Israel's Labor Party, fought a vigorous campaign and regained power. Both were in favor of talking to the PLO and making peace with the Palestinians.

THE OSLO ACCORDS

The Declaration of Principles

In the summer of 1993 negotiations were held in Oslo between representatives of Israel and the PLO, hosted by the Norwegian Foreign Minister Johan Joegen Holst. The negotiations concluded with an exchange of letters between Prime Minister Yitzhak Rabin of Israel and President Yasser Arafat of the PLO. These letters became known officially as the Declaration of Principles (DOP), which both Rabin and Arafat signed on the White House lawn in the presence of U.S. President Bill Clinton on September 13, 1993. Under the DOP, the PLO recognized the right of the state of Israel to "exist in peace and security," and the government of Israel recognized the PLO as the legitimate representative of the Palestinians and agreed to work together to negotiate peace. While difficult issues such as refugees, settlements, water rights, security and borders were postponed, the Declaration provided guidelines for future negotiations and for a five-year interim autonomy period in the West Bank and Gaza Strip, followed by a permanent agreement based on United Nations Resolutions 242 and 338.

Oslo I (Gaza-Jericho) Agreement

The DOP was followed by several additional agreements popularly known as the Oslo Accords. These were based on UN Security Council Resolutions 242 and 338, which call for Israel to withdraw from the areas it occupied in the June War of 1967. The vision of the Oslo Accords was for Israel to return the land of the West Bank and Gaza Strip to the Palestinians in stages. As such, Oslo I (also known as the Gaza-Jericho Autonomy Agreement) was signed on May 4, 1994 outlining the first stage of Palestinian autonomy in Gaza and Jericho. The agreement included Israeli redeployment (military withdrawal) from Gaza and Jericho and the establishment of a Palestinian self-governing authority. Israel was to maintain control of settlements, military areas and security matters.

In accordance with Oslo I (Map 9), the Israeli army pulled its troops out of Jericho and most of Gaza, granting Palestinians formal limited autonomy in those areas. The transitional period was not to exceed five years, with "permanent status negotiations" beginning no later than the start of the third year of the interim period. The agreement proclaimed, "It is understood that these [permanent status] negotiations shall cover remaining issues, including Jerusalem, refugees, settlements, security arrangements, borders, relations and cooperation with other neighbors, and other issues of common interest."[67]

Rabin, Clinton and Arafat at the White House during the signing of the Oslo Accords. April 2004

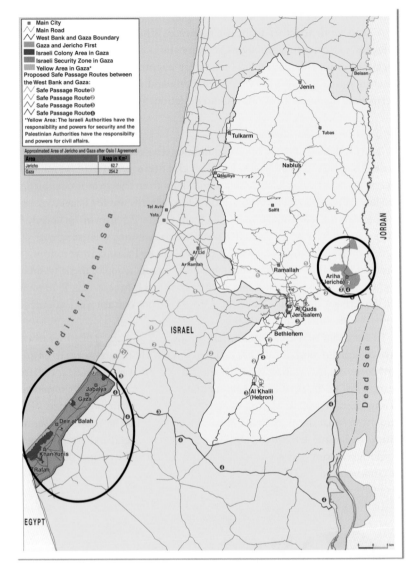

Map 9: Oslo I Gaza-Jericho

Oslo II Interim Agreement

The Oslo II Agreement, signed on May 28, 1995, also known as the Interim Agreement on the West Bank and Gaza Strip, outlined the second stage for Palestinian autonomy, extending it to other sectors of the West Bank. This was to be done by dividing the West Bank into three different categories; labeled A, B and C. In Area A, both civil jurisdiction and security control would be granted to the Palestinian Authority. In B areas, only civil jurisdiction would be given to the Palestinian Authority, while Israel would retain security control. Finally, those areas labeled C would be under complete Israeli jurisdiction, both civil and security. The Palestinians hoped that the Israeli troop withdrawal would proceed smoothly, that is, they expected C areas to become B areas, which, in turn, would become A areas. Eventually, the expectation was that all of the West Bank would be under full Palestinian control.

With great struggles and many delays (which will be explained further in the next section), Palestinians gained limited autonomy over the areas in red visible on *Map 10*. Area A consisted of major city centers and amounted to 3% of the West Bank. Another 24% of the West Bank was designated as Area B and the remaining 73% of the West Bank was defined as Area C.

There were other negotiations after Oslo II resulting in Israeli military withdrawals from further sectors of the West Bank, in effect increasing the "A" areas and decreasing the "C" areas. At the time of writing (2012), the Palestinian Authority has Area A status in approximately 17% of the West Bank, but Israel still retains ultimate authority over movement both into and out of these areas. The practical implication of this reality is that Israel can, and frequently does, impose arbitrary "closures" on the population centers contained within Area A, effectively turning them into large "Bantustans" or ghettos.

"B" areas now comprise 22% of the West Bank. Residents in these areas are, if anything, worse off than those in Area A, as they have no police protection and little civil representation, and their access to roads and resources, such as water, is even more compromised. Area C, approximately 60% of the West Bank, still remains under complete Israeli occupation.[68] *Map 11* shows how the West Bank has effectively been carved into noncontiguous sections, making it virtually impossible for Palestinians to achieve their aspirations for a future Palestinian state. Some Palestinians sarcastically refer to this as the "Swiss Cheese" state.

The average Westerner has no frame of reference for the words "checkpoint" and "closure." For Palestinians, the terms go hand in hand and have become a daily fact of life since the Oslo Peace process. While the stated objective of the Oslo Accords was to bring peace, the Oslo agreement was actually perverted by Israel into a tool to increase the persecution of Palestinians.

Breaking up the West Bank into different zones allowed Israel to justify the creation of hundreds of checkpoints throughout the West Bank. Checkpoints are military-controlled posts separating Palestinian towns and cities from one another and from Israel proper. The Israeli Defense Forces (IDF) man the checkpoints and have total authority to determine who is allowed through. On days when the Israeli military enforces a complete closure, no Palestinian is permitted to pass. Palestinians are often made to wait for hours in long lines at checkpoints before being told whether they will be allowed through, and they are often denied passage. Further, they are frequently interrogated, verbally and/or physically abused, or otherwise humiliated. Young soldiers experience the intoxicating power of having ultimate authority over the Palestinian population, and consequently many abuse this authority.

The following excerpts are from essays by Palestinian students at An-Najah University in Nablus relating their experiences living and moving in a "carved up" Palestine. These incidents occurred during the Israeli incursion into Palestinian cities in 2002:

> The partition of Nablus into three separated parts is among the greatest challenges we face daily. Before the Israeli Occupation, An-Najah University students used to live with their families and we could reach the University in about 15 minutes from Nablus, usually by taking a taxi and paying about one dollar. Now we are forced to take two or three taxis and to pay triple the fare.
>
> The first taxi drives us through a rough road by the mountainside and then we continue by foot through the mountain. In the winter we face the slippery mud and in the summer the hot dust.

After we make it to the second taxi we queue in lines between the rocks and hide from any passing tank or soldiers. When we are in the second taxi we sway back and forth as we come down a path that isn't even a road and we are living targets that can be shot at any moment. Sometimes while we are walking to reach our destination the soldiers appear and make crude statements and lift their guns to us. Sometimes they shout and shoot shells and bullets, and we must stand quietly. If we ignore orders we will be killed. We do whatever they ask and hear their crude statements, while saying or doing nothing. Our goal is to make it to our classes and we must always keep that first in our mind.

The greatest torment lies at the checkpoint that keeps us from our Palestinian cities. Teachers, students, employees, employers, men, women and children are stopped. From ambulances you can hear loud shrieks of pain coming from someone who is giving birth, or a patient in pain from a gunshot wound groaning. At these checkpoints we are treated as herds of cattle.

Inside the University campus there is also terror. Only about thirty percent of the students can manage to reach the University in bad weather and through dangerous streets. During times of curfew we even have to arrange to do our lessons "secretly."
—*Nael, student of English*

—

When you look at the military barriers at the entrances of our cities and the small towns and on almost every road, you will see the many kinds of humiliation that we, as college students just trying to make our way to the University to study, will carry in our memories all of our lives.
—*Hamad, student of Business Administration*

—

I decided to visit my family in Hebron... It took us more than 17 hours from Nablus City to Hebron City [a trip which would normally have taken no more than two hours]. There were about thirty Israeli checkpoints on the road; they inspected everything and even forced us to open our pants and sometimes to take them off. We were so embarrassed and had done nothing to be treated so roughly and so crudely by the soldiers. After they inspected us, and after waiting for hours, we were often forbidden to pass a checkpoint and told we must return from where we came. We would then search for another way.

Once they ordered us to lie on the ground, and our clothes were filled with mud and dirty water. It was very cold and they told us that they wanted to humiliate us. They hit a Christian Palestinian woman who was very old. She spoke kindly with them and asked them to allow her to pass, but a soldier pushed her away.

Every time and in every checkpoint we were forced to take off all of our clothes and even, I must say with shame, our underwear too. We were forced to take the back roads and go over the rough roads in the mud for hours.

I ask: What is this? I want someone to answer me. Where are the United Nations and the laws about humanity? Where is the human rights organization that will look out for the right of each human to live in peace? I wish that someone could come and live here and hide and stay among us and move with us from one city to another, with the Palestine people, so that they will hear and know what we are experiencing.

When I saw the soldier hitting the old woman I felt that he cut my heart, but I stood helpless and quiet, forlorn and heartbroken. I could do nothing but witness his cruelty. How can we keep such anger and our pain so quiet inside of us? There is no fairness, and we know that we are not human in their minds.

—*Feras, student of Engineering*

(The complete essays can be viewed on
http://www.najah.edu/english/reports/report11.htm)

Many hoped that from the Oslo peace process there would emerge, enough trust and confidence among both Israelis and Palestinians, to achieve the compromises necessary to resolve the thorniest issues. Although Palestinian hopes were partially realized in the Oslo Accords, major setbacks hindered the vision of peace set forth in Norway.

First, there were delays in the form of Israeli parliamentary politics. Many of the Oslo peace agreements made between Israeli negotiators and the Palestinians were signed without the approval of the Knesset, the Israeli Parliament. Thus, the task of Israeli negotiators was to return to their legislature and argue for the approval of the treaties they had signed, but the forward-looking Israeli leaders in favor of "land for peace" faced fierce opposition. While several treaties were eventually passed, it was often by the smallest of margins.

Another serious setback was the assassination of Prime Minister Yitzhak Rabin on November 4, 1995, shortly after he had spoken at a Tel Aviv peace rally. Rabin's assassination by a right-wing Israeli, Yigal Amir, was the outcome of a hate campaign by Jewish extremists against anyone who sought to "give away" so much as a square inch to the Palestinians. It was a campaign fueled by elements within the Likud leadership and an ultra-religious community unhappy with concessions being made towards Palestinians in the Oslo peace process. Anger and a sense of betrayal festered within the settlement communities, whose populations felt that they were being abandoned. This sentiment gradually attracted other segments of Israeli society and lead to the creation of Jewish extremists such as Yigal Amir.

Another consequence of this right-wing campaign was a shift in the mindset of the Israeli public, leading to a decline in the popularity of the Labor Party. Labor, the party that initially signed the Oslo Accords, was defeated in the 1996 Israeli elections, and the newly-elected Likud Party, then headed by Benjamin Netanyahu, was far less conciliatory towards the Palestinians. It tried its best to halt the process of returning any land. These factors ensured that any movement in the peace process, and certainly any actual return of land, slowed to a crawl.

As a result of these delays, the original time-frame for implementation of Oslo began to stretch beyond what was outlined in the agreements.

Meanwhile, illegal Israeli colonization of the West Bank and Gaza Strip continued relentlessly. All this made it increasingly difficult for Palestinians to perceive – or even to believe – that the Israelis were truly interested in peace.

Israeli settlements and bypass roads now choked the Palestinians on all sides. Vast amounts of West Bank land had been confiscated for the colonies and the bypass highways that connect them. Though the Palestinians had hoped that the Oslo Accords would end, or at least reduce, such oppression, they did not. In fact, Israeli colonization actually increased during the so-called "peace process": during the relatively short course of the Oslo negotiations, the settler population *doubled*, reaching over 125,000 settlers. In addition, a vast, 300-mile-long network of 29 highways and bypass roads was constructed (each road involving confiscation of an adjacent corridor three to four football fields wide), gobbling up more and more Palestinian land. These major roads which crisscross the West Bank are completely closed to private Palestinian vehicles.[69]

Thus, instead of being used to build confidence between the Israelis and Palestinians, the interim period established in the DOP was utilized by the Israelis as a cover for further colonization, with the intention of leaving as little as possible to the Palestinians in the event that final status talks should somehow actually occur. Although the Palestinians gained some autonomy in Areas A and B, they often discovered that the "areas" scheme they had agreed to only served to facilitate and legitimize Israel's control over and isolation of the Palestinian people. They were granted a quasi-government, but soon realized that this government (admittedly plagued by corruption and mismanagement) was, in effect, more of an agent for Israeli/American interests than a source of empowerment and self-determination.

Grab the Hilltops'

"Everybody has to move, run and grab as many hilltops as they can to enlarge the settlements, because everything we take now will stay ours. Everything we don't grab will go to them."
—*Ariel Sharon*
(then Foreign Minister), in a speech to Tsomet Party November 15, 1998

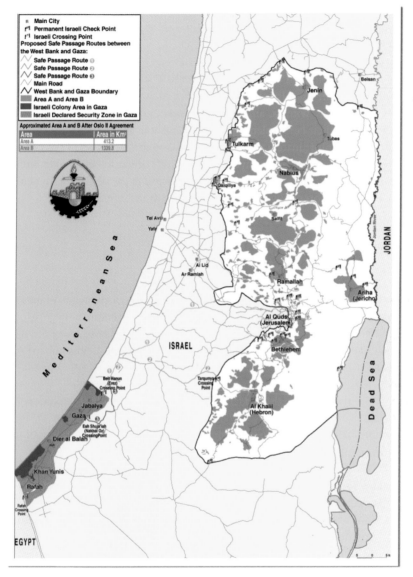

Map 10: Oslo II Interim Agreement

Map 11 depicts the severity of encroachment on Palestinian land. Since 1967, approximately 150,000 Israeli housing units have been built on occupied Palestinian territory. Meanwhile, the Israelis have systematically *destroyed* some 11,000 Palestinian homes; fewer than 600 of the houses demolished belonged to individuals accused of terrorist activities or their families, the oft-used Israeli justification for such actions.[70] Each and every day Palestinians witness, among other injustices, their farms and houses being razed, their land stolen, and even their water siphoned off and denied to them.[71] Unfortunately most of them, lacking the resources to fight back legally, are powerless to do anything but watch their land being taken from them piece by piece. At the same time, Palestinians are denied permits for new construction of any sort, even in their own neighborhoods.

CAMP DAVID 2000

In light of the breakdown of the Oslo peace process, new negotiations for peace began at Camp David, Maryland in July 2000. Palestinian negotiators accepted U.S. President Clinton's invitation to Camp David, even though they had been given little time to prepare and despite being put off by Barak's "Four 'No's" circulated widely prior to the talks:

- "No" to a return to the borders of 1967 (as required by UN Resolution 242)
- "No" to the return of Palestinian refugees (as stipulated by UN Resolution 194)
- "No" to even a partial withdrawal from East Jerusalem or to accepting any form of Palestinian sovereignty over it (as required by UN Resolutions 194 and 242)
- "No" to dismantling or "freezing" Jewish settlements in the Occupied Territories (despite UN resolutions and other international calls for this activity to cease and labeling the settlements as illegal "obstacles to peace")

Not surprisingly, the Palestinians went to the negotiations with legitimate reservations and with the feeling that Barak's "no go" areas were too rigid to work with on an equitable basis. When the two parties placed the most

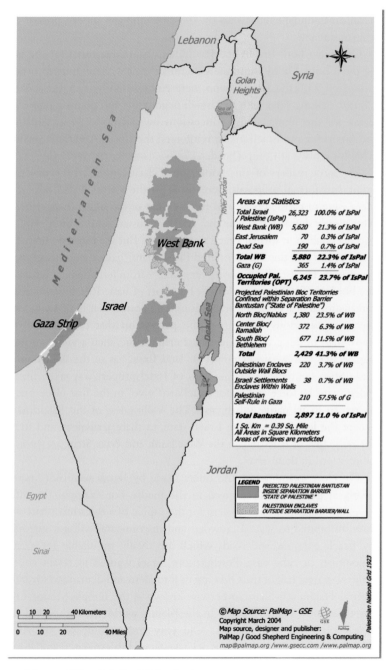

The following statistics appear on the map:

Areas and Statistics

Total Israel / Palestine (IsPal)	26,323	100.0% of IsPal
West Bank (WB)	5,620	21.3% of IsPal
East Jerusalem	70	0.3% of IsPal
Dead Sea	190	0.7% of IsPal
Total WB	**5,880**	**22.3% of IsPal**
Gaza (G)	365	1.4% of IsPal
Occupied Pal. Territories (OPT)	**6,245**	**23.7% of IsPal**

Projected Palestinian Bloc Teritorries Confined within Separation Barrier Bantustan ("State of Palestine")

North Bloc/Nablus	1,380	23.5% of WB
Center Bloc/ Ramallah	372	6.3% of WB
South Bloc/ Bethlehem	677	11.5% of WB
Total	**2,429**	**41.3% of WB**
Palestinian Enclaves Outside Wall Blocs	220	3.7% of WB
Israeli Settlements Enclaves Within Walls	38	0.7% of WB
Palestinian Self-Rule in Gaza	210	57.5% of G
Total Bantustan	**2,897**	**11.0 % of IsPal**

1 Sq. Km = 0.39 Sq. Mile
All Areas in Square Kilometers
Areas of enclaves are predicted

LEGEND
PREDICTED PALESTINIAN BANTUSTAN INSIDE SEPARATION BARRIER "STATE OF PALESTINE"
PALESTINIAN ENCLAVES OUTSIDE SEPARATION BARRIER/WALL

© Map Source: PalMap - GSE
Copyright March 2004
Map source, designer and publisher:
PalMap / Good Shepherd Engineering & Computing
map@palmap.org /www.gsecc.com /www.palmap.org

Palestinian National Grid 1923

Map 11: What is left of Palestine!

significant, fundamental issues on the table, the gap indeed proved to be insurmountable.

Of course, both Israelis and Palestinians blame the other for the failure of the Camp David Summit. Palestinian voices were muted, however, compared with the Israelis, who were empowered by U.S. President Bill Clinton's taking sides with the Israeli negotiators and pouring praise upon Barak for the "courageous" concessions he had made. In addition, both the American and Israeli media reinforced the Israeli/American version of what took place at Camp David.

For most readers of this book, some clarification is necessary at this point. No formal proposals were made in the Camp David talks, rather ideas were just tossed back and forth. None of the offers from either side were clearly defined. It is true that Barak discussed issues which, until then, had been taboo in formal Israeli negotiations. But the claim by both Barak and Clinton that the Israelis offered Palestinians "generous concessions" is a big stretch. The Israeli offers on every issue – from Jerusalem, to refugees, to the borders of a Palestinian state – fell short of basic Palestinian needs and international peacekeeping resolutions. The notion that Israel's concessions were magnanimous stems from the perception that considers anything more than nothing to be generous. Furthermore, such a view ignores the perspective that whatever power or land Israel has in the West Bank and Gaza Strip (and even in large areas of Israel proper) was taken from the Palestinians by force and is not Israel's to "give" in the first place, but only to return to its native inhabitants. The willingness of the Palestinians to accept the legitimacy of the Israeli state, to share Jerusalem, and to settle for only 22% of Palestine, in the West Bank and Gaza Strip, are enormous concessions in themselves.

On close examination, the offers made by Barak were not, in reality, nearly as generous as portrayed in the media. For example, the offer of neighborhoods in East Jerusalem for the capital of a Palestinian state would have amounted to several crowded and disconnected villages surrounded by Israeli colonies, and roads which are totally unsuitable for a capital, Palestinian or otherwise. Furthermore, Israel wanted to retain complete control of over half of the Old City of Jerusalem and demanded sovereignty over al-Haram ash-Sharif, otherwise known as the Temple Mount. One of the three most important sites in the Islamic world, the compound covers nearly one-sixth of Jerusalem's Old City and encompasses the Al-Aqsa Mosque and the Dome of the Rock. Arafat and Palestinian negotiators said conceding al-Haram ash-Sharif to Israel was out of the question because that particular piece of land is not just an issue among Palestinians but also a pan-Arab and pan-Islamic one. The Palestinian team insisted that even if they were to accept Israeli demands, their implementation would not bring peace to the region but would instead prolong the conflict for future generations. Arafat warned that the Israeli positions were "dangerous and destructive," and that such ideas could "throw the region into an age of new religious conflict."[72]

Barak's supposed offer of 94% of the West Bank was equally disingenuous. When Israeli officials speak in percentages they do not usually include the territorial waters of the Dead Sea or the strip of "No Man's Land" in their calculations. This deliberate strategy has two purposes: First, it advances the false assumption that these specific areas are not part of the West Bank but actually part of Israel. Second, by decreasing the size of the West Bank in their calculations, Israeli officials are able to inflate their withdrawal percentages. However, including these areas, Israel's claim of 94% is in actuality only 88.9%. Then, taking into account the accomplished fact of Israeli annexation of occupied areas into what they call "Greater Jerusalem," the unilaterally expanded city limits which include illegal settlements built since 1967, the percentage shrinks again to 86.5%. Moreover, Barak insisted on retaining security control over the Jordan Valley for an unspecified number of years. The Jordan Valley amounts to another 10% of the West Bank, leaving only 76.5% of the West Bank for a semi-sovereign Palestinian state. In essence, the Israeli negotiators presented the Palestinians with two potential offers, amounting to Israeli annexation (not counting the Jordan Valley) of either 10% or 13.5% of the West Bank (again, depending on how one defines "West Bank").

Within the Palestinian territory, the Israeli plan proposed three blocks of Jewish settlements, all subject to future expansion: one in the north, one in the center, and one in the south. These settlements would be connected with bypass roads constructed on Palestinian land that would span the bulk of Palestinian territory. From a Palestinian perspective, the roads would serve as an Israeli security belt choking Palestinians and undermining their independence.

Arafat and the Palestinian team at Camp David expressed a willingness to accept 95% of the West Bank, with an exchange of territory from Israel proper that would compensate for the 5% already populated by Jewish settlers. The Palestinian negotiating team sought an exchange ratio of 1:1

whereby the Palestinians would be compensated an equal area of land for each piece of territory in the West Bank to be retained by the Israelis. Barak's offer, however, called for a ratio of 9:1, so that for every *nine* units of land the Israelis kept they would compensate the Palestinians with *one* unit.[73]

Barak and the Israeli team also failed to offer just concessions on the issue of refugees. Dr. Mahdi Abdul Hadi, Director of the Palestinian Academic Society for the Study of International Affairs (PASSIA), reported:

> *The Israeli team refused to acknowledge any moral or legal responsibility for the Palestinian refugee problem, merely offering a willingness to point out their "sorrow" for what "happened" to the Palestinians during the first Arab-Israeli War. They simply refused to accept the "right of return" equating it with a "war for the destruction of Israel" and therefore rejecting the notion of creating any kind of timetable or program for the implementation of that right.*[74]

A surprisingly positive element did arise, however, when the Israelis expressed a willingness to allow an unspecified number of Palestinians to return over a period of ten years, though only for humanitarian concerns, such as a family reunion. On the other hand, they refused to consider any Israeli compensation for Palestinian refugees.

The final nail in the coffin of the Camp David talks was the Israeli refusal to relinquish control over water resources, and ease other economic strangleholds. This could only be taken as an effort to keep the envisioned Palestinian "state" in a position of crippling subjection. To add insult to injury, Barak insisted that, in the event of Arafat signing an agreement, any further Palestinian claims and grievances would be null and void.

When Arafat rejected the proposals made by the U.S. and Israel, both nations attacked him publicly, further pushing the Palestinians into a political corner. Throughout the peace process many Palestinians have felt they were treated as if it were their fault that they lived in Palestine. While other countries stood by, Israel not only demanded that the Palestinians cease fighting them but insisted they make concessions – as though the Palestinians were the ones aggressively colonizing someone else's land and retaining it under military occupation. But for negotiations to ever truly function and someday bring peace to the Middle East, they must stop being a platform for Israeli and American political bullying and instead reflect a genuine effort toward justice; justice for all concerned parties.

Instead of sharing and exposing his objections to Camp David with his people and the Israeli public, as well as with the international community, with all the media potential that implies, Arafat took his case only to Arab and Islamic leaders. In both Islamic and Arab capitals Arafat predictably received a great deal of support for his position and for the ongoing Palestinian resistance to occupation. But these capitals and their leaders, while granting much-needed financial and moral support to Arafat and the Intifada, provided him with little leverage which might impact the negotiating positions of the Israeli/American team.

This lack of communication on the part of Palestinian negotiators, combined with incomplete media coverage, left much of the world with, at best, a skewed and incomplete understanding of the nature of the negotiations, especially the reasons for the Palestinian "rejection" of Israel's terms. Palestinians did not support the Camp David Accords because they did not believe Israel should be given any more than the 78% of historic Palestine that they had already taken, and they were frustrated that the years they had spent working for peace ended with such a one-sided deal. Thus, many felt little hope for a just and reasonable solution. The Israeli public accepted the inaccurate summation – the spin – offered by their official Israeli information agencies which simply stated that Barak had offered the Palestinians 95% of the West Bank in exchange for peace with the Jewish state, which Arafat rejected, opting instead for violence. This infuriated the Israeli public, leading many in Israel to the conclusion that Israel could never make peace with the Palestinians.

A Christian Delegation Visits President Arafat (June 2004)

By the author

We made our way through several Israeli checkpoints and crowded streets and alleys of Ramallah, the de facto commercial and political capital of Palestine, to President Yasser Arafat's compound. Even before arriving at the half standing Muqataa (Mr. Arafat's headquarters) they were moved at the visible suffering and incredible hardships of the Palestinian people. They observed the blocks and slabs of concrete that now lie alongside the main road from Ramallah to Jerusalem soon to be erected as the barrier fence that will separate Palestinians from their family members and loved ones on the other side of the street. The visitors were a Christian delegation led by Rev. Jim Hoogenboom from Arizona. I was invited to accompany the delegation representing the Council of Local Evangelical Churches in the Holy Land.

The American delegation was warmly welcomed by the beleaguered President Yasser Arafat, who took time to explain and illustrate the difficult conditions of the Palestinian people under Israeli occupation. None of them however could have predicted that within less than one year, their host would die. He related how Palestinians are prisoners of the guardians of an unjust occupation. This includes Mr. Arafat himself, who was not permitted to visit Bethlehem on Christmas Eve and most recently was denied a visit to Jerusalem to join Christians for Easter celebrations. The delegation was overwhelmed to see the strength of Arafat's commitment to a peaceful solution in the face of the incredible daily humiliation that he and his people experience. Mr. Arafat presented the group with his vision for peace between Israelis and Palestinians and answered several of the delegation's questions.

Rev. Hoogenboom asked Mr. Arafat what the Christian community in the United States can do to help the situation in Palestine. "The only thing we are asking our brothers and sisters in the United States to do is to stand for truth and justice." Mr. Arafat said. "Peace-loving and fair-minded Americans would be appalled to see what the Israelis are doing to us. We welcome Christian leaders from the United States who come and visit us in order to discover the truth themselves."

Near the end of the visit I asked Mr. Arafat the question that many American friends were asking me when I give lectures on the Arab Israeli conflict. I put the question to him exactly as I heard it. I said, "Mr. President, why did you reject Israel Prime Minister Barak's generous offer in the failed 2000 Camp David Peace Talks?" Mr. Arafat took a big breath, then chuckled with a huge smile on his face as if to express unbelief and then said to the entire delegation, "Mr. Barak claimed that he generously offered us Al Aqsa Mosque. But he only offered us the existing mosque's structure. Meaning the land upon which the building stands will not be included in the deal neither the sky over the building. In the future if something happens to the building, we cannot rebuild it because they (the Israelis) would own the ground and the sky above it." Arafat continued, "I immediately called President Husni Mubarak of Egypt, King Abdullah of Jordan and the rest of the Arab Kings and Presidents to ask them about their opinion of Barak's offer, they all, one by one, rejected the offer." Arafat then looked directly at me and said, "Could I accept an offer that no decent Arab or Muslim leader would accept and that the vast majority of my people would consider an insult and treason?" Arafat then looked at the delegation and said, "If Barak truly desired peace, he would not hurl at us something so ridiculous."

Mr. Arafat further explained that while the Israeli team was willing to return what seemed a reasonable percentage of Palestinian land, they expected to keep the larger Jewish settlements in the heart of the Palestinian entity and to keep control over the water resources, of the sky and of all the borders. "How could we have a sovereign state with all these limitations? Still, in spite of all of these setbacks, I never gave up on the possibility of continuing the negotiations and we did achieve progress in future negotiations (Taba and Sharm El-Sheik). But with the arrival of Sharon we were pushed back to square one because what little Barak had conceded to us, Sharon considered it to be too much. We continue to reach out to the Israelis with genuine peace on our hearts and on our minds. It's up to them if they want to reciprocate," said Mr. Arafat.

Mr. Arafat made mention of several American eyewitnesses to the negotiations who wrote extensively, highlighting the great effort that Palestinian negotiators made to bridge the gap with Israelis during the Camp David negotiations.

The Christian leaders ended their meeting with a prayer for the President, for the Palestinian people and for the restoration of peace to all the people who live in this land. On the way home, the delegation was treated to a sample of what Arafat had relayed as they spent two and a half hours waiting at the Kalandia checkpoint before they could make the usual 20 minute trip across to East Jerusalem.

Top: Author and Christian delegation discuss Middle East Peace with President Yasser Arafat.
Bottom: Author in dialogue with President Arafat. April 2004

CHAPTER FIVE

THE AL-AQSA INTIFADA

When will our conscience grow so tender that we act to prevent human misery rather than avenge it?
–Eleanor Roosevelt

A twisted sort of thinking developed in the minds of Israelis during the Oslo years. According to this warped thinking, the Palestinians would accept a situation of coexistence in which they were on an unequal footing vis-a-vis the Israelis and in which they were ranked as persons who were entitled to less, much less, than the Jews. However, in the end, the Palestinians were not willing to live with this arrangement.
–Amira Hass "The mirror does not lie", Ha'aretz, November 1, 2000

It was in the context of the failed Camp David talks that Likud opposition leader Ariel Sharon made his notorious visit to the third holiest site in Islam, the al-Haram ash-Sharif (the Temple Mount). On September 28, 2000, flanked by 1,000 armed policemen and protected by over 3,000 Israeli troops deployed throughout the city of Jerusalem, Sharon entered the mosque compound. The failure of Barak and his Labor government to come to an agreement with the Palestinians had paved the way for Sharon to seize the political spotlight before his Likud archrival, Benjamin Netanyahu, could be cleared of suspected offenses and regain political momentum. Sharon's entry into the al-Haram ash-Sharif compound was intended to send a calculated message to the Likud leadership and constituency.

Sharon's message to both the Israelis and Palestinians was clear. To Israelis, his visit announced that he was the one who could be trusted to ensure Israeli sovereignty over Jerusalem in its entirety, including the most holy sites. His message to Palestinians, and to Arabs and Muslims globally, was one of provocation and challenge. The average Palestinian heard him say, "I stand on your holy place as an invader and an occupier. What can you do to save your holy place from my hands?" Many leaders warned of the consequences of such provocation, but Sharon insisted on going ahead with the visit.

Had Sharon made the visit at a time of lessened tension, or had he chosen a less sensitive site than al-Haram ash-Sharif, the bloodshed that began in September 2000 likely would have been avoided. Instead, his actions agitated millions of Muslims around the world, but especially Palestinian Muslims.

THE BEGINNING OF THE SECOND INTIFADA

In reaction to Sharon's provocative entry into the al-Haram ash-Sharif mosque compound, Palestinians began throwing stones at the Israeli soldiers inside the compound. In response, soldiers fired their machine guns at the protestors, killing some of them. The next day there was another clash at the site, leaving still more Palestinians dead. After the first two days, five Palestinians had been killed and more than 200 injured. In the days that followed, thousands of enraged Palestinians threw stones at Israeli soldiers stationed at checkpoints all over the West Bank and Gaza Strip. Israel again reacted harshly, with heavy weaponry, killing many more Palestinians. Not only were unarmed demonstrators shot fatally, but many Palestinian bystanders not involved in the demonstrations at all, including several children, were also killed.

The deaths of unarmed demonstrators, bystanders and children only exacerbated Palestinian anger and encouraged more Palestinians to take to the streets with stones. Israel again reacted, using helicopter gunships, snipers and machine guns against Palestinian civilians. Within two weeks, over 100 Palestinians had been killed and more than 3,000 injured. But the violence continued and the number of dead and injured continued to rise. Arab Israelis, equally outraged, expressed their sentiments in a large, nonviolent demonstration in Nazareth. Here the Israeli police and civilian settlers opened fire on the demonstrators, killing 13 of them. Outrage at the slaughter of so many Palestinians and Israeli Arabs spread across the Arab world and reverberated throughout many Islamic countries.

A Personal Reflection: "Al-Aqsa Martyr"

September 30, 2000 is a day I will never forget. Two days earlier Sharon had entered the Al Aqsa Mosque, our holy place. After that many innocent people were killed. The next day I went to my University as usual. There were protests and noise and all over the campus students wanted to go out and protest what Sharon had done. Everyone was full of anger and ready to face the Israeli soldiers. I saw Jihad, a friend of mine. I will never forget his face as he wished me good morning.

"Where are you going, Jihad?" I asked. "With the other guys of course." "Oh Jihad, don't do this – it's so dangerous," I said. "What will a stone thrown at these well-armed soldiers mean? Don't be a fool." His reply was firm. "No matter what, I will not stand here watching them re-occupy my homeland and do nothing. We have no guns to fight them, but a stone in my hand is better than nothing and I must make them understand that we will not give up our land, never. No, only over my dead body." I asked him to take care and said I would see him the next day. The next day never came.

In the evening I heard rumors that Jihad had been shot. Then the rumors became truth. He was shot in the head and leg. I called the hospital to ask about his situation and I prayed for him. The next day Jihad was martyred. They shot to kill him, killed him for nothing but trying to protect his land with his naked hands. How brave they are facing our stones protected by their heavy military equipment.

I saw Jihad's funeral on television. I saw his calm, white, peaceful face sleeping like an angel but with no soul left. I cried along with all of his friends. I cannot remove his picture from my mind. Jihad has left us forever. This we must accept. But his soul, his smile, and his patriotic self lives on among us and his voice echoes in our minds.

How heartbreaking you are, Death!
How unmerciful you are, Occupation!
How cheap are our lives in their eyes.
Sleep in peace, Jihad.
And be safe.
I shall never forget.
I shall never give up.

From an essay by Duha, a student at An Najah University in Nablus when the Al-Aqsa Intifada broke out. The complete essay can be found on http:// www.najah.edu/english/reports/report11.htm

UNDERLYING CAUSES OF AL-AQSA INTIFADA

Sharon's visit to al-Haram ash-Sharif was the spark that kindled the second Palestinian uprising, now known as the Al-Aqsa Intifada. But while the immediate cause of the uprising was Sharon's visit and Israel's excessive response against Palestinian protestors, there was an underlying cause, namely the continued Israeli occupation of Palestinian territories and the resultant anger and frustration among the Palestinians as a people.

The Israelis allege that Yasser Arafat was to blame for the months of bloodshed following September 2000. They propose that he incited

Palestinians to commit acts of violence against the Israelis when he did not get what he wanted at the Camp David talks of the previous summer. According to this Israeli narrative, Arafat reasoned that violent tactics might achieve what peaceful negotiations had not, and Israel effectively mobilized its multimillion-dollar public relations machine to help communicate this version of events.[75]

Yet no balanced assessment of the causes of the Al-Aqsa Intifada can be made without listening to the Palestinian perspective as well. The Palestinian National Authority (PNA) had no desire to resume hostilities, but once the popular uprising took hold throughout the West Bank and the Gaza Strip, the PNA had little choice but to support it. Arafat had no magic wand to make an angry populace stop its revolt, without some promise of a just political solution. The Israeli claim that the Al-Aqsa Intifada was a premeditated, coordinated war masterminded by Arafat contradicts the chronological order of events. The facts show that the PNA and Arafat had little to do with the beginnings of the Intifada. Rather, it was a spontaneous, popular uprising.

The author visited Arafat on several occasions, as part of various Christian delegations. In every visit, Arafat spoke with us proudly about the "peace of the brave" which he signed with his "friend" Prime Minister Rabin. Arafat considered the Declaration of Principles reached during the Oslo Agreements, and signing them in the presence of President Clinton on the lawn of the White House, to be his crowning achievements. He desired a resumption of the Oslo Accords, which he believed would lead to an independent Palestinian state. But Sharon and the Likud had a different agenda, as they despised both Arafat and the Oslo Agreements.

Israel has claimed repeatedly that in the Intifada it was always fighting a defensive war against Palestinian terrorism. Yet the first lethal mass attack by Palestinian militants against Israelis happened on November 2, 2000, more than a month after the beginning of the Intifada, at a time when over one hundred Palestinians had already been killed. Then, after a lull of several weeks in suicide bomb attacks, a renewal of such attacks did not occur until the third month of the Al-Aqsa Intifada, when the Palestinian death toll already stood at over three hundred.[77] The only reasonable explanation for this phenomenon is that after the death and injury of hundreds of Palestinians, not to mention continuous oppression of Palestinians under Israeli forces, the most desperate of the militants were finally pushed over the edge. They had been pushed to hate and anger and, unfortunately, responded lethally.

Within the first two months of the Al-Aqsa Intifada, Israeli forces had killed some two hundred Palestinians, and Palestinian militants had killed approximately twenty Israelis. These figures underscore the excessive force of Israel's tactics in trying to quell demonstrations. Many of the Palestinians who were killed were in fact young boys.

Numbers of Israelis and Palestinian killed during the al Aqsa Intifada

	Population	Citizens Killed*	U.S. Equivalents**
Israeli	6,116,533	908	43,101
Palestinian	3,512,062	3,141	259,667

* Number of people killed during the al-Aqsa Intifada, from September 29, 2000 to date (August 11, 2004).

** Based on a total U.S. population of 290,342,554. Total Population numbers from the CIA World Factbook.

INTERNATIONAL EFFORTS TO CALM THE SITUATION

American and European mediators began pouring into the area hoping to break the cycle of violence and prevent it from spreading regionally. Urgent talks, at the request of U.S. Secretary of State Madeline Albright, were held in Paris and then moved to Sharm e-Sheikh, Egypt in order that an agreement might be signed in the presence of Egyptian president Hosni Mubarak. Arafat accepted the invitation, demanding that the international community conduct an inquiry and hold Israel accountable for excessive use of force and for its role in starting the hostilities. Barak, in turn, placed the blame on Arafat and the Palestinian leadership.

The Sharm el-Sheikh Summit, held in October 2000, organized an inquiry into the causes of the Al-Aqsa Intifada, and sought ways to restore security cooperation and to return to peace negotiations. To this end, the Mitchell Commission was established as part of the agreement reached at the close of the talks. On October 17, U.S. President Bill Clinton made a statement declaring that both sides had reached agreement on three key points, starting with, and based on, a truce. First, both sides agreed to make statements denouncing violence and calling for an end to hostilities. Second, both sides accepted the formation of a U.S.-led "fact finding" mission to investigate the causes of the current Intifada. Third, both sides agreed to find a way to resume negotiations towards final status agreements.

But all efforts to mediate between Arafat and Barak failed. In an interview with CNN's Wolf Blitzer on October 15, Barak declared, before the start of the summit: "With this leadership [i.e. Arafat's leadership] … we cannot make peace."[77] In essence, even before the peace talks had started, Barak had already admitted that the peace process was dead. Additionally, nothing emanating from the summit could quench the fire that was raging in the hearts of Palestinians all over the West Bank and the Gaza Strip: "Palestinian negotiators stressed that all that had happened at the summit had been to please President Bill Clinton's desire not to leave empty-handed once again."[78] Thus the Mitchell Plan was marginalized.

SHARON ELECTED PRIME MINISTER

On February 6, 2001 Ariel Sharon defeated Ehud Barak and became the 15th Prime Minister of Israel. This was not the first time Israelis had turned to Sharon in a time of political crisis: Sharon had seen Israel through several wars and military endeavors, and now many Israelis viewed him as the tough general who could help them withstand the challenge of the Al-Aqsa Intifada.

With Sharon in the highest position in the Israeli government, and the failure of all avenues to peace, the Palestinian population sensed that the worst was yet to come. Three days after Sharon's election, Barak made the comment to U.S. President George W. Bush that "nothing is agreed until it's all agreed," insinuating that concessions Barak had made with Arafat did not commit Sharon to the same.[79]

This was a concern felt by most Palestinians. While much of the population was already exhausted from years of struggle, Palestinian resistance groups such as Tanzim (militias), militant Islamic organizations, and other nationalist groups readied themselves for what they expected would be a long confrontation with Sharon and his right-wing government.

Indeed, the first two years of Sharon's reign unleashed the bloodiest era in the history of the Palestinian-Israeli conflict, excluding the major Arab-Israeli wars. Between September 28, 2000 and August 11, 2004 more than 3,000 Palestinians were killed and more than 30,000 injured by live Israeli ammunition, heavy weapons, or assassination attacks (the so-called "targeted killings"). According to UNICEF estimates, 448 children were among the Palestinian dead, and more than nine thousand Palestinian children were injured.[80]

Palestinians were not altogether passive under Israel's newest hard-line leadership. At the height of the Al-Aqsa Intifada, Palestinian militants hit Israeli targets anytime and anywhere they were able to penetrate Israel's tigh security. Lacking the weaponry and trained military personnel to fight a conventional war, Palestinians targeted the soft underbelly of Israeli society in a wave of suicide attacks. Thus, Israeli civilians became the most accessible target of militant Palestinians.

One of the most deadly suicide attacks occurred during a Passover dinner in a hotel in Netanya on March 27, 2002. Twenty-two Israelis were killed and more than 100 wounded when a suicide bomber blew himself up

Israeli security officials and medics on the scene after a Palestinian suicide bomber blew himself up - killing himself and scores of Israeli citizens.

in the Park Hotel shortly after guests had sat down to dinner. On October 21 of the same year, 14 Israelis were killed and over 50 injured when a car packed with explosives rammed into a bus at a junction near Hadera and Pardes Hannah. These and other suicide attacks, bus bombings and drive-by shootings created a spirit of fear and panic in the hearts of many Israelis. By this stage in the Intifada, over 900 Israelis had been killed and more than 6,000 injured in such attacks.[81] Most of the victims were civilians, and according to UNICEF, 92 children were among the dead.[82]

Essay: "Feeling Their Pain"

By the Author

We live so close to each other and yet we do not feel one another's pain. When a homicide bomber succeeds in killing Israelis in Jerusalem, I can sometimes hear the sirens of ambulances and emergency vehicles from my apartment in Beit Safafa. I then rush to the TV to watch the horrible details unfold.

I do not like what I see or hear, but somehow that doesn't seem enough. I feel strangely numb to the pain of my Jewish neighbors who lose their lives or are burned, injured, or traumatized due to the bombings. It is a real issue for me, because as a practicing Christian I am called to love my enemies. I think one way to express that love is to truly share the pain of others when they suffer.

When innocent Palestinians are assassinated by Israeli attacks in Gaza, Jenin, Hebron, Bethlehem and elsewhere in the West Bank, my

---

A charred and burned Israeli bus, the work of a Palestinian suicide bomber, stands in the heart of an Israeli city.

heart goes out in sorrow to them. I wish I had the same level of compassion for innocent Israelis who are killed or hurt.

This is a spiritual dilemma, which is further complicated by the fact that I am a pastor of a Christian congregation in East Jerusalem and, therefore, often preach peace and reconciliation and call on members of my congregation to love their enemies regardless of racial or political realities. I confess it is much easier to speak about forgiveness than to actually forgive, and it is much harder to practice love than to preach it. Then I think: If I, a Christian pastor, cannot truly love my enemies, what must it be like for the average Palestinian?

I have tried to examine my heart in an attempt to understand why I feel the way I do. Why do I care less when innocent Jews are killed?

The answer to this question is found not so much in my heart as in my mind. Although I am religious and care much for my spiritual well-being, I am also rational. Rationality, mingled with a sense of patriotism, overcomes my spiritual motivation and desire to love my enemies. Reason tells me that for every innocent Israeli killed in these cycles of violence, at least three innocent Palestinians are also annihilated. It also tells me that even if the death on both sides of the conflict were numerically equal, the day-to-day suffering of the average Palestinian far outweighs the suffering of the average Israeli. Palestinians cannot order curfews and imprison Israelis in their homes and cities. Palestinians have no power to establish checkpoints on the borders of Israeli cities. Palestinians cannot employ bulldozers to demolish Israeli homes. Again, reason tells me that a nation who occupies another should expect the pain resulting from the desperate lashing out of an occupied population.

I cross the Bethlehem checkpoint on a daily basis. My eyes, which are windows to my intellect, see injustice every day. I see demolished homes, a collapsing economy, the masses under perpetual and suffocating closures and the daily suffering of an entire population.

When I look eastward, near the checkpoint, the settlement of Har Homa built on land Israel confiscated from Palestinians after 1967 (on what Palestinians call Jabal Abu Ghnaim), stares me in the face. Turning to the West I see the Aida Refugee Camp, one of three refugee camps in Bethlehem, which is home to Palestinians who were forced to flee their villages in 1948 in what is now called Israel. Then I look straight ahead and see Rachael's Tomb, a holy place turned into a prison-like fortress. Looking behind me it is impossible to avoid the settlement of Gilo that was also built on Palestinian land that Israel annexed to Jerusalem after 1967.

The realities I view, along with the stories I hear, are imprinted on the walls of my soul and influence my entire person, including my spiritual outlook. Injustice makes me exceedingly upset and definitely affects my attitude. Consequently, when pictures of innocent Jews, slaughtered by a Palestinian homicide bomber are shown on TV, I rationalize instead of empathize. I continue to blame Sharon, the occupation, or the latest Israeli bombing that snuffed out the lives of a number of Palestinians.

I long for the day when, deep in my heart, I can feel the pain of my Jewish neighbors in their time of calamity as much as I feel the utter despair of my people. I long for the day when we, on both sides of the political divide, can step into each other's shoes and understand the anguish and hopelessness that the other side is feeling. Perhaps then we can become better aware of our common humanity, cry together, and express forgiveness to the other. Only then, perhaps, will we triumph over those – on both sides – who thrive on violence, destruction and bloodshed.

Published in an edition of Ha'aretz. January 2003

The Day After, an Israeli Home Demolition by Zaki Baboun

CHAPTER SIX

ISRAEL'S MILITARY OFFENSIVE ON THE WEST BANK AND GAZA

If words have meaning, Mama,
        What is Is-ra-el?
What does a word mean
if it is mixed
        with another—
If all soldiers, tanks, planes and guns are
Is-ra-el-i
                What are they doing here
In a place I know
        In a word I know—(Palestine)
                In a life that I no longer know?

-From the poem, "Hadeel's Song", by Hanan Ashrawi

It would take volumes to record the chronology of events following Sharon's election and the stories of human suffering inflicted on both Israelis and Palestinians as a result of endless cycles of violence and rounds of retaliation and counter-retaliation. Sharon clearly intended to crush the Intifada by using excessive force, perhaps hoping this would bring Palestinians and their leadership to their knees. His military assault against the Palestinians climaxed in March 2002 in an incursion which Israel dubbed "Operation Defensive Shield."

186

Israel's
Military
Offensive
on the
West Bank
and Gaza

OPERATION DEFENSIVE SHIELD: AN ATTACK ON PALESTINIAN CITIES

Beginning in February 2002, Sharon launched attacks against several Palestinian refugee camps in the West Bank, causing major physical damage and destruction. Within two weeks, 180 Palestinians had died in the attacks. On March 29, 2002, after declaring Arafat an "enemy," Israel attacked his compound headquarters in Ramallah.

From March 29 to May 1, Israeli tanks invaded all major towns in the West Bank, with the exception of Hebron and Jericho, wreaking major destruction on the civil infrastructure. Towns were placed under 24-hour curfew, and more than 250 Palestinians died. The Israeli government then launched a second large-scale invasion on June 19 into every West Bank town and village (except Jericho), in a complete re-occupation of the West Bank. For the first few weeks, almost two million Palestinians were placed under 24-hour curfew.[83]

The following is a summary of the key events which unfolded in several Palestinian cities under "Operation Defensive Shield." It is only a small sample of the death and destruction that took place in the West Bank during the Al-Aqsa Intifada. Violence and oppression swept the land on a level not seen in Palestine since the War of 1967.

Ramallah

Five Palestinians were killed and 50 wounded in the March 29 attack on Arafat's headquarters. Israeli troops seized most of the buildings in his compound, confining Arafat to a few rooms. They then prevented ambulances and paramedics from evacuating the wounded; plus they destroyed electricity networks and other sectors of the infrastructure. Various buildings were turned into Israeli military outposts.[84]

Nablus

In early April thirty Palestinians were killed within 48 hours when Israeli forces rumbled through the city of Nablus, the largest city in the West Bank, and encircled three adjacent refugee camps. Palestinians resisting the Israeli invasion in the casbah (old section) of Nablus refused to give themselves up to IDF troops and vowed to "fight until the end".[85] On April 18, the bodies of over 70 Palestinians, including women and children killed during the Israeli incursion, were buried in a mass grave during an easing of the curfew.

Students at An-Najah University in Nablus wrote about their experiences under the 2000 "Defensive Shield" incursion:

> The siege started from city to city until it arrived in Nablus. On that day silence covered all the people in the city and you could not hear anything but the roar of the helicopters striking everything and hundreds of military machines and tanks knocking down anything in their path. The darkness of those nights was terrifying with no electricity, no water and no telephones. Children were crying and frightened for themselves, not knowing what would happen to their families or if they would become homeless.
>
> - *Nagham, Fine Arts student*

—

> On April 3, 2002 the Israeli tanks invaded Nablus City; they demolished and killed and rampaged …the first night was the most terrifying as the Israeli tanks showered us with bombs and bullets. Electricity was cut and water pumps exploded. We could see nothing but bullets, shells and flashes of light. We were deprived from any communication. Fifteen days elapsed without water or electricity and many of our historical buildings were demolished and even old trees were not left standing.
>
> We were terrified. The tanks were invading the streets and we lived in a "double prison" as our homes were not safe either. The soldiers watched us always and they were everywhere and even came in-

188

Israel's
Military
Offensive
on the
West Bank
and Gaza

side our homes. There were soldiers living in occupied houses near us. They searched our furniture and rooms thoroughly and in many homes they destroyed everything. After that it was as though our homes were filled with terror since they could enter any time, day or night, and simply break up all that we had saved to build. As they destroyed our homes they destroyed our present and our future.

Many of the families who lived in flats that the soldiers took over still suffer, constantly reliving the fear of being trapped in one room and not permitted to even leave the room to go to the toilet. Even now that the troops have left some of those homes the children still suffer. They have nightmares and fears. The aggressive manner and the cruelty have registered in the children's minds forever. All over the West Bank children live in fear and confusion.

During the depressing curfew we risked being killed if we even tried to peep out the door, but bit-by-bit our people started to move. So many people were faced with such grave problems even as they tried to take their children to the doctor. The soldiers laughed at them and did not allow them to pass. Any human could see the suffering of the child but still it was impossible for the children to be treated for their illnesses. We felt they wanted us all to die.
- *Nael, English student*

———

During the nights I could not sleep because of the noise of the tanks and the gunfire. On one night they bombed and destroyed three houses, leaving all of the families homeless.
- *Feras, engineering student*

———

During the first months of the siege, no one could think of anything, we were so afraid and worried. There was nothing that anyone could do. There was no electricity in most places and we could only use candles. There was no television to see what was going on outside. We listened to the radio to hear the news about our situation. Everyone was waiting for breaking news and only sorrow filled our free time.
- *Wafa, interior design student*

(The complete essays can be found at:
http://www.najah.edu/english/reports/report11.htm)

An elderly Palestinian negotiates the right to cross a checkpoint with Israeli troops.
N. Hashlamoun

Palestinian Muslim religious leaders confront obstacles on their way to worship.
N. Hashlamoun

Jenin

Israeli troops entered the Jenin Refugee Camp in April, demolishing dozens of homes and killing and injuring many of its inhabitants. On April 11, the United Nations Relief and Works Agency for Palestine Refugees in the Near East (UNRWA) said that at least 3,000 Palestinian women and children were homeless in the Jenin area. After touring the camp on April 18, UN envoy Terje Roed-Larsen said the scene was "horrifying beyond belief," calling it a "blot that will forever live on the history of the State of Israel" and stressing the urgency for "immediate access" by international humanitarian agencies. Two days later U.S. Middle East envoy William Burns toured the ruins of the camp and said, "I just think what we are seeing here is a terrible human tragedy."[86] Alaa, a student from An-Najah University during the time of the Israeli incursion into West Bank cities, describes her experience:

> *In Nablus and Jenin there were hundreds of people murdered. The children were killed in the streets and doctors and press photographers were injured. Israeli tanks destroyed cars and we spent the most horrible time in our lives with no fresh water to drink, no electricity and no phone lines. There was no medicine for the sick people. This was our life in that period. We couldn't study or remember any thing. I am not sure that anyone can study when there is only bad news about the death or imprisonment of friends and relatives and the country and the city that you love is being destroyed.[87]*

The United Nations Security Council (UNSC) approved Resolution 1405 which designated a delegation to look into the matter and demanded that Israel allow free access to humanitarian and medical organizations for the beleaguered Palestinians. Resolution 1405 also called for the implementation of three previous resolutions, 1397, 1402 and 1403, calling for a ceasefire and Israeli withdrawal from the West Bank. The UN report criticized both sides for putting civilian lives at risk. According to the report, 52 Palestinians and 23 Israeli soldiers were killed during the invasion of Jenin.

Bethlehem

When Israeli troops stormed into Bethlehem on April 2, 2002, more than 150 people – the vast majority of them unarmed civilians – took refuge in Bethlehem's Church of the Nativity, one of Christianity's most sacred sites. Those who ran inside became hostages in a 38-day standoff during which

190

*Israel's
Military
Offensive
on the
West Bank
and Gaza*

Israeli forces frequently shot into the church. Over the course of the siege on the Nativity church, Israeli army snipers killed seven and wounded more than 40 of those inside.

The Israeli version of events was that a large group of armed "terrorists" had entered the church and taken dozens of civilians, including Christian priests, as hostages, using them as human shields. All of the so-called "hostages" within the church, including Father Ibrahim Faltas, Christian lawyer Tony Salman, and the governor of Bethlehem, Mohammad Almadani, denied this account. They confirmed that the vast majority of people inside were civilians who ran into the church to save their lives. While there were some Palestinian gunmen among those who had entered the church, they did not fire a single shot from within the church. Most of the armed persons who entered the church were PNA tourism police and policemen from the adjacent police station who were targeted as enemies by the invading Israeli army.

During the siege on the Church of the Nativity, Israel blocked efforts from humanitarian organizations to deliver food and medicine to those inside. Under pressure from peace activists and humanitarian groups around the world, Israel finally reached an agreement on May 10 in which 13 of the Palestinians in the church were deported to other countries, 26 were transferred to Gaza, and the remainder were released.

Steeple at Mar Elias Monastery near Bethlehem

By the Author, April 2002

192

Israel's
Military
Offensive
on the
West Bank
and Gaza

Bethlehem, home of the Prince of Peace, has seen better days. Since March 29, 2002, its people have been subjected to unimaginable tyranny and hardship. Many of its citizens are boiling with anger and frustration. They are outraged over the month-old curfew that the Israeli army has forcefully imposed over their city and all the neighboring suburbs and refugee camps, including the towns of Beit Jala and Beit Sahour. A population of over 100,000 people is directly or indirectly affected by this unprecedented, county-wide curfew.

Those who have never lived under military incursion may find it difficult to understand the depth of humiliation that the average citizen of Bethlehem feels. Unfortunately, the media focuses on certain hot spots and ignores others. As one journalist put it, "If it bleeds, it leads." In other words, where blood is not spilled and where destruction cannot be portrayed via vivid and dramatic video footage, the story is placed on the back burner or neglected altogether. Thus, the tragic events in and around Manger Square, where over 150 people are held prisoner inside the Church of the Nativity by Israeli tanks and sniper fire, is getting far more media attention than the plight of the 100,000 people *outside* the church who have been imprisoned in their homes for over a month.

To shed some light on the dark but non-televised saga, come with me to visit an average Palestinian home in the Bethlehem area. We will accept the hospitality of the Rishmawi family who live in Beit Sahour (Shepherd's Fields). In spite of the fact that it is early Monday morning, the Rishmawis give us a warm welcome. It is 7:30 am. In normal circumstances, Mrs. Rishmawi wakes up the children, fixes them breakfast and gets them ready for school, and then Mr. Rishmawi drives them from their home in Beit Sahour to Talitha Kumi School in Beit Jala. But due to the curfew, Mrs. Rishmawi has no reason to wake her children early. It is neither a holiday nor a vacation, but today – like every day for the past month – all schools, colleges and learning centers are closed. Instead of buses and parents transporting children to school, armored vehicles and tanks are roaming the streets bringing fear and anguish to the hearts of all citizens.

On Tuesday, Mr. Rishmawi cannot go to work for the same reason that his children cannot get to school. A curfew means that people must stay in their homes around the clock. If they leave, they do so at tremendous risk to their lives and well-being. Israeli snipers are perched on surrounding rooftops watching for any individual that would dare even to go to church, to celebrate the Resurrection of Christ. Later, if the curfew is lifted for a few hours, they gather for a special meal with members of the extended family, and in the afternoon they visit friends, neighbors and family members. This Easter the Rishmawis are not in the mood to celebrate, and even if they were, they are prevented from doing so by Israeli tanks and armored vehicles roaming their streets. Fear and terror continue to be inflicted on the entire population, while news of death and destruction is reported daily from the besieged Church of the Nativity.

A month-long siege of any city in the world is a crime against humanity no matter who inflicts it. To place tens of thousands of people under house arrest for such a long period of time is a reflection of the moral bankruptcy of Sharon and his government. Why should all the inhabitants of Bethlehem be sentenced, without trial, incarcerated in their homes, traumatized beyond reason and impoverished, all for the activities or misdeeds of a few militants?

Guardians of the Military Occupation patrol a street in Hebron.
N. Hashlamoun

School boys subjected to searches and humiliation at the hands of heavily armed IDF troops on their daily commute to school. - N. Hashlamoun

CHAPTER SEVEN

A REIGN OF TERROR

I don't know if many of the children here have ever existed without tank-shell holes in their walls and the towers of an occupying army surveying them constantly from the near horizons. I think, although I'm not entirely sure, that even the smallest of these children understand that life is not like this everywhere.
-Rachel Corrie, Februry 7, 2003

Peace cannot come from punishing the Palestinian people.
-Nick Rahall, U.S. Congressman

How can we talk of human rights and ignore them for the Palestinians? How can Israel talk of Jewish rights to a homeland and deny one to the Palestinians?
-I.F. Stone, late Jewish journalist

The military assault on Palestinian cities and refugee camps during the height (2000-2004) of the Al Aqsa Intifada - informally referred to as the second uprising - was only one among many facets of Sharon's and Israel's war on Palestinians. In its continued and systematic plan to rid the land of Palestinians, Israel targeted civilians and their leader in the following ways:

1. Humiliating and liquidating Palestinian Leadership

Israel did its best to weaken the Palestinian National Authority (PNA) and other Palestinian leadership, largely through targeted political assassinations and through the destruction of the PNA's infrastructure, a strategy of devastating the body by crushing the head. In its military incursion into the West Bank, Israel bombarded the PNA headquarters, police stations, radio and TV stations, prisons, security buildings and offices. What had taken years for the Palestinians to build, with the help of the international community, overnight became prime targets for Israeli F-16s and Apache helicopters. The Palestinian Economic Council for Development and Reconstruction (PECDAR) estimated that the rebuilding costs for the destruction inflicted during Operation Defensive Shield alone would reach $450 million.[88] Much of the damage occurred to infrastructure paid for in part by the United States and the European Union.

By Sharon's order, scores of Palestinian leaders were either assassinated or imprisoned. On March 22, 2004, Israel assassinated the highly respected Hamas spiritual leader, Sheikh Ahmad Yassin, in a move that outraged millions of Palestinians as well as Arabs and Muslims around the world. The 68-year-old, wheelchair-bound Yassin was coming out of a Gaza mosque following morning prayers when Israeli helicopters fired three missiles at him, instantly

Common street scene in a West Bank city: Heavy armed IDF troops ready to shoot during curfew. - N. Hashlamoun

killing him and six other Palestinians and injuring at least 15 more.

Many Israelis at various times called for the assassination of Arafat himself, but Arafat was always spared, most likely because Israel could not risk the international backlash that would result from the assassination of an elected leader. In addition, it suited them to demonize the leader, and to keep him as an "address" at which to level criticism, all the while effectively restricting his movements and depriving him of any real power – and demanding that he "do more" to curb Palestinian violence.

2. War on the Palestinian economy

The Palestinian economy has been a casualty of the Israeli occupation, in the West Bank and the Gaza Strip, from the time the occupation started in 1967 until the present. For example, Israel has always maintained control over the main water aquifers and other vital natural resources of the Occupied Territories. In fact, thirty percent of Israel's water comes from the West Bank and Gaza Strip, leaving the West Bank only 20% of its own water resources for the 2.5 million Palestinian inhabitants.[89]

If this were not enough, Sharon and his government hit the economy even harder, perhaps hoping Palestinians would be forced to beg, subsist on international charity, starve – or leave. In addition to the standard Israeli practice of destroying property, Sharon and his government implemented sweeping curfews and closures that by definition immobilized the Palestinian work force. On account of these closures, the UN estimates that at least 80% of the 125,000 Palestinians who used to work in Israel lost their jobs.[90] In addition, Israel continued its policy of tightly limiting the opening of Palestinian banks and businesses and impeding their licensing and inspection. It has also hindered the planting and marketing of Palestinian crops.[91]

In a report issued in May 2003, the World Bank estimated total losses to the Palestinian Gross National Income (GNI), after 27 months of the Intifada, to have reached $5.2 billion.[92] In August 2002 UN Special Envoy Terje Roed-Larsen commented that Israel's military clampdown was causing an economic disaster in the West Bank and Gaza Strip, and was directly responsible for "breeding chronic violence."[93]

The economic losses caused a 51% drop in the GNI and forced 59% of Palestinian firms to either shut down or reduce production. 75% of Palestinians were reduced to living in poverty (less than $2 a day), with an unemployment rate of 67% in Gaza and 48% in the West Bank.[94]

3. Maximum incarceration of the Palestinian population, through curfews, sieges and widespread travel restrictions

Palestinians were subjected to the most severe and sustained set of restrictions on movement since the beginning of the occupation in 1967. In fact, during the first twenty years of the occupation, a relatively benign period by comparison, Israel imposed *no* internal impediments to travel within the West Bank. Suddenly, however, besides repeatedly invading areas under Palestinian control and placing towns and villages under prolonged curfew, Israel also imposed road closures that still daily affect the now three million Palestinians. One hundred and twenty permanent Israeli checkpoints in the West Bank and (until 2005) in the Gaza Strip, along with hundreds of permanent roadblocks, divide the West Bank into 300 separate clusters and the Gaza Strip (again, until 2005) into three enclaves.[95] Palestinian towns and cities are thus effectively cut off from one another through these completely *internal* closures. In addition, the forced closure of Gaza International airport in February 2001 and Israeli-imposed border closures with neighboring countries combine to further isolate Palestinians from the rest of the world. Besides the extreme economic impact already discussed, the closures, curfews and restrictions negatively affect *all* aspects of life, including the medical and educational concerns of Palestinians. By 2004, some 432 reported incidents of denied access to ambulances at roadblocks occured, resulting in the deaths of at least 76 people. Closures also caused shortages of food, water and gas. The following accounts are from essays by Al-Najah University students on life under curfew during the Israeli incursion into Nablus[96]:

Soup lines are a direct consequence of a prolonged military occupation.
N. Hashlamoun

Living under curfew is yet another story. Although it is called a curfew it is actually like being in a huge jail. It is remarkable that someone in their youth can simply be forced to stay home, locked in the house against their will. I tried to read books during the curfew but felt that I was out of strength. How could I stay home doing nothing, not helping my country?

When they would lift the curfew for a few hours we would rush to check on family and friends and try to get food to allow us to survive. We were like caged animals suddenly given a brief freedom.

I heard shooting most of the time and the tanks always passed by my house. I thought that all the birds had died and that the sky would not be there anymore. I was very careful not to look out the window because they were out there waiting to shoot at my head. What kind of life do I have? In fact it is not living, but only surviving.

—*Samah, business administration student*

—

During the longest curfew, which lasted almost ninety days, we spent the time becoming increasingly frustrated. We could not leave our house without being shot, so we tried to speak with neighbors, or watch television for news bulletins or play games and sometimes if we could concentrate we would try to read a book. But we never knew if we could even finish that book.

Four months of my life passed in vain and I lost that time for no reason. I was simply kept in a cage. One cannot imagine what it is like to stay home for months without living a normal life or seeing your friends. We only heard news of people dying, or people trying to leave for the mosque to pray and being killed.

—*Firas, science student*

—

As the curfew continued for a long period, I had to learn to cope. I couldn't visit family or friends, even though they were close to our house. I cannot imagine how I passed those days.

The whole situation is bad. Everyone is suffering. There is such a high rate of unemployment and people have no income. The future is unclear and this makes people think that the only future is outside of Palestine. Must we leave our home for any hope in life at all?

—*Wafa, interior design student*

—

My friends and I are not able to meet to walk the streets or to celebrate birthdays or go to movies or to do any of the things that young people usually do. Whenever there is a curfew I sit at home and do nothing. To pass on the road means to be shot, harassed or arrested. I feel that my whole life is being wasted while I am doing nothing to fulfill my simplest dreams.

—*Rawan, fine arts student*

—

We were kept inside and I although I was ready to go to the university I could not. We were forbidden to leave the flat where I stayed with other students. I spent the days without eating anything. Finally after four days I decided to leave the house and snuck my way to a friend's house. I took some bread and food and returned the same way. On the fifth day people decided to break curfew and left their houses. I went to the university but it was closed for an unknown period of time. I asked some of my friends about the situation and found out that a great number of students couldn't graduate because of the closing of the university and the delay of the exams.

—*Feras, engineering student*

—

During the curfew we tried to sleep when we could, but the nights were long and filled with explosions and gunshots. We always worried about finishing the semester and the financial problems that we face because there is no work. These are all things that go through our mind, as we stay in our houses unable to even take a walk.

> Who are the terrorists? We who are living in our land and making every effort to live free in the land of our fathers and grandfathers? Who are the terrorists is a question that needs to be answered quickly. I ask God to help us live our lives in a land that is free.
> —*Najwan, science student*

4. *Attacks on emergency medical personnel, services and hospitals*

During the Israeli incursion, Operation Defensive Shield in 2002, the Israelis attacked hospitals and medical clinics throughout the West Bank, wounding patients and cutting off electricity and water. The IDF shelled both the French and Al Hussein hospitals in Bethlehem. Indeed, on several occasions they fired live ammunition at various hospitals in Bethlehem, Hebron and Ramallah. Settlers shot a security officer at Augusta Victoria Hospital in Jerusalem in an attack that lasted for several days.

There were 197 attacks on Palestinian ambulances with live ammunition, rubber-coated steel bullets, and on some occasions, with stones thrown by Israeli settlers. Thirty-six ambulances were destroyed in these attacks, in many cases killing and/or wounding medical personnel. Overall, during the first three years of the Al Aqsa Intifada, 25 medical personnel died while on duty and 425 medical personnel were injured. Staff of the Union of Palestinian Medical Relief Committees (UPMRC) were stopped, detained and denied access up to three times daily during the March/April 2002 invasion, and even afterwards, their mobile clinics were seriously violated. Seventy-one emergency medical personnel and volunteers were arrested during the invasion.[97]

5. *Education restrictions*

Midway into the Al Aqsa Intifada, 185 Palestinian schools and universities had already been shelled and fired upon by Israeli soldiers, 11 of which were completely destroyed. Fifteen schools were occupied and used by the IDF as detention centers and army barracks. In addition, at least 580 other schools were closed due to Israel's policies, curfews and closures. During the school year 2002–2003, UNRWA reported a sum total of 1,475 lost school-days, just in its own schools across the West Bank and Gaza.[98] On October 2, 2002 United Nations Children's Fund Special Representative Pierre Poupard issued a statement that "a generation of Palestinian children is being denied their right to an education," referring to over 226,000 school children (out of one million in the West Bank) and 9,300 teachers who were being denied access to their schools.[99] Of even more concern, 132 Palestinian students were killed and 2,500 injured on their way to or from school.[100]

School boys and girls confront heavily armed IDF troops on their way to school. - N. Hashlamoun

Essays (excerpts) by students of Al-Najah University in Nablus, during the incursion into that city

Since April 2002, the way to Nablus, where my university is located, has been blocked from my village, Dier Sharaf, which is only 11 kilometers (about 7 miles) away. From that date my life has become very difficult. My daily struggle is how I can make it to the university the safest way possible. The soldiers at the army checkpoint do not always allow me to pass.

Sometimes the soldiers require that we do the absolutely unacceptable, such as take off our clothes to pass through their checkpoints and go to study. We are often stopped in the cold, rainy weather. Once, the soldiers tore my university identification card. They shout terrible things at us and we tolerate their daily anger and insults.

I have tried going through back mountain roads to reach the university. These roads are long and difficult to pass. I have to wake up before sunrise to arrive at the university at the correct time and it can take me hours. During the rain, the land becomes slippery and my clothes and shoes become muddy and dirty. I have to take some time to clean myself to appear at school. Sometimes the soldiers have stopped me on the mountain roads. Sometimes they force me to return home and I cannot study. The soldiers have shot at me before, and one day they detained me for eight hours in the cold weather for trying to pass to the university.

Any student facing these problems would be unable to study properly. I arrive home after another long and stressful day and only want to sleep. My university day sometimes takes eleven hours, I lose so much time on the road passing from my university to my home. I am in the engineering college so it takes a long time to study, but that time is not available and I can see how this has affected my study results.

I tried living in the city near the university, but it did not work out. It required a lot of money that my family didn't have and it was also not a safe place to live because the soldiers came to the flat many times to make problems for us students. Three or four students live in a small room and there is always so much noise and worry. For that reason I wanted to live back in the village with my family.

I try to think about the future. It is as if things just seem go from bad to worse. Sometimes I think my dreams might be too big. I look for some development to happen in the world and hope that technology and the media can make our lives easier. But this seems to be impossible. I feel like a man trying to cross the ocean without a ship. I feel that I have enough inner strength to help the world but I also fear that I am reaching a stage where the future will have no meaning for me.

—*Sabri, engineering student*

—

Over the past two years there have been frequent periods when the Israeli army has occupied my city of Nablus. On June 20th, 2002 all of the students living outside of the city had a difficult time. I was happy to finish my exams but many of the other students could not make it to the city to complete their final exam. There was always a rumor that the curfew would be lifted but it lasted for a very long time. The students were kept out of the university and the city for two months.

This semester before I get ready to go to the university, I check from my window to see if there is shooting or a tank in the street, anything that means "curfew." I sometimes return because there is a tank at the university with speakers announcing, "Curfew enforced." If we do not obey, the soldiers can easily shoot or arrest us. They can then simply say that we are "terrorists." Sometimes we try to find any way to get to our university and we become stronger, as we feel that we should not surrender and that no one should prevent a student from going to class.

—*Mona, engineering student*

One day I woke up as usual and passed by the checkpoint. I walked alone for about half an hour carrying my books and with one hand in my pocket to keep it warm. I was only minutes away from reaching Nablus and I was beginning to feel the sense of relief that in just a few more minutes I would be just another student sitting safely at my desk like all students around the world.

But I heard jeeps and a tank coming behind me. I did not dare look. The noise moved closer and suddenly I heard the sounds of guns being prepared to shoot at me. Then the soldiers yelled, "Stop, hands up!" The soldiers came to me and checked every little part of me and had me take off much of my clothing. I felt so humiliated standing there before them being insulted.

They told me that I am a savage, a terrorist and a killer of children. They used many dirty words. I carefully took my books back and stood beside the tank amidst their guns and filthy words. I found it ironic: I am a victim accused of being a killer. I felt how unfair life is. They kept me from six o'clock in the morning until six in the evening. Finally, they allowed me to return home.

This is not only a period of occupation but also of humiliation. This is how the Palestinian student is living.

—*Mohammad, ITM student*

—

I saw on television that the Israeli students were studying in their universities and walking and moving everywhere safely and laughing and playing with their families and friends. Our position was just the opposite. We were filled with depression and sadness, and news of the death of our friends was everywhere.

—*Nagham, fine arts student*

—

The university announced that we would begin studying, but not at the university. We started going many places outside of the university. We needed a lot of money to travel to these different places, each time in a different area – a hotel, a Red Cross center, or a mosque. Because of my financial situation, sometimes I could not arrive where the other students were studying, and always there was the danger of being shot for breaking the curfew.

—*Feras, engineering student*

—

Along with all of the problems that we face to get here our families also have a terrible problem financially. Many families can no longer work and are not able to provide the students with enough money to register for a new term. Even bread has become too expensive to buy, and students who live in the surrounding villages have had to rent rooms to protect themselves from the daily torment at the checkpoints. Life has become so difficult and sometimes it feels impossible.

—*Nael, English student*

—

There is a feeling of extreme fear and of being lost. There are times that there is no way to concentrate when our mind is filled with scenes of blood, killing and destruction. The military forces have said that we are renegades, and there is no respect for a student, a professor, or even the university. Despite these conditions the students have tried hard to continue our education, by renting flats close to the university campus and coming to the campus when there is no curfew. Yet as soon as we find one solution another problem starts. We must worry about money to continue our education. The financial factor has kept many of us from studying and we are forced to delay some semesters to collect the funds to continue. Some of our homes are not so far from the university but still it is almost impossible to make it through the checkpoints and to go from one city to another. And so studying is even more difficult. All of this kills our hope.

But despite all of these hardships we students are working hard to obtain our education so that we can change the future. We would hope to give a message to the entire world that we are not savage or uncivilized as some people say. We are dedicated students searching for an education just like any other student you would find all over the world.

—*Hammad, business administration student*

(Complete essays are available at http://www.najah.edu/english/ reports/report11.htm)

School boys and girls subjected to searches and humiliation at the hands of heavily armed IDF troops on their daily commute to school. - N. Hashlamoun

6. Confiscation of Palestinian land and property damage

A Gallup survey published by the Israeli newspaper *Ma'ariv* on May 26, 2001 revealed that most Israelis agreed with not only an unconditional freeze on settlement construction but also with an end to all settlements. The Israeli government, however, obviously has a different opinion. Thousands of dunams (1 dunam = 0.25 acre) of Palestinian land have been expropriated to expand Jewish settlements or to build bypass roads. From the beginning of the Al Aqsa Intifada until May 2003, Israel confiscated 848,155 dunams of Palestinian land and razed another 18,521 dunams.[101]

Israeli acquisition of Palestinian land and the building of settlements are politically and economically motivated, and are *not* due to a shortage of housing. According to an Israeli Housing Ministry report published on April 16, 2001, most of the housing units constructed in public projects in the Israeli West Bank settlements of Givat Ze'ev, Ma'ale Adumim and Har Homa (all in the immediate Jerusalem area) over the previous six years remained *unsold and empty*. Of 3,470 units in Ma'ale Adumim, 1,610 (47%) remained unsold; 790 (97%) of the 810 units constructed in Givat Ze'ev remained unsold; and 2,200 (76%) of the housing units offered in Har Homa between 1999–2000 remained unsold.

In contrast, Israel has had a history of confiscating and destroying Palestinian land and property. Since 1967 over 11,000 Palestinian homes have been destroyed in the West Bank and Gaza, 4000 of which have been destroyed since September 2000, with dozens of new demolition orders issued each month by the Israeli authorities.[102] On November 23, 2001 The UN Committee Against Torture condemned Israel's house demolition practices as violating Article 16 of the UN Convention Against Torture and other Cruel, Inhuman or Degrading Treatment or Punishment.[103] The committee stated that the Israeli government's house demolition and closure policies "May, in certain instances, amount to cruel, inhuman or degrading treatment or punishment." Israel's attacks on residential areas only increased during the first 15 months of the Al Aqsa Intifada, costing the Palestinians over $305 million in physical damage. The toll of the damage done in the West Bank (in 2000–2001) totals as follows:[104]

- 720 homes completely destroyed, affecting 73,600 people
- 30 mosques destroyed
- 12 churches destroyed
- 134 water wells destroyed
- 34,606 olive and fruit trees uprooted
- 14,339 dunams of land bulldozed or burned

In the Gaza Strip:

- More than 600 houses destroyed
- Approximately 16,000 dunams of land, mostly agricultural, razed by the Israeli army

Then in the March/April 2002 invasion, a further $361 million worth of property was destroyed and looted by the Israeli army. This shelling and demolition amounted to:

- 881 homes destroyed
- 2,883 houses in refugee camps damaged, affecting 22,500 people

Still later, in May 2004 the Israeli army launched a massive attack on the Rafah refugee camp in the Gaza Strip. During the course of the operation, more than 40 Palestinians were killed, the vast majority of them civilians. But the focus of the assault was home demolition on a vast scale, which left almost 4,000 Palestinians homeless.

The destruction wreaked by the Israeli army was strongly condemned by UN Secretary General Kofi Annan, who urged "Israel to uphold its obligations as an occupying power by immediately halting such actions, which are tantamount to collective punishment and a clear violation of international law."[105]

Palestinian woman mourns the demolition of her home.
N. Hashlamoun

Home demolition in Hebron.
N. Hashlamoun

by the Author

For years the family of Tony Nassar, a graduate of Bethlehem Bible College where I serve as Dean of Students, has been striving to hold onto their ancestral land. The story of the Nassar family is typical of many Palestinians living in the Gaza Strip and the West Bank, whose greatest nightmare is to wake up one day to see their land fenced off and confiscated by Israeli settlers.

The Nassar family purchased a 100-acre vineyard near Bethlehem – Daher's Vineyard, as the family call it today – in 1924 and 1925. They have paid taxes on the land since the British Mandate over Palestine, and from the very beginning have worked diligently to plant grapevines, fruit trees and olive trees.

At various times they have applied to the occupying Israeli government for municipal water and electricity, but all of their requests were denied. The Israeli army, on several occasions, blocked the only road to the vineyard, preventing the family from using tractors to plough the land. One time, a mule used by the family to work the land was shot and killed by Israeli settlers.

Daher's Vineyard first came under threat of appropriation in October 1991, when the Israeli authorities determined to confiscate 75% of the land for future Israeli projects. To prepare the way for the appropriation of Daher's Vineyard, the Israeli authorities issued an order in 1990 for the demolition of two small buildings used by the family for storage, claiming that the structures were built without a permit, but the family succeeded in blocking that overture through the courts.

Repeated infringements took place at various times over the next decade, but the Nassar family, fueled by their faith and long historical connection to the land, refused to give up. They sought to prove legitimate ownership of the land within the Israeli court system, and did achieve brief respites from Israeli aggression.

Then, one evening in February 2003, Tony Nassar called me with news that settlers from a nearby Jewish settlement were once again using giant bulldozers and heavy tractors to carve a new road through the land. I wondered how I, Tony's teacher and pastor, could be of any help in such a matter, but I promised Tony my prayers and a visit to the land the following day.

The next day I took a group of six – Christian attorneys Jonathan Kuttab and Sani Khoury, a visiting Danish pastor, a local land surveyor, Tony and myself – to the Nassar land. Upon our arrival we saw the bulldozers at work and Jonathan, speaking in Hebrew, tried to persuade the settlers to cease their bulldozing, but they continued their work on the land unimpeded. Finally, Jonathan challenged us.

"The only way to stop them is to stand before the digging tractor. Who will stand with me?"

Three of us joined Jonathan, standing right where the tractor was cutting the earth to finish the road. The settler operating the machine cursed and threatened us as he continued digging at our feet. The situation became very tense. Soon there was a big hole dug in the earth under Jonathan's feet causing him to pitch forward and lose his footing. Standing next to him, I quickly helped pull him back to level ground.

As soon as he regained his balance, Jonathan stood back in front of the giant digger and shouted to the operator that no matter what happened, he would not move. Astounded by such a display of courage and fearing that our nonviolent resistance could seriously hurt one of us, the operator called his boss to the settlement, who gave him the order to stop clearing the land. Within 15 minutes, police arrived and with difficulty convinced the settlers to go. The Nassar family was joyful that we were able to stop the settlers.

It was another small, though uncertain victory for the Nassar family. The next day we had a prayer meeting on Daher's Vineyard seeking God's protection over the land. A Jewish Rabbi and other peacemakers joined with us to stand in solidarity with the Nassars and to develop a strategy for protecting the Nassar land against future theft and confisation. The case of the Nassar family is still an ongoing saga and a final decision on ownership is still pending in the Israeli court.

Tony's story is one of thousands of its kind that are all too familiar to Palestinians. Many landowners have been injured and even killed trying to protect their land from confiscation. In March 2003, an American peace activist, Rachel Corrie, was killed as she stood before a military bulldozer in solidarity with a Palestinian landowner in Gaza.

7. Restraint of and assault on journalists

On March 31, 2000 Israel declared Ramallah and El-Bireh closed military areas, preventing journalists from entering the area and demanding that those within the area exit immediately. In April 2002, the International Press Association declared the West Bank the second most dangerous place for journalists to work after Afghanistan. At least 20 press centers were shelled, vandalized or damaged. At the height of the Al-Aqsa Intifada eight journalists had been killed, one of them Italian, and at least 167 journalists had been attacked by Israeli soldiers.[106] Many journalists were beaten or detained and/or had their equipment confiscated or destroyed. Five Palestinian journalists were arrested and are currently in administrative detention.

More Than Just a Journalist

"What do I want from this life? What makes you happy is not enough. All the things that satisfy our instincts only satisfy the animal in us. I want to be proud of myself. I want more. I want to look up to myself and when I die, I want to smile because of the things I have done, not cry for the things I haven't done."
—Tom Hurndall

British photographer and activist fatally wounded by an Israeli sniper while trying to get two small Palestinian children to safety.

8. Arrests and routine detention of Palestinians

Over a period of approximately four years, the Israelis arrested over 40,000 Palestinians, incarcerating them for varying periods of time in Israeli prisons and detention centers. As late as August 2004, 7,500 were still in prison, 700 of these under administrative detention. Four hundred and seventy of the prisoners were less than 18 years old.[108] Many of the prisoners were subjected to torture and were not given adequate medical care. Under so-called "administrative detention," individuals are routinely imprisoned for months or years without receiving a trial – or even being charged with a crime.[109]

9. Construction of the Separation Barrier

A separation barrier – in many places taking the form of a wall standing eight meters tall, twice the height of the Berlin Wall – is touted by Israel as a "security fence" and is the most recent measure by Israel to siphon off Palestinian land, part of the Israelis' own ongoing, latter-day "Partition Plan". The barrier is being rapidly constructed by Israel almost totally *beyond* the so-called Green Line, Israel's internationally recognized border along the 1949 Armistice Line – that is, *within* the West Bank – against the wishes of Palestinians and despite international opposition.

The Israeli rationale offered for the separation barrier is that it is intended to keep Palestinian suicide bombers away from Israeli civilians. It is implied that the wall keeps "them there and us here." While this arguably may be a secondary effect, the implications of the wall reach much further. By the time of its projected completion in 2008, the wall will be more than 450 miles long and, according to the *Palestine Monitor*, will, in effect, annex as much as 45% of the West Bank to Israel. This would leave Palestinians with only 12% of historic Palestine.

Not only does the construction of the wall uproot tens of thousands of trees and destroy hundreds of fresh-water wells, but it also cuts off the land's inhabitants from their groves, their agricultural land, and from one another. One hundred Palestinian villages will be separated from their agricultural lands, much of it rich and ideal for olive growing.[109] The route that the wall takes, as it snakes tortuously between Palestinian villages and Israeli settlements, exposes the real reasons for its erection: 1) it siphons off prime Palestinian natural resources, 2) it keeps all the Jewish settlements in the West Bank intact and allows the settlers free movement to and from Israel, and 3) it squeezes Palestinians into small enclaves, or confined pockets of land.

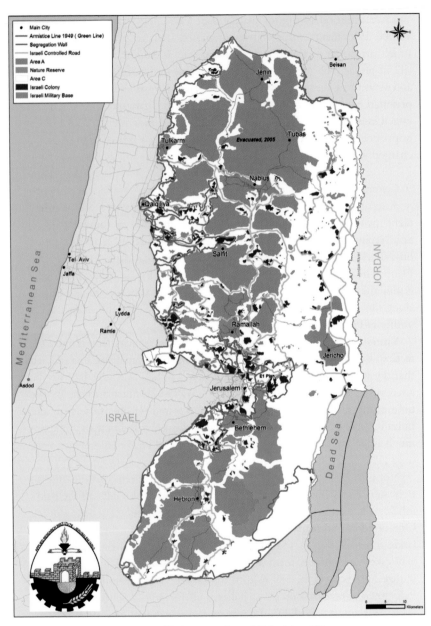

Map 12: The Wall of Separation (in blue) Zigzags through Palestinian Cities, Towns and Villages – 2012

The barrier, which Israel claims will prevent Palestinians from entering Israel "illegally," also cuts off some 12,000 Palestinians from social services, schools and farmland and serves to isolate Palestinian towns and villages from one another. The Palestinian cities of Qalqiliya and Tulkarm are already completely encircled by the wall. The fence has been referred to as an "Apartheid Wall," as it will clearly lead to the "bantustanization" of Palestinian towns and villages (recalling the many black homelands established under South Africa's former apartheid regime). Eventually 875,000 Palestinians will be either permanently confined to small, encircled enclaves and isolated from wider West Bank society, or enclosed in West Bank cantons.

International, Israeli and Palestinian peace advocates have tried to peacefully protest the construction of the wall, and continue to do so to this day, but to no avail. In most cases, the Palestinian protestors have lacked the freedom to even approach the wall in order to express objections to its building. Nearly all parties who have dared to demonstrate against the wall's construction have been faced with heavily-armed Israeli troops, frequently responding with bullets, tear gas and incarcerations.

10. Elusive Permits

Even before beginning construction of the security barrier, Israel's tactics have long served to separate Palestinians from one another and limit their freedom of movement within the West Bank. Since the start of the Oslo peace process, the West Bank and Gaza have gradually fallen under permanent closure. This takes the form of 120 permanent checkpoints, hundreds of earth mounds or other obstructions, and hundreds more non-

Olive picking season in Palestine. N. Hashlamoun

Clockwise from top left: The 8-meter high separation wall cuts through the Palestinian town of Bethany. - By the author.

Palestinian teenager expresses feelings about the wall. - N. Hashlamoun.

Members of international solidarity group demonstrate to protest the wall placing themselves between Israeli troops and Palestinians affected by the construction of the wall.
- N. Hashlamoun.

The wall in Bethany cripples Palestinian life on both sides of the wall.
- N. Hashlamoun.

permanent checkpoints, all serving to control Palestinian movement among the some 300 separate enclaves which these barriers create.

This means that most Palestinians cannot even travel from town to town within the West Bank without a permit from Israeli authorities, a system enforced at hundreds of checkpoints throughout the West Bank. Palestinians know how humiliating and time-consuming applying for a permit can be. The rejection rate is high. And even when Palestinians have permits to travel within the West Bank, they are not allowed to travel using their own vehicles but must go on foot or use public transportation. Moreover, the Israelis can, and often do, deny passage – capriciously and without explanation – even when Palestinians do present a perfectly valid permit.

With this grave injustice already in place, the separation barrier is now tightening the noose even more, further isolating Palestinians from their loved ones, from essential services, and from much of their land. It is already having a devastating effect on the daily life of the great majority of Palestinians. As the wall dissects the Palestinian heartland, parents living on one side of the wall are prevented from visiting their children who live on the other side – without a permit from the Israeli authorities. The wall is only adding to the anguish and sorrow of a population that has been in distress for over half a century.

Life in Palestine

By Lucy Mair

How do I describe what life is like here – of the sadness in the eyes of my colleagues, of the exhaustion that results when every daily action requires an extraordinary effort, when perseverance is no longer enough and futility and despair fight for a place on the proud faces carrying bags and babies and the burden of poverty through checkpoints, over dirt piles, past soldiers and tanks and the bombed-out shells of buildings. On rainy days the muddy water swells around the feet, slowing passage. The soldiers stand in shelters and never seem to get wet under their helmets and uniforms and weapons, protected by arrogance and hatred and a state and an army and the world's superpower. They pull people out of the battered Ford Transit vehicles that always seem to drive too fast to make up for lost time, jostling the school children and old men and mothers who ride in them, if

A peaceful demonstration against the Separation Wall. N. Hashlamoun.

Palestinian art conveys a message of protest. (By the author).

Palestinian expresses outrage at IDF soldier at checkpoint. N. Hashlamoun.

they can afford the 3-shekel fare and if they are not males between the ages of 18 and 35 and if they have permission to enter Jerusalem and if there is no curfew or closure. The soldiers line them up, face to the wall, make them sit in the dirt or stand in the rain or the scorching sun for minutes or hours while they chat on their mobile phones, joke with their friends, eat, smoke, laugh, abuse, with words and with actions.

How do I explain that when the wind blows it does not bring respite from the heat, but rather fills the mouth and the nose with grit, ripe with the smell of sewage and garbage and exhaust fumes. An Israeli woman asks "Why don't they clean up their streets? Why do they live like animals?" And the children play in the refuse that can never be collected in villages and towns and cities that remain for hours and days and weeks and months under crippling curfews. Curfews that are enforced with a shoot-to-kill policy. Curfews that are not lifted during school hours. Curfews that prevent pregnant women from giving birth in hospitals, which stop ambulances in their tracks, which forced a Bethlehem family to live with the decaying corpse of their family member for days.

How can I express the feeling of death that lurks around every corner—of the children shot on their way home from school, of the old woman killed while sitting on her porch, of the people in Gaza killed in their homes when the bomb was dropped on their apartment building, of the refugees killed in their homes in Jenin when the tanks and the bulldozers ate up their camp, razing houses on top of their inhabitants, of people killed in taxis and on sidewalks when the Israelis carry out "preventive pinpointed killings".

How do I tell the story of refugees made homeless for the third or fourth time, of the woman who throws up her hands, in the middle of her house, with the gaping holes from the bulldozers in the wall, and the windows shot out by snipers, and the rooms filled with the debris of a family's life, and begs me to tell the people of the U.S. to please make it stop, this terrible nightmare. And wipes away my tears which I am ashamed to shed, and hugs me and gives me some of the precious drinking water that is so hard to come by in Rafah these days since the wells have been destroyed. And the people next door who invite us in for coffee, while sewage washes past the steps of their battered home which is sure to be demolished, standing as it is on the front line of Rafah, empty land where the next row of houses once stood. And the farmers chased from their olive trees by armed settlers and the people in Hebron who live with sandbags blocking their windows because the settlers have shot the glass out so many times, and my colleague who only sees his four adoring children once a week, because the closures make the distance between his home and his work, just 30 km apart, a four-hour journey.

How can I show the faces behind the statistics—70% unemployment, 75% poverty, 13% malnutrition in children under five? The number of dead and injured and blinded and handicapped, in wheelchairs and hospital beds, and orphaned and homeless. The children that play 'funeral in the schoolyard', or 'ambulance stopped at the checkpoint', or 'soldier abusing passersby'. The number of school days missed and the number of schools invaded and closed and the number of teachers who can't get to work and the number of students who can't afford to return to university. And the number of people in administrative detention, held without charge, without trial, without lawyers, without family visits, in tents without adequate food and water and sanitation and protection from the elements. And the number of trees uprooted, and dunams of land razed and kilometers of bypass roads built and wells destroyed. And of the courage and the dignity and the determination and the family who rebuilds their house again and again, each time it is demolished. And of the fear and the loss and the humiliation and the despair that has robbed even the living of their lives.

[Lucy Mair, then a worker for Grassroots International, wrote this piece during the Al-Aqsa Intifada, in February 2003; since 2005 she has been a researcher for Human Rights Watch.]
Published on http://gush-shalom.org/diary/diary51.html

Top: Bread distribution at an NGO relief center in Hebron. N. Hashlamoun.

Center: This bougainvillea, which graces a Palestinian fence, absorbs the sun's rays, despite the suffocating presence of the Wall. (By the author).

Bottom: The cross on a local Bethlehem church defies imprisonment within the wall. (BBC Mass-Media Department.)

The Flight to Egypt, Palestinian Artist Zaki Baboun offers a
contemporary rendition of the Holy Family's escape to Egypt.

CHAPTER EIGHT

THE ROLE OF AMERICA

When a just cause reaches its flood tide - whatever stands in the way must fall before its overwhelming power.
-Carrie Chapman Catt

The policy of the United States in the Middle East is not an American policy but an Israeli one. It is not American because it does not represent the values and concerns of most Americans. It is Israeli because it has been manipulated by the Israel lobby in the U.S. and by Christian Zionists, who together place the interests of the State of Israel over the interests of America and the American people. My wife Brenda and I lived in the United States for many years, and in connection with our work as United Methodist missionaries we have visited churches and stayed in people's homes in at least twenty-five different American States. We have spoken in churches, colleges and universities, in high schools and elementary schools, and to various social clubs. We have learned from this broad exposure over a period of many years that Americans, for the most part, are peace-loving people who have a strong sense of justice and fair dealing. Thus many U.S. citizens acknowledge the moral gap that has developed over the years between who Americans are as a people and the behavior of their government as it deals with Israel and the Palestinians.

Regrettably, many Americans have resigned themselves to the notion that the power of the lobbies is too strong to challenge and that the damage they have done is impossible to repair. Nevertheless there are still those Americans who will not keep silent in the face of the mounting injustice of American policies in the Middle East. Some Christian denominations, however, are experiencing a new awareness and hence a spirit of disenchantment with the injustices not only sanctioned but actually funded by their government, and they are beginning to speak out.

It is my opinion, or even a fact, had it not been for an entrenched American foreign policy that has consistently favored one party in the conflict in the Middle East over the other, the Arab-Israeli disputes would

Palestinians watch as George W. Bush announces his new peace initiatives.
N. Hashlamoun.

have been resolved many years ago. The Palestinian people lost their battles first in the Oval Office and in the Halls of Congress before they ever lost them on the ground, as they fought to stop the Zionist takeover of their country.

In spite of all of this, an American visitor to the Palestinian territories will discover that most Palestinians genuinely like and welcome Americans. Palestinians, however, are forced to view Americans through two lenses. With one they see America as the champion of democracy, freedom and human rights the world over, while with the other lens they see an America which, through the government's policies, denies to Palestinians all of the above.

For me this is a very difficult chapter to write, because my family and I love America and are grateful to the country that received us and granted us citizenship and freedom, in a land of great opportunities. All of my siblings, with the exception of one sister, are now U.S. citizens. My mother and her two brothers, with all of their children, have all likewise migrated to the U.S. in the last 40 years. My mother was very proud when, for the first time in her life, she stood before an American judge in 1978 and pledged allegiance to the American flag – her flag.

Indeed, it is my love for *both* America and for Palestine that prompts me to present this perspective on America's role in the Arab-Israeli conflict.

WHY ARE THE UNITED STATES AND ISRAEL SUCH STRONG ALLIES?

The rise of U.S. strategic interests in the Middle East corresponded with the emergence of the oil industry in many Arab countries and U.S. dependence on this vital resource. The United States had two primary goals in the Middle East: to secure the oil resources of the Arab states for its own domestic use and to prevent the region from falling within the Soviet sphere of influence. During the Mandate period, the Zionists had been assiduously courting U.S. favor, and by the end of World War II they had convinced the American government that the emerging Jewish state was a strategic asset in the region.[110] Upon Israel's declaration of independence on May 14, 1948, the U.S. immediately recognized it as a state, though it was not at all clear in the first decade of Israel's history that the country was firmly in the

American camp. Indeed, at times the American government's need to court the oil-rich Arabs was an obstacle to its relationship with Israel.

From the end of the Second World War until the late 1980's, the Cold War framed the context of the American-Israeli alliance. In the 1950's the relationship was shaky, but by the end of the 1950's Israel was firmly under the wing of the United States. Israel's main role as an ally to the U.S. was to provide intelligence from inside the Soviet Union by way of those Jews still living there. Eventually, Israel became America's key ally in its paranoid war against the spread of communism, helping mainly in the area of covert operations, not only in the Middle East but also in Africa and Latin America. Whenever America was unable to become directly involved politically in countries like Angola, South Africa, Columbia or Guatemala, it simply had the Israelis step in. By the start of the 1967 Arab-Israeli War, their relationship had been sealed.

As the alliance grew, the two countries became entangled in a booming weapons trade, trapping each other in a web of dirty secrets. Additionally, the powerful lobbies of the weapons industry allied themselves with certain Jewish lobbies and together they became a major source of money and information for figures in both the Republican and Democratic parties. These forces, with powerful allies in both the Israeli and American governments and the media, have succeeded in shaping Israel's image and issues surrounding the Arab-Israeli conflict into an almost unquestioned political narrative.

While today the Cold War is over, the U.S.-Israel relationship is not. In fact, America's moral and material support for Israel has only increased since the fall of the USSR, as the two countries have found new mutual enemies in the form of "terrorist threats" and "rogue states" such as Iraq. Thus, support for Israel remains a given within the American political system. Beyond the obvious political and economic ties between the two countries, popular support for the State of Israel – automatic and uncritical – has become woven into the social fabric of the United States. In short, it is now a part of American culture. Thus, today an American politician has little hope of winning an election espousing a platform that is in any way critical of Israel – unless it is for Israel's government not being tough *enough*, as with the 2005 withdrawal from Gaza.

One major reason for this is the central place given to Israel in the understanding of many within the growing American evangelical movement. As a committed evangelical Christian myself, this is a cause of real concern. For many of my fellow evangelicals, a national homeland for the Jewish people in Israel is strategically important in their views of prophecy and how God works in the different periods or dispensations of history. The formation and expansion of the State of Israel is considered to be a necessary step in the fulfillment of God's will and a pre-condition for the second coming of Jesus Christ. Not surprisingly, many Jewish Israelis have a great antipathy toward the evangelical movement with its stress on Jesus as the Christ and Savior of all peoples, and because it seeks their conversion to Christianity. Nevertheless the Israeli government has not passed up the opportunity to tap this rich human and financial resource supporting the cause of colonizing Palestine.

Being friends with Israel continues to have a place in the American liberal mindset as well. This bond is in part a natural expression of the remorse and perhaps guilt people still feel over the horrors of the Holocaust, and also a response to the anti-Semitism that not only led to that profound tragedy but indeed still infects our world. However, in today's discourse, *any* perceived criticism of the State of Israel is often automatically equated, deliberately and many times unfairly, with anti-Semitism.

In sum, America's relationship with Israel is the result of over fifty years of perceived common interests in the realms of geo-politics, economics and culture. This kinship did not form spontaneously but grew out of many years of intentional effort among the political, economic and religious figures of both countries. Though much of this courtship occurred behind closed doors and in the corridors of power, it is important not to interpret the relationship through the lens of a simplistic conspiracy theory. It is a much more complex and nuanced linkage. In fact, the American-Israeli alliance has never been a completely open and trusting one, and both governments have in fact kept each other in the dark when it suited their interests. Arms dealers, for instance, are first and foremost interested in profits, not friendship.

Still, there are a few influential people in both countries who, as dissenting voices from the status quo, do question the integrity of the relationship and its strategic advantage to the United States – *and* to Israel. These people, however, are in the minority, and until they receive more support from their colleagues and the public they will remain powerless to challenge the U.S.-Israel alliance.

The Nixon, Ford, and Carter administrations all concurred with international opinion that Israeli settlements in the Occupied Territories of the West Bank and Gaza are illegal. Since then, subsequent administrations have toned down their condemnation of settlements, but still opposed their expansion. They refer to them as "obstacles to peace," but have refrained from labeling the settlements illegal. Yet in spite of its seeming disapproval, the U.S. has offered increasing support to Israel on this issue in recent years. Indeed, America has repeatedly vetoed UN Security Council resolutions calling for the halting of settlement construction. The U.S. is one of five countries granted the power to veto such resolutions (the others are the UK, France, Russia and China). Since the UN's founding, the U.S. has exercised this power nearly 80 times, the overwhelming majority of these vetoes being in opposition to resolutions favored by the majority of the world's nations. Approximately half of these vetoed draft resolutions directly concerned the Israeli-Palestinian conflict and either criticized Israel for its human rights violations or called on it to comply with previous UN resolutions and the Geneva Convention of 1949.

For a list of UN Security Council draft resolutions directly condemning illegal Israeli settlements and the confiscation of Palestinian land which were vetoed by the U.S., see _Appendix III._ There can be found also a list of twelve resolutions insisting that Israel comply with the Fourth Geneva Convention relative to the Protection of Civilian Persons in Time of War (August 12, 1949), under which such settlements are illegal – again, all vetoed by the U.S.

DISPROPORTIONATE AID: U.S. SUPPORT OF ISRAEL

Every year the United States gives _billions_ of dollars in foreign aid to Israel. This enormous influx of funds bloats the Israeli government's budget, freeing up funds for colonization through the confiscation of Palestinian land and the construction of Israeli settlements on it.

U.S. financial assistance to Israel officially began in 1949, largely as economic aid. Economic aid comes in the form of both loans and grants allocated by the Economic Support Fund (ESF), and is provided on a direct-transfer basis without any U.S. governmental oversight. Military aid in the form of loans began 10 years later and increased substantially between 1966 and 1970, to make up almost half of the then $102 million in yearly aid to Israel. Since 1985, this Foreign Military Financing (FMF) has come solely in the form of grants used to improve Israel's defense capabilities by financing the purchase of U.S. military equipment, services, and training. By 1971, it became a practice of Congress to designate specific amounts of foreign aid to Israel, which for the next few years averaged $2 billion per year and from 1985 has averaged in excess of $3 billion per year. Two-thirds of this assistance is military aid.[111]

This yearly figure, comprising one-third of America's total foreign aid budget, makes Israel the largest recipient of U.S. aid in the world and has helped build Israel into the third largest military power in the world.[112] Israel – a country smaller than Hong Kong in both area and population – makes up just one-tenth of one percent (.001) of the world's population and has one of the world's highest per capita incomes, comparable with that of many European countries. All other worldwide U.S. aid recipients are developing nations that have either been devastated by poverty or natural disasters or are somehow strategic to U.S. interests. Many U.S. aid recipients, for example, make their military bases available to the U.S. or are key members of international alliances favored by the U.S.

Another interesting case, and one directly linked to Israel, is that of Egypt. Egypt became the *second*-highest U.S. aid recipient in 1979 when it signed the historic peace agreement with Israel. That very year, aid to Egypt jumped to $2.2 billion per year, compared to a combined total of $4.2 billion for the preceding 26 years. This means that Egypt and Israel together are the recipients of *more than half* of U.S. grants worldwide. There is an acknowledged link between this sudden skyrocketing of U.S. aid to Egypt and the U.S.'s relationship with Israel. As the late Yale University Law School Professor Charles Black, Jr. put it, "Truly huge grants are made only in the interest of Israel. If anyone can think of a better reason for this altogether astonishing out-sized largesse to Egypt, starting just when the separate peace was coming into sight, I would be glad to hear it...."[113]

However, the actual total of U.S. aid to Israel – its true cost to U.S. taxpayers – is easily *twice* the published amount of $3 billion per year. By some estimates the figure is closer to $10 billion per year! These latter estimates take into account a variety of other U.S. aid channels, separate from the foreign aid budget, as well as billions in loan guarantees to Israel for which the U.S. has waived payment before the loans' maturity dates. By these means, almost all of these loans are converted to grants, a fact verified by congressional researchers. Since 1974, repayment of almost all U.S. military loans to Israel has been waived, bringing the total from 1974 to 2002 to $42 billion. In effect, the vast majority of U.S. loans to Israel have long amounted to outright grants. In addition to U.S. government-backed loans, Israel receives up to $1 billion annually in commercial loans. The State of Israel (that is, the Israeli government) also receives in the neighborhood of $1 billion annually from Americans in tax-deductible donations through Jewish charities, making Israel the only foreign government Americans can contribute to in this way.[114]

Israel not only receives special treatment in the form of waived loan repayments and tax-deductible contributions, but also in the *way* it receives U.S. aid. Thanks to a bill passed by Congress in 1982, Israel is the sole recipient of aid in one lump sum during the first month of the fiscal year, rather than in four quarterly installments. This allows Israel to invest the funds in the U.S. markets and earn interest. Meanwhile, the U.S., since it must borrow the aid funds from future revenues, *pays* interest on these funds which it has granted to Israel in advance – yet another handout, cleverly buried in bureaucratic logistics!

Thus, despite the fact that the State of Israel breaks numerous international laws and conventions, and despite Israel's brutal policies condemned by the UN, the European Union, the National Council of Churches, Amnesty International, the International Red Cross and numerous other international bodies, the U.S. has maintained its uniquely generous and uninterrupted financial support over the last five decades. The former U.S. senator from South Dakota, Jim Abourezk, wrote: "What drives much of congressional support for Israel is fear – fear that the pro-Israel lobby will either withhold campaign contributions or give money to one's opponent."[115]

AMERICA'S ROLE IN PEACE TALKS

While there are many reasons for the failure of these diplomatic activities and no one party should shoulder all the blame, the United States truly holds the greatest responsibility for the collapse of most peace initiatives, especially in the last fifty years. First, it is important to stress that successive U.S. governments have seemingly worked very hard to bring peace to the region. Moreover, several U.S. presidents invested much time and personal effort trying to bring the warring parties to reach a peace settlement. It is therefore ironic that the country that has invested so much time, effort and funds in bridging the gap between the opposing sides is also the country most responsible for *widening* the gap.

For a long time Israel trusted no party to mediate peace except for her strong ally, the United States, and hence both Israel and the U.S. bullied or out-maneuvered every other possible mediator, to their exclusion. The Israelis did not trust the UN or the Europeans, nor did they have confidence in the former U.S.S.R. or the post-Soviet Russian Federation.[116] The Palestinians never had any say in who could or couldn't take part in peace talks, despite the fact that they are the other significant party to the conflict. Arab countries have often been consulted, or invited to endorse the final peace proposals, but in the negotiation process these Arab governments could only politely accept or reject what Israeli and American diplomats presented to them via numerous envoys and shuttle diplomats. Whenever other parties like the UN or European Union have been formally invited to participate, Israel and the U.S. quickly made every effort to keep their involvement marginal.

The fact that the U.S. made herself the sole broker in negotiations is at the root of the failure of all attempts to end the conflict. The U.S. was obliged to show the international community that it was capable and worthy of such a mission, thus America always created the impression that it was keeping busy working for peace in the Middle East. With every new political crisis, the U.S. sent a new envoy or launched a new diplomatic initiative, often knowing ahead of time that the plan was doomed to failure and the diplomat would return empty-handed. For the majority of U.S. administrations, "failure" in their Middle East role was for the world to *perceive* that they were doing nothing – whether their efforts were in reality achieving anything or not.

It is not that the U.S. does not yearn for peace in the Middle East. Every American president since Harry Truman would have been greatly honored to go down in history as the mediator of a Middle East peace agreement. However, the utter failure of most U.S. efforts is due to the American government's unquestionable bias toward the pro-Israel lobby and an unwillingness, or inability, to openly confront that lobby.[117]

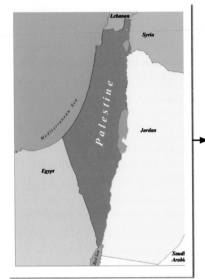

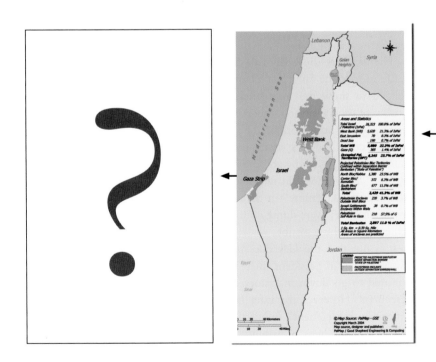

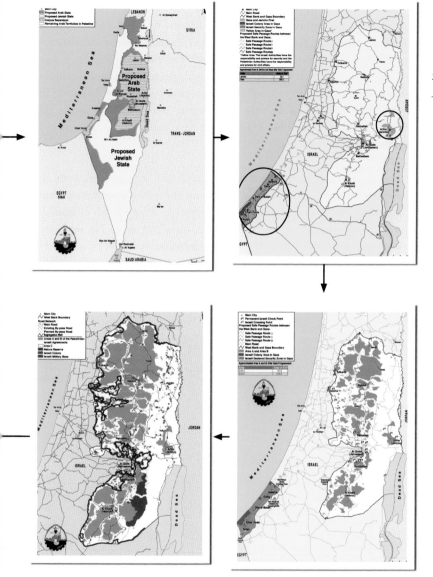

These maps tell the story of the systematic
conquest of Palestine. Please follow the arrow
starting at top left and go clockwise

The majority of American citizens are unaware of the vastly disproportionate amount of U.S. aid that goes to Israel each year. This does not change the fact that the U.S. government – and, by extension, all Americans – are supporting what amounts to ethnic cleansing, carried out by a government which has long received widespread international criticism for its poor human rights record and its political policies. By financing this government, the U.S. is directly encouraging Israel's actions and is thus responsible for the way in which Israel uses these funds. According to Middle East expert Professor Black:

> *Such a pattern of material, political and diplomatic support sends forth a message beyond itself – a message of approval of Israel's actions; it would be something like insane to furnish all this support for a regime such as Israel's while at the same time not approving the actions of that regime. The world at large must draw the inference that we do approve, that our weak protests over a few things cannot be seriously meant. The least possible inference would have to be that we don't care very much for human rights.*[118]

CHAPTER NINE

FURTHER PEACE PLANS

If you want to make peace, you don't talk to your friends. You talk to your enemies.
-Moshe Dayan

If you assume that there's no hope, you guarantee that there will be no hope. If you assume that there is an instinct for freedom, that there are opportunities to change things, there's a chance you may contribute to making a better world. That's your choice.
-Noam Chomsky

Peace is not something you wish for; it's something you make, something you do, something you are, something you give away.
-Robert Fulghum

The myriad attempts to resolve the Arab-Israeli conflict are – to put it in biblical terms – like "the number of the stars in the sky." Most of these diplomatic efforts to usher in peace during the last 100 years have failed, and instead of bringing about the much-desired peace, many of these attempts in fact hindered the resolution of the conflict or actually spun off yet another round of violence.

Many of the post-1967 Arab-Israeli peace plans were doomed to failure from the start because they didn't address the most heated issues – the occupation and the Israeli settlements – which were at the root of so much of the violence to begin with. For example, the Palestinian National Authority (PA) has repeatedly insisted that a freeze on settlement construction is necessary for peace to happen. Thus, many of the proposed peace plans have been recipes for peace without the key ingredients. Any plan that calls on Palestinians to cease all violence and terrorism, without also seeking to eliminate the conditions that have caused the violence to erupt, is merely addressing the symptoms rather than the disease. In Chapters 4 and 5 we mentioned briefly the Madrid Conference, the Oslo Accords, and the Sharm el-Sheikh Conference. Yet two more peace plans have been proposed since the eruption of the Al-Aqsa Intifada in 2000, the Mitchell Report and the Tenet Plan.

THE MITCHELL REPORT

The Mitchell Report, published on May 20, 2001, called for an immediate ceasefire, a freeze on Jewish settlements, and more determined action against terrorism by the Palestinian Authority.[103] Ariel Sharon, however, stated that Israel would not accept the settlement freeze recommended by the commission.

Meeting with an E.U. delegation in Jerusalem, Sharon refused to drop his own demand for "one week of quiet" before implementing the Mitchell Report recommendations, and he repeated his accusation against Arafat as leading "a coalition of terrorism in cooperation with Hamas, Islamic Jihad, Hezbollah, Fatah, Tanzim, and Force 17."[119]

CIA director George Tenet proposed what became known as the Tenet Plan. It was a ceasefire and security plan aimed at helping Israel and the PA to resume security cooperation, take measures to enforce a ceasefire, and share information on terrorist threats, thus intending to prevent acts of violence. In turn, Israel was to lift internal closures and barriers in the Palestinian territories; reopen external border outlets, including Gaza's seaport and airport; and re-deploy to positions held before September 28, 2000. While all parties agreed to the Tenet Plan which took effect on June 13, 2001, it was never implemented in any meaningful way. Its most obvious weak spot was focusing on reducing the violence and terrorism while neglecting to address the ongoing confiscation of land and building of settlements.

THE SAUDI PEACE INITIATIVE

In March 2002, Saudi Crown Prince Abdullah presented an eight-point peace proposal to the Arab League summit in Beirut, Lebanon promising "normal relations" with Israel in exchange for recognition of a Palestinian state and the refugees' right to return. On the second day of the summit, the Arab states approved the final draft of this Saudi peace initiative.

The main points of the plan were: an Israeli withdrawal from Palestinian areas, an end to the then-current Israeli siege on Ramallah, deployment of an international peacekeeping force, reconstruction of damaged Palestinian areas, renunciation of violence, talks on a political settlement to Israeli-Palestinian issues (as opposed to pending security issues), an end to Israeli settlement activity in Palestinian areas, and U.S. leadership in implementing UN Resolution 242, in exchange for Arab recognition of Israel's borders.

The Saudi peace proposal was endorsed by Yasser Arafat and approved by all Arab states, as well as by U.S. Secretary of State Colin Powell, E.U. Foreign Policy Chief Javier Solana, and Israeli Foreign Minister Shimon Peres, but it was rejected by Sharon and his Likud government.

The so-called Quartet was a panel formed in April 2002 and given the task of designing a "road map" for achieving an Israeli–Palestinian permanent status agreement, including the establishment of a Palestinian state. The panel was comprised of the foreign ministers of the U.S. and Russia and senior representatives from the E.U. and U.N. The Quartet met in New York in July 2002 to discuss a plan of action to end Israel's occupation and achieve the vision of two states within three years. The U.S. refused to acknowledge Yasser Arafat as leader of the Palestinians and stuck by its decision to cut off all contact with him, even though the U.N., E.U. and Russia all recognized Arafat as the legitimate head of his people's statehood movement. Thus, the Road Map plan was not issued until April 30, 2003, after Mahmoud Abbas had been sworn in as the first Palestinian prime minister.

THE ROAD MAP (See Appendix IV for Full Document)

The Quartet's Road Map aimed at a comprehensive settlement of the Israel-Palestinian conflict by 2005. While it offered no timetable as such, it included target dates and benchmarks for dismantling Jewish settlement outposts, implementing thorough reform of the PA, and the creation of a Palestinian state by 2005, with monitoring groups present under the auspices of the Quartet.

Implementation of the Road Map stalled due to the ongoing construction of Israeli settlements and the unwillingness or inability of the U.S. to maintain impartiality as a mediator. U.S. President George W. Bush all but promised Israel in April 2004 that the Road Map would not require Israeli withdrawal from settlements in the West Bank. Jim Winkler, General Secretary of the United Methodist Church General Board of Church and Society, framed the issue this way: "Instead of telling Prime Minister Sharon that it's okay now to violate international law and United Nations resolutions, President Bush should be pressuring both sides to stem the violence and start talking again. President Bush has effectively told the world that what Israel has taken by force from the Palestinians is now acceptable. This is a road map to war."[120] With the kind of cautious and one-sided American support enunciated by Bush, nothing was able to save the Road Map, and by the end of April 2004 Sharon himself had announced that the Road Map was dead.[121]

THE GENEVA ACCORD

In the fall of 2003 a "virtual" peace agreement was signed by moderate Israelis and Palestinians, an unofficial plan launched at a ceremony in Geneva amidst a flurry of publicity.[122] The blueprint was the brainchild of former Israeli Justice Minister Yossi Beilin and former Palestinian Information Minister Yasser Abed Rabbo, who had previously served as official negotiators for their respective governments.

The Accord met with a mixed response, ranging from condemnation by the Israeli government and numerous Palestinian factions to enthusiastic support from some peace groups and international diplomats. Israeli officials refused to publicly endorse even one of the Accord proposals in its entirety. In any event, what distinguished the Accord from other peace proposals was its recognition of the need for both parties to accept compromise, and to seek a political settlement before demanding a total cessation of hostilities. Despite the initial excitement generated in some quarters by the Geneva Accord, as so often happens, it was overshadowed by real-world events which, in the eyes of many, have rendered the agreement irrelevant. Nevertheless, the framers' real point was made: that the outlines of a final-status agreement acceptable to both sides are already well-known (and in some detail), requiring only the element of genuine compromise activated by the political will of forward-looking leaders.

The international community, including the U.S., wanted to calm the situation in the region, perhaps not so much for the benefit of the Israelis and Palestinians themselves but now in the larger cause of countering the forces of militant Islam. These extremist groups, motivated in part by the ongoing injustices against the Palestinians, were ready to strike against U.S. and other Western interests in Iraq, Afghanistan and elsewhere around the globe. America's support for Sharon, and now their own military adventures in Iraq, served only to further damage the reputation of the U.S. in the eyes of the Arab and Islamic world, and also of some European countries. As a result, Sharon was pressured from the U.S. and the International community to engage in some kind of peace process. Sharon's inability to accept any of the peace plans put forward – forced him to find an alternative, one that would buy him time and sidestep the mounting international pressure against his government. The result was Ariel Sharon's plan to unilaterally disengage from the Gaza Strip.

THE DISENGAGEMENT PLAN

> I don't know if it will be done in one go, or gradually, but over the course of time, it will not be right to continue Jewish settlement in Gaza.
> —Ariel Sharon

On 2 February 2004, Israeli Prime Minister Arial Sharon announced to the Likud Party his plan to dismantle the Israeli settlements from the Gaza Strip. This turned out to be a unilateral plan, since Sharon chose not to discuss or coordinate his moves with the Palestinian National Authority. Sharon's frequently expressed claim was that there was no party on the Palestinian side with whom Israeli officials could deal – there was "no one to talk to."

Soon after Sharon's announcement, opposition in the Likud Party began to mount against his withdrawal plan. On May 2, 2004, the Likud party voted overwhelmingly against the plan, the pullout rejected by a ratio of 60% to 20%. Strong opponents of the pullout, such as senior Likud cabinet ministers Netanyahu, Shalom and Livnat, called for a referendum, however the Knesset by a vote of 72 to 39 rejected the referendum proposal. This seemed to confirm what the polls were already attesting to – the fact that a majority of the general Israeli public, over 60%, were for the pullout.

Sharon set the month of August 2005 as the target date for carrying out the transfer of the settlers, and the following two months as a timeframe for the completion of the pullout. On August 14, 2005 the period of voluntary evacuation of the settlements expired, and three days later the forced eviction of all the remaining settlers took place. By August 21, all 21 Israeli settlements in the Gaza Strip, plus four in the West Bank, were evacuated with little resistance. Soon after the pullout the Israeli army embarked on the demolition of all the settler homes and community buildings in the evacuated areas. Though all housing units were destroyed, some would say senselessly, in the Gaza Strip, the international community had arranged for many of the agricultural greenhouses to remain intact for the future use of Palestinians. Finally, on September 12, 2005, the last of the Israeli troops pulled out of the Gaza Strip, thus ending 38 years of Israeli occupation.

The Gaza pullout naturally caused jubilation among the Palestinians and received general approval worldwide. However, the stated intention of the Israeli authorities to maintain control over the borders, air space and water resources of Gaza served to both dampen the excitement locally and temper international optimism. Many feared that Israel's intent to continue dominating the Gaza Strip – now by "remote control" – would turn it into a large detention camp plagued with poverty and discontent. Israel, however, contends that security issues, especially its concern over Palestinians smuggling weapons across the Egyptian border at Rafah, are the reasons behind their ongoing control over all of Gaza's borders.

Why did the Israelis pull out of Gaza after 38 years of occupation?

Firstly, the decision to let go of the narrow strip came as a response to mounting international pressure, especially American, for Sharon to somehow demonstrate to the world Israel's willingness to take steps towards peace. Sharon knew that, politically, Israel must make some compromise for – or in place of – peace. He did not want that compromise to be made by sacrificing the major settlement blocs in the West Bank, thus the Gaza pullout was intended to buy time, silence criticism, ease the pressure from the international community, and divert attention away from the continued and rapid Israeli colonization of the West Bank.

A second impetus for the disengagement had to do with demographic realities. A study conducted by *Ha'aretz*, a leading Israeli newspaper, showed that the proportion of Jews living in all territory under Israeli control (including Israel proper) had dropped below the halfway mark, standing at slightly more than 49%. However, after the pullout from Gaza, with its 1.38 million Palestinians, the proportion of Jews in areas under Israeli control suddenly jumped to nearly 60%, guaranteeing a Jewish majority for at least 15 years. With such a strong Jewish majority in Israel and the West Bank, Israeli politicians hope, among other things, to achieve a more favorable outcome for Israel in any future peace negotiations.

Perhaps the above assessment seems too cynical and dismissive. Is it not possible that the Israeli pull-out from Gaza was a magnanimous gesture made, at least in some measure, out of pity, love or feelings of guilt towards the Palestinian people? Consider the following: In the midst of the public discourse over the Disengagement Plan, Ariel Sharon's chief advisor, Dov Weisglass, gave a media interview which was published on 6 October 2004. Speaking with a cynical candor rarely heard from a public official, Weisglass laid out clearly the true purpose of the Disengagement: "It is the bottle of formaldehyde within which you place the president's [Road Map] formula so that it will be preserved for a very lengthy period... It supplies the amount of formaldehyde that's necessary so that there will not be a political process with the Palestinians... The political process is the establishment of a Palestinian state... the evacuation of settlements, it's the return of refugees, it's the partition of Jerusalem. And all that has now been frozen."[123]

Any fair appraisal of the Disengagement would have to allow that the removal of Israeli settlements and military forces from Gaza, taken in isolation, was a positive move and long overdue. However, as we have seen, it was conceived and carried out for all the wrong reasons. Moreover, as a purely unilateral move, and leaving intact the regime of absolute Israeli control over Gaza's borders, including the option of future incursions, it certainly did nothing to bring genuine peace in the region any nearer. Yet there was one undeniable if unintended by-product: it proved how easily even longstanding Israeli settlements can be evacuated and their residents relocated within Israel proper, given the political will to do so.

CHAPTER TEN

THE BIBLE AND CHRISTIAN ZIONISM

Blessed are the peacemakers for they shall be called the children of God.
-Matthew 5:9

The wheels of justice - they're square wheels.
-Barbara Corcoran

Did the prophets of the Old Testament, and the Apostles of the New Testament, predict the creation of the modern State of Israel? Is the Zionist enterprise in the land once called Palestine an act of divine intervention in the history of humanity? Has the seeming endless turmoil, violence and bloodshed in Israel/Palestine been preordained by God and predicted by his prophets thousands of years ago? Is God indeed behind all the hostility, discord and aggression that have resulted from the atrocities that have taken place in Palestine, Israel and the Middle East over the last one hundred years? This chapter is an attempt to answer these questions, and to provide a Biblical alternative to the claims of Christian Zionism.

CHRISTIAN ZIONISM

Christian Zionists support the creation and sustenance of a Jewish homeland in Palestine (and all that implies), out of the belief that such historical events are predicted in the books of the Bible and central to God's plan – and his end-of-days arrangements – for all humanity. In practical terms, it translates into strong support for the State of Israel and its official policies as an expression of one's Christian faith. Admittedly, most Christians who embrace these ideas may never have heard of the term we choose to use, "Christian Zionism." By contrast, secular Zionism (or simply "Zionism") is a movement first established in 19th century Europe, by mainly non-religious Jews, with the political objective of creating a Jewish homeland.

The Zionist project in Palestine would most likely never have succeeded had it not been for the efforts of incalculable numbers of Christians who believed that the endeavor was divinely predicted by biblical prophets and apostles. Many of these Christians began nurturing the Zionist movement from its infancy, and today like-minded believers are still some of its staunchest supporters. Indeed, British clergymen and Bible scholars were preaching and promoting the necessity of the Jewish return to Palestine long before Herzl ever thought of organizing the Zionist Movement. Lord Balfour, for example, the architect of the 1917 Balfour Declaration, was a later adherent of this Zionist school, and British Zionists were instrumental in prodding the British government to take control of Palestine as a prelude to the creation of a Jewish state. Throughout, Christian Zionists contributed to the Zionist enterprise through both their financial gifts and active political advocacy.

In more recent times, some of the more zealous Christian Zionists have established a self-styled "International Christian Embassy in Jerusalem." Set up in September 1980, it serves to promote their causes from a base in the Holy Land and to solicit worldwide Christian support for the Jewish state. On certain occasions, Christian Zionists have preached their gospel directly to Arab-Palestinian Christians living in Israel/Palestine. Here is one example, from my own experience:

One Sunday afternoon in July 2000, many members and pastors of local Evangelical congregations from the Palestinian territories and Arab East Jerusalem had gathered at the Bethlehem Hotel in Bethlehem in order to celebrate the formation of a new council. An American woman who was present at the meeting approached one of the pastors and asked permission to say a few words to the assembly. The pastor, desiring to show courtesy to the unknown guest, asked the emcee, likewise a Palestinian pastor, if the lady could say her few words. The moderator, totally unaware of what the woman might say, nonetheless agreed to let her talk. When the lady took the microphone, neither I nor the others present could believe the words that came out of her mouth! She declared to the Palestinian Evangelical Christians assembled that she had a "word from the Lord" for them: "God," she said, wanted them all to "leave Israel and go to other Arab countries." She added that they must leave to make room for God's chosen people, the Jews. Moreover, she warned the pastors and the audience that if they did not listen to the instructions which God had given through her, God would pour out his wrath on them. As soon as the lady's outrageous agenda became clear, one of the pastors came and whisked her away from the pulpit, but not before she had delivered to the whole assembly a dose of what many Palestinians regard as Christian Zionist propaganda.

This is not an isolated example of an overzealous and aggressively obnoxious Christian Zionist. Every one of the pastors gathered in that assembly could tell similar stories. Here is a comparable episode from America, again from my own experience:

In Kansas City, Missouri, Campus Crusade for Christ once invited an Israeli official and me to engage in a live TV debate on the Arab/Israeli conflict. When the time came for phone-in questions from the viewers, a man, having learned that I was an Arab-Palestinian Christian pastor, called to tell me that if I were truly a Bible-believing Christian and a true follower of Jesus, I would know that God had given the Holy Land to the Jews and that I and other Palestinians Christians should peacefully leave the country!

I am certain that most Christian Zionists are not as radical and confrontational as the woman and man in these examples. Still, many Christians in the United States and around the world do cling to these ideas, without ever critically examining them and holding them up to the light of reason, justice and genuine biblical truth.

Influential TV evangelists such as Pat Roberson and the late Jerry Falwell, both strong advocates of Christian Zionism (though, again, they may not use the term), have warned and threatened U.S. presidents against carrying out policies that would pressure Israel to make concessions to the Palestinians on the pathway to concluding a peace agreement. Pat Robertson went so far as to say that Ariel Sharon's debilitating stroke in 2006 was a punishment from God for carrying out Israel's disengagement from Gaza. While labeling Muslims as "worse than Nazis,"[124] Robertson, Falwell, Rev. John Hagee and other influential Christian Zionists have done their utmost to manipulate U.S. presidents and their policies, in particular cautioning them repeatedly against forcing Israel to abandon Jewish settlements in the West Bank as part of any "land for peace" deal.

Many adherents of Christian Zionism, having unthinkingly embraced a set of beliefs that seem, at least on the surface, to be biblically grounded, are not aware of the destructive theological, religious and political implications of these ideas.

THEOLOGICAL IMPLICATIONS

Christian Zionism is a contradiction in terms. Zionism is a secular political movement with political goals, most of which center around the creation of a Jewish state in Palestine. Because of the political and moral positions of Zionism, millions of people around the world have equated it with racism; therefore it is not to the advantage of Christianity to be in union with Zionism. Zionism deviates from the heart of the New Testament. New Testament Christianity proclaims, "For God so loved the world," while Christian Zionism proclaims, 'for God so loved the modern political State of Israel'. According to the book of Acts, Jesus made clear to Peter in a vision that God no longer favors one nation over others:

"Then Peter began to speak: "I now realize how true it is that God does not show favoritism but accepts men from every nation who fear him and do what is right." (Acts 10:34–35)

In his epistle to the Galatians, St. Paul confronted a faction in the churches of Asia Minor that wanted to drag the new believers back to Judaism. Paul stood firmly against this group, teaching the churches that in Christ there is no difference between Jew and Greek but that both have equal access to God through Christ. Paul wrote to the Galatians:

"You are all sons of God through faith in Christ Jesus, for all of you who were baptized into Christ have clothed yourselves with Christ. There is neither Jew nor Greek, slave nor free, male nor female, for you are all one in Christ Jesus. If you belong to Christ, then you are Abraham's seed, and heirs according to the promise." (Gal. 3:26–29)

RELIGIOUS IMPLICATIONS

Christian Zionism is adding fuel to the tension between Muslims, Christians and Jews. Many Christian Zionists, especially after 9/11, began to view Muslims as enemies of God, again led into this thinking by influential TV evangelists who went on the air publicly denouncing Muslims and Islam. Christian Zionists continue to talk about reaching the world for Christ while at the same time, by embracing such rhetoric, they are building walls of mistrust and alienation between themselves and over a billion Muslims worldwide. Likewise, when Christian Zionists embrace wholeheartedly the Israeli agenda with regard to the Palestinian people, they engender the same kind of suspicion and hostility. The esteemed American pastor and speaker Tony Campolo has raised this very issue when he wrote: "How can we expect to win our Arab brothers and sisters to Christ when our interpretation of the scriptures calls for an unjust assessment of their rights to land that was held by their fathers for centuries?"[125]

Arabic-speaking Christians have existed in the Holy Land since the day of Pentecost and have kept the torch of Christianity burning faithfully for the past two thousand years. (It is interesting that the very first Arabic-speaking Christians were probably Jews! – see Acts 2:5, 11.) If the Christian Zionists' agenda is realized, it will mean the death of Palestinian Christianity in the Holy Land. The erosion of Christianity in its very birthplace is already a tragic loss for the body of Christ everywhere. Can we imagine the Holy Land totally devoid of any Christian presence, without a Church which has been a faithful witness for Christ since the day the Church was born?

Zionism is militarizing the church. The influence of Zionism on U.S. Christians has helped alter Christians' perceptions of both the Arab-Israeli conflict and the war in Iraq. Christian Zionists overwhelmingly supported the war in Iraq and continue to support oppressive Israeli measures in the West Bank. For example, the slaughter of tens of thousands of Iraqi men, women and children in Iraq goes virtually unnoticed and unchallenged because of their belief that President George W. Bush is a dedicated Christian who is carrying out the will of God. Likewise, Israel's disproportionate use of force against Palestinian civilians in refugee camps in Gaza, the West Bank and Lebanon is usually accepted by Christian Zionists. If it is condemned at all, the response is equivalent to a slap on the wrist, while a disproportionate amount of blame is placed on the Palestinians themselves. Lying almost wholly within the "blind spot" of Christian Zionists is the fact that the Palestinian people, every day and in every aspect of their lives, are living under an oppressive military occupation. The Anglican minister and academic Dr. Stephen Sizer notes how Christian Zionism, because of its uncritical, unfailing support for Israel, tends to justify any and all actions taken against Palestinians, however oppressive they may be: "Christian Zionists have, therefore, sanctified this relationship [with Israel] while demonizing Arabs and Islam; they have defended Israel's right to live within secure and expanded borders, while encouraging the ethnic cleansing of Palestinians from their land."[126]

Unlike the prophets of the Old Testament, Christian Zionists have no prophetic words of reprimand for the State of Israel. They are silent when the Jewish state indulges its appetite for oppression. Christian Zionists do not call for Israel to uphold principles of justice, nor even to live by the generally-accepted norms of civilized behavior, of human decency. Thus Israel, with seeming impunity, routinely confiscates Palestinian land, demolishes the homes of the poor, destroys their agricultural land and siphons off their water resources – while Christian Zionists blindly and fervently continue to "bless Israel" and sing her praises.

There are Israelis today, however, like the brave prophets of ancient Israel, who do not hesitate to call upon their compatriots to pursue justice. Jeremiah reflected that courage when he wrote:

" ...O house of David, this is what the LORD says:
"Administer justice every morning;
rescue from the hand of his oppressor the one who has been robbed,
or my wrath will break out and burn like fire
because of the evil you have done,
burn with no one to quench it." (*Jer. 21:12*)

THE BASIC BELIEFS OF CHRISTIAN ZIONISM

Palestinian Christians are, for the most part, appalled by the great flood of support that numerous Western Christians have poured into the Zionist project during the last 120 years. This, sadly, has turned some Arab Christians throughout the Middle East and North Africa totally against the Old Testament – the Hebrew scriptures – and the eternal truths and rich heritage they embody. But other Arab Christians, including this author, have come to a different perspective. They instead determined, through a thorough study of the Biblical record in both the Old and the New Testaments, to find out for themselves whether the Bible supports the Zionist claims. In the following pages the reader will find the result of my study of Old Testament prophecies about 'the land' in light of New Testament teachings.

Christian Zionists generally hold to the following doctrines which are also endorsed, either in part or the whole, by many Christians who take for granted popular views of prophecy or the covenants:

- Jews have special favor with God, and he gave them the Holy Land. It belongs to them by divine decree and it always will. Neither history, nor the passing of centuries, nor the religious or moral condition of Jews can alter this fact.
- God will bless those individuals and nations who bless the Jews and their State, and God will curse or punish those who do otherwise.
- Jews today are a direct extension of the Israelites in Biblical times. Therefore, just as the nations during the Old Testament era were judged as to how they treated ancient Israel, the same is true today.
- Old Testament prophecies, although uttered thousands of years ago, are being fulfilled in Israel today and have been since 1948 when the Jewish state was born.

- God's 'end time' plan is directly connected with the modern State of Israel, and Christians can speed up the coming of Christ by helping bring about the fulfillment of prophecies pertaining to Israel.
- The creation of the Jewish State is a miracle of divine intervention on behalf of the Jewish people and a visible sign of the end times and the soon coming of Jesus Christ.
- The current conflict in the Middle East is caused by Palestinians, Arabs and Muslims who are out of touch with the will of God as it concerns the Land of Israel.
- There will be no peace in the Middle East until Christ comes back. All the efforts of Jews, Arabs, the United Nations and the United States to broker peace between Arabs and Jews are futile and will not produce peace.
- The Jews will build a Jewish Temple in Jerusalem in the place of the Al-Aqsa Mosque and/or the Dome of the Rock, where they will resume offering animal sacrifices to God.
- A great (and literal) war, 'Armageddon', will break out in the last days between Israel and the surrounding nations. Jesus will come back from heaven to rescue the Jews who now believe in him, after one third of them get slain in the final war.

The above concepts are held in the hearts and minds of millions of Christians around the world. Some adherents of the Christian Zionist movement have been United States presidents such as Ronald Reagan[127] and George W. Bush. Possibly these politicians embraced the Zionist agenda – or appeared to – in order to win the support and vote of Evangelical Christians.

When I speak to groups of Christians from the United States or from Europe, I am often asked: "But what about prophecy, didn't God give the land to the Jews? Why do Arabs and Muslims want to thwart the plan of God?"

AN ALTERNATIVE BIBLICAL PERSPECTIVE ON THE THEOLOGY OF THE LAND

There are many Biblical references in the Old Testament that state that God gave the Holy Land to Abraham and his descendants, among whom are the ancient Jewish people. In Genesis 12:1–5 God promises Abraham that he will give the land of Canaan to him and his descendants. Similar promises are repeated throughout the Old Testament. The challenge today is to search for answers to the following questions:

- Are God's promises to ancient Israel unconditional?
- Are these promises perpetual, i.e. never-ending?
- Do Old Testament prophecies relating to 'the land' in the Old Covenant continue to have significance and fulfillment within the framework of the New Covenant?
- Does God have a special plan for the Jewish people, different from that for other peoples?

Are these promises unconditional?

The Old Testament is full of evidence that these promises are conditional on the faithfulness and obedience of the people of Israel to God. Examine the following references:

"And if you defile the land, it will vomit you out as it vomited out the nations that were before you." (*Lev. 18:28*)

"Keep all my decrees and laws and follow them, so that the land where I am bringing you to live may not vomit you out. You must not live according to the customs of the nations I am going to drive out before you…" (*Lev. 20:22*)

"When Abram was ninety-nine years old, the Lord appeared to him and said, "I am God Almighty; walk before me and be blameless. I will confirm my covenant between me and you and will greatly increase your numbers" (*Gen. 17:1*)

These and many other verses clearly show that ancient Israel's possession of the land was conditional upon Israel's obedience to God, and when Israel failed to obey God, the people were driven out of the land. The Babylonians exiled the Jews from Israel about 600 years before Christ, and then in 70 AD the Romans conquered and destroyed Jerusalem and expelled the Jews again. These are two examples of the Jews being removed from the land because of ancient Israel's rebellion against God.

Today, the majority of the Jews in Israel and around the world are either secular or non-religious traditionalists. Only 20% of the Jewish population categorize themselves as religious.[128] Indeed, many leading Zionists who were among the visionaries and founders of the State of Israel were atheists, and modern Israel today is not a nation under God nor does it claim to be one. The trail of violence and injustice in Israel in the last 60 years is clear evidence that the State of Israel today is not the Israel of the Bible or the Israel of the covenant. Again, God's promise to ancient Israel was conditional upon Israel's obedience. Evangelicals in particular should be concerned that modern Israeli society continues to reject its Messiah, bans missionary activities, and often condemns those who attempt to share the good news of Jesus Christ. To idealize the religious significance of the State of Israel is to close one's eyes to the spiritual, religious and moral realities of the modern Jewish state.

Are these promises perpetual, i.e. never-ending?

In the past, God promised ancient Israel the land and he gave it to them, thus fulfilling his promises. Some Christians read in the Old Testament of promises and prophecies that were given three or four thousand years ago and they strive to find modern fulfillment of those prophecies, prophecies which in actuality have already been fulfilled. Some of these prophecies were given to the Jews when they were living in exile in Babylon. For example, Isaiah promised his exiled contemporaries, and those who were on the verge of exile, that God would have mercy on them and bring them back to the land. He wrote:

> "For a brief moment I abandoned you,
> but with deep compassion I will bring you back.
> In a surge of anger
> I hid my face from you for a moment,
> but with everlasting kindness
> I will have compassion on you,"
> says the LORD your Redeemer." (*Isaiah 54:7–8*)

Indeed, God kept his promise and he did restore the Jewish people to the land after some 70 years of exile. The prophets preached a message of hope for the exiles, a message that was also a means of preparing them to be restored to the land. But those prophecies do not address today's Arab-Israeli conflict and the current situation in the Middle East. How unfortunate it is that these verses are taken out of their historical context and taken to apply to the present-day conflict between Jew and Arab, because manipulating the Word of God in this way is not only unfaithful to the Biblical record but is, in its implications, exceedingly harmful to all Palestinians and especially to the Palestinian Christian community. How long will the Bible be used as a manual to promote military occupation? And how often must the Palestinians be subjected to the cruelties and brutalities of military conquests sanctioned by theories of divine involvement?

Do Old Testament prophecies relating to 'the land' in the old covenant continue to have significance within the framework of the new covenant?

To respond to this question it is necessary to point out the similarities and differences between the two covenants. Biblical scholars have written volumes on this theme but to briefly address this question, I will point out and compare six major elements in the two covenants, namely, the nation, the land, the city, the temple, the priesthood, and the sacrifice. The comparison is illustrated in the chart below.

The Two Covenants – Chart of Comparision		
	OLD COVENANT	NEW COVENANT IN CHRIST
NATION	Israel	All Believers
LAND	Promised Land	Kingdom of God
CITY	Jerusalem	New Jerusalem
TEMPLE	Mount Zion	Hearts of Believers
PRIESTHOOD	Levitical	Christ and Believers
SACRIFICE	Animal	Jesus Christ

According to the old covenant, God chose a specific family to be a light to all the nations: Abraham and his descendants. God created nations from that family and selected one to be used as a vehicle through which all the other nations of the world would be blessed. The people of that nation, Israel, from which the prophets and the law were derived, became known as God's chosen people, as illustrated in the following verses:

"I will bless those who bless you,
and whoever curses you I will curse;
and all peoples on earth
will be blessed through you." (*Genesis 12:3*)

"For you are a people holy to the LORD your God. The LORD your God has chosen you out of all the peoples on the face of the earth to be his people, his treasured possession." (*Deuteronomy 7:6*)

"Yet the LORD set his affection on your forefathers and loved them, and he chose you, their descendants, above all the nations, as it is today." (*Deuteronomy 10:15*)

"If you fully obey the LORD your God and carefully follow all his commands I give you today, the LORD your God will set you high above all the nations on earth." (*Deuteronomy 28:1*)

With the death of Jesus Christ on the cross, and the ushering in of the new covenant, the gates of God's grace were opened to the entire human race. Jews and Gentiles now have equal access to all the privileges and responsibilities of being people of God. Who are God's people according to the new covenant? The following verses provide the answer.

We first start with Paul's declaration to the Church in Ephesus:

"For he himself is our peace, who has made the two one and has destroyed the barrier, the dividing wall of hostility, by abolishing in his flesh the law with its commandments and regulations. His purpose was to create in himself one new man out of the two, thus making peace, and in this one body to reconcile both of them to God through the cross, by which he put to death their hostility. He came and preached peace to you who were far away and peace to those who were near. For through him we both have access to the Father by one Spirit. Consequently, you are no longer foreigners and aliens, but fellow citizens with God's people and members of God's household, built on the foundation of the apostles and prophets, with Christ Jesus himself as the chief cornerstone. In him the whole building is joined together and rises to become a holy temple in the Lord. And in him you too are being built together to become a dwelling in which God lives by his Spirit." (*Ephesians 2:14–22*)

In the above verse Paul announces to Gentiles believers that in Christ they are now:

- One with the people of God
- Citizens with God's people
- Members of the household of God
- Built on the foundation of the apostles and prophets
- A dwelling in which God lives

Believing Gentiles and believing Jews together comprise one body, the body of Christ. Paul repeats this same theme when he addresses the Gentiles in the city of Colossi:

"Therefore, as God's chosen people, holy and dearly loved, clothe yourselves with compassion, kindness, humility, gentleness and patience." (*Colossians 3:12*)

Peter also speaks to both Jews and Gentiles scattered throughout the Roman Empire and declares to them that they are God's chosen people and a holy nation when he writes:

"But you are a chosen people, a royal priesthood, a holy nation, a people belonging to God, that you may declare the praises of him who called you out of darkness into his wonderful light. Once you were not a people, but now you are the people of God; once you had not received mercy, but now you have received mercy." (*1 Peter 2:9–10*)

It is obvious from the verses above that the concept of nationhood was modified in the new covenant. Whereas in the old covenant God's people were the Jewish nation, in the new covenant all those who receive the grace of God through Jesus Christ become the people of God. The apostle John states this fact clearly in the following verses:

"He came to that which was his own, but his own did not receive him. Yet to all who received him (Jews and Gentiles), to those who believed in his name, he gave the right to become children of God, children born not of natural descent, nor of human decision or a husband's will, but born of God." (*John 1:11–13*)

Thus Israel as a nation annulled its privilege as God's chosen nation by rejecting God's ultimate plan for the redemption of humanity in Jesus Christ. Yet God still fulfilled his purpose through them and blessed all the nations of the world through Abraham's seed, that is, Jesus Christ. In calling the old covenant "obsolete" (Hebrews 8:13), the writer did not mean to imply that God had banned Jews from receiving all the blessings of the new covenant. Rather he meant that God had a greater plan for the Jews, as he had for all people, which was his son Jesus Christ who by his death redeemed all of mankind, Jews and Gentiles.

THE LAND

In the old covenant the land was important in order to house and shelter God's chosen people, and provide a place for a central temple where the priesthood could function. But, since the basic features of that covenant were changed, there was no longer any need for a specific land or territory to "house" the new covenant. For this reason the concept of a Promised Land was modified in the new covenant to a new reality, a reality which Jesus and his followers called the 'Kingdom of God'. When contemporaries of Jesus asked him about the place of that kingdom, he responded by saying, "The kingdom of God is within you." By localizing the kingdom in the hearts of the faithful, Jesus made that kingdom of God both spiritual and global. And a kingdom that is thus present throughout the world need not – cannot – be limited to a specific plot of ground. Luke wrote:

> "Once, having been asked by the Pharisees when the kingdom of God would come, Jesus replied, 'The kingdom of God does not come with your careful observation, nor will people say, 'Here it is' or 'There it is', because the kingdom of God is within you.'" (*Luke 17:20–21*)

The Samaritan woman who met with Jesus at the well also had difficulties with the concept of "sacred" territory. Upon discovering that Jesus was the Messiah, she immediately presented him with a subject that had puzzled Jews and Samaritans for years: "Sir," the woman said, "I can see that you are a prophet. Our fathers worshiped on this mountain, but you Jews claim that the place where we must worship is in Jerusalem" (John 4:19–20). Essentially, she had asked, "Which is the right place? Which real estate does God favor?" The reply she received from Jesus is worth examining. He told her,

> "Believe me, woman, a time is coming when you will worship the Father neither on this mountain nor in Jerusalem. You Samaritans worship what you do not know; we worship what we do know, for salvation is from the Jews. Yet a time is coming and has now come when the true worshipers will worship the Father in spirit and truth, for they are the kind of worshipers the Father seeks." (*John 4:21–23*)

Jesus' response to this question is of utmost importance to all who continue to be confused about the issue of 'the land'. First, Jesus did not tell the woman that Jerusalem, where Jews worshiped, or Gerizim, where Samaritans prayed, were exclusively the right places of worship. Second, he directed her attention to a new era in God's dealing with humanity. Jesus said, "Yet a time is coming and has now come." He was referring to the new covenant, a time when God will no longer be concerned about a specific piece of land, territory or a centralized place of worship but rather in the spiritual attitude of the worshipper.

To overemphasize the importance of 'the land' is to live in the old covenant. God's *terra sancta* is the human heart! For this reason, in reading the Gospels it is clear that significance is given *not* to the land but rather to the kingdom of God. I do not wish to undermine the significance of the Holy Land as a testimony to God's revelation through the Old Testament prophets, as a witness to the acts of incarnation, crucifixion, resurrection and ascension, and as the place God chose for the birth of the Church on the day of Pentecost. I wish rather to emphasize that the land is significant only because God chose it to become the cradle of his acts of salvation to humanity. The Holy Land was God's launching pad for the kingdom of God, a realm that truly has no address and no geographical boundaries.

Jesus also de-emphasized the issue of the land in the dialogue that took place between him and his disciples just before his ascension. We read in the book of Acts:

> "So when they met together, they asked him, 'Lord, are you at this time going to restore the kingdom to Israel?' He said to them: 'It is not for you to know the times or dates the Father has set by his own authority. But you will receive power when the Holy Spirit comes on you; and you will be my witnesses in Jerusalem, and in all Judea and Samaria, and to the ends of the earth.'" (*Acts 1:6–8*)

The disciples showed concern over a physical and territorial kingdom of God on earth, with Jerusalem as its capital and Christ as its king. Jesus responded to his disciples' query by telling them it was not needful for them to have this knowledge and only the Father in his authority had access to information of unspecified times and dates in the future. He immediately directed their attention to the task at hand – spreading the Good News of the kingdom of God, beginning in Jerusalem and reaching to the uttermost parts of the world. Thus, Jesus de-emphasized the territorial concept of the kingdom of God, while stressing the spiritual and global aspect.

What does all of the above have to do with the current Arab-Israeli conflict? Its connection lies in the fact that the Arab-Israeli conflict is mainly a conflict over land possession. And many Christians, embracing a confused concept of sacred territory in both the old and the new covenants, hold that even under the new covenant the land is not only highly significant but belongs exclusively to the Jewish people. Acting out of this mistaken belief, these Christians not only support, both financially and politically, the State of Israel's overriding claim to "The Land," but they also refrain from calling Israel to account when it engages in acts of terrorism and injustice against the Palestinian population. Sadly, for them certain skewed notions of biblical prophesy such as arcane prophetic theories, take precedence over real-world justice and mercy. Consequently their hearts are not moved with compassion over the plight of millions of Palestinian refugees, the demolition of their homes, the confiscation of their land, the destruction of their lives and economy, and their daily suffering under a brutal occupation.

Should speculative interpretations of prophecy have precedence over the clear teachings of justice and mercy? Perhaps we can deduce the answer to this question from the words of Jesus to the religious folk of his times:

> "Woe to you, teachers of the law and Pharisees, you hypocrites! You give a tenth of your spices – mint, dill and cumin. But you have neglected the more important matters of the law – justice, mercy and faithfulness. You should have practiced the latter, without neglecting the former. You blind guides! You strain out a gnat but swallow a camel..." (*Matthew 23:23–24*)

It is clear that Jesus Christ, Paul, and all the other writers of the New Testament promoted The Kingdom rather than The Land. Promoting the Kingdom of God *brings about* that Kingdom and its fruits, whereas promoting 'the land' produces hate, strife, anger, violence, wars, bloodshed and untold suffering as we have seen in the Middle East in the last one hundred years.

THE CITY

From the time King David moved his capital from Hebron to Jerusalem; the city became a symbol of the spiritual and political life of the nation. As Jerusalem went so went the fortunes of the Jewish nation. The old covenant underscored the significance of Jerusalem as the spiritual core of the Jewish nation:

> "King Rehoboam established himself firmly in Jerusalem and continued as king... and he reigned seventeen years in Jerusalem, the city the LORD had chosen out of all the tribes of Israel in which to put his Name..." (*2 Chronicles 12:13*)

> "So the name of the LORD will be declared in Zion and his praise in Jerusalem" (*Psalm 102:21*)

Pray for the peace of Jerusalem:

"May those who love you be secure.
May there be peace within your walls
and security within your citadels."

For the sake of my brothers and friends,

"I will say, "Peace be within you."
For the sake of the house of the LORD our God,
I will seek your prosperity." (*Psalm 122:6–9*)

No doubt Jerusalem had the distinction of being the most prominent city—far above all others—in the old covenant. The prominence begins to erode with the dawn of the new covenant. Although Jesus, during his ministry on earth traveled often and ministered to many in Jerusalem, his reflections on the Jerusalem of his days were neither positive nor favorable. Jesus knew that Jerusalem would be the place of his suffering and death:

"From that time on Jesus began to explain to his disciples that he must go to Jerusalem and suffer many things at the hands of the elders, chief priests and teachers of the law, and that he must be killed and on the third day be raised to life." (*Matthew 16:21*)

Jerusalem's tragic history is predicted by Jesus:

"O Jerusalem, Jerusalem, you who kill the prophets and stone those sent to you, how often I have longed to gather your children together, as a hen gathers her chicks under her wings, but you were not willing. Look, your house is left to you desolate. For I tell you, you will not see me again until you say, `Blessed is he who comes in the name of the Lord.'" (*Matthew 23:37–39*)

Paul and the other writers of the New Testament did not place their contemporary Jerusalem on a high pedestal. Paul wrote:

"Now Hagar stands for Mount Sinai in Arabia and corresponds to the present city of Jerusalem, because she is in slavery with her children.

But the Jerusalem that is above is free, and she is our mother."
(*Galatians 4:25–26*)

The writer of the Epistle to the Hebrews clearly deemphasizes the significance of the earthly Jerusalem as he glorifies the heavenly one:

"But you have come to Mount Zion, to the heavenly Jerusalem, the city of the living God. You have come to thousands upon thousands of angels in joyful assembly." (*Hebrews 12:22*)

The writer of the book of Revelation compares earthly Jerusalem with the wicked city of Sodom:

"Now when the (the two witnesses) have finished their testimony, the beast that comes up from the Abyss will attack them, and overpower and kill them. Their bodies will lie in the street of the great city, which is figuratively called Sodom and Egypt, where also their Lord was crucified." (*Revelations 11:7–8*)

The same writer describes the heavenly Jerusalem as the place where God dwells with his people:

"I saw the Holy City, the New Jerusalem, coming down out of heaven from God, prepared as a bride beautifully dressed for her husband. And I heard a loud voice from the throne saying, "Now the dwelling of God is with men, and he will live with them. They will be his people, and God himself will be with them and be their God." (*Revelations 21:2–3*)

Jesus and his apostles did not sing the praises of an earthly Jerusalem, rather, they spoke of a heavenly Jerusalem. As we focus on the priesthood, the sacrifice and the temple in the next few paragraphs, we will realize that a central city to house a central temple was no more needed for humans to enjoy the benefits of the new covenant.

I love the city of Jerusalem which is both my physical birthplace and the birth place of my Christian faith. However, the sanctity of Jerusalem and the Holy Land is not contained in the soil, stones, rocks, sand, shrines, churches, mosques and synagogues of which the city is made. Jerusalem's holiness is contained in its spiritual heritage as the city where God chose to perform his acts of redemption to all humanity. Today, many Muslims, Christians and Jews have made Jerusalem the greatest obstacle to world peace as a result of too much emphasis on real-estate and too little awareness of the spiritual message of peace and reconciliation that Jerusalem has for all humanity.

THE PRIESTHOOD

God instituted the Old Testament priesthood when Aaron, Moses' brother, became the first High Priest. In the Pentateuch, detailed instructions are given for the management of the institution of the priesthood. The writers of the New Testament, however, described a new type of priesthood, the priesthood of all believers. The Apostle Peter, in his first epistle, addressed new converts – Jews and Gentiles – and called both of them, "a royal priesthood" when he wrote:

"But you are a chosen people, a royal priesthood, a holy nation, a people belonging to God, that you may declare the praises of him who called you out of darkness into his wonderful light. Once you were not a people, but now you are the people of God; once you had not received mercy, but now you have received mercy." (*1 Peter 2:9–10*)

The writer of the book of Revelation focused on the same theme when he wrote to both Gentile and Jewish believers and referred to all of them as "a kingdom of priests":

"To him who loves us and has freed us from our sins by his blood, and has made us to be a kingdom and priests to serve his God and Father, to him be glory and power forever and ever! Amen." (*Revelation 1:5–6*)

The priesthood in the old covenant was limited to one of Israel's tribes, the Levites. In the new covenant, however, it is clear that all who believe are members of a royal priesthood. In comparing the priesthood of the old covenant with that of the new, the writer of the book of Hebrews explains that the old priesthood must diminish to make way for a new and permanent one, declaring:

> "But because Jesus lives forever, he has a permanent priesthood. Therefore he is able to save completely those who come to God through him, because he always lives to intercede for them. (*Hebrews 7:24–25*) By calling this covenant "new," he has made the first one obsolete, and what is obsolete and aging will soon disappear." (*Hebrews 8:13*). See also Jeremiah 31:31.

Very clearly, the author of the book to the Hebrews announces that the priesthood of the Old Testament expired, making way for a new priesthood of both believing Jews and believing Gentiles.

THE SACRIFICE

In the old covenant animal sacrifices were an essential part of worship, but in the new covenant Jesus became the eternal sacrifice to atone for all sins. The author of the book to the Hebrews says:

> "The blood of goats and bulls and the ashes of a heifer sprinkled on those who are ceremonially unclean sanctify them so that they are outwardly clean. How much more, then, will the blood of Christ, who through the eternal Spirit offered himself unblemished to God, cleanse our consciences from acts that lead to death, so that we may serve the living God!" (*Hebrews 9:13–14*)

> "Day after day every priest stands and performs his religious duties; again and again he offers the same sacrifices, which can never take away sins. But when this priest (Jesus) had offered for all time one sacrifice for sins, he sat down at the right hand of God." (*Hebrews 10:11–12*)

These verses, and many others like them, reflect a dramatic change in the concept of sacrifice as demonstrated in the two covenants. Whereas the sacrifices in the old covenant demanded the regular, ritual slaughter of animals, the new covenant presents Jesus as the ultimate and perfect sacrifice to atone for all sins, for all people, and for all times. Thus, the sacrificial order of the old covenant was terminated to make room for the new order. Christians who become euphoric over the possibility of the restoration of the Jewish sacrificial system should earnestly seek divine understanding to make sure that they are not stepping out of the will of God, as his will has been made clear to us in the writings of the New Testament.

Not only did the new covenant terminate the need for animal sacrifices and cancel the Levitical priesthood, but it also abolished the need for a central temple. Instead of the temple in Jerusalem, the Church of Jesus Christ – the redeemed from all nations – became the temple of the Holy Spirit.

Notice the words of Jesus in response to his disciples' amazement at the grandeur of the Jerusalem temple:

> "Some of his disciples were remarking about how the temple was adorned with beautiful stones and with gifts dedicated to God. But Jesus said, "As for what you see here, the time will come when not one stone will be left on another; every one of them will be thrown down"" *(Luke 21:5–6)*

Paul, in the following three passages, explains to early believers that they themselves are the temple of God:

> "Don't you know that you yourselves are God's temple and that God's Spirit lives in you? If anyone destroys God's temple, God will destroy him; for God's temple is sacred, and you are that temple." *(1 Corinthians 3:16–17)*

> "Do you not know that your body is a temple of the Holy Spirit, who is in you, whom you have received from God? You are not your own; you were bought at a price. Therefore honor God with your body." *(1 Corinthians 6:19–20)*

> "What agreement is there between the temple of God and idols? For we are the temple of the living God. As God has said: "I will live with them and walk among them, and I will be their God, and they will be my people."" *(2 Corinthians 6:16)*

The above verses contain two messages: first, that God's grace period for the temple in Jerusalem had expired and the temple was condemned to destruction. In order for a new temple to be established, the old one had to be destroyed. Second, the new temple is no longer a building but is comprised of the body of Jesus Christ, the Church.

DOES GOD HAVE A DIFFERENT PLAN FOR THE JEWISH PEOPLE?

Some may say that while the above argument is true for Gentile believers it is not true for Jews. They may also argue that God has a special plan for the Jews that differs from God's plan for the Gentiles. I do not accept this concept for the following reasons:

1   God's plan in the new covenant includes both Jews and Gentiles, providing salvation and blessing for both. In the new covenant the two are reconciled to make one. To promote an additional plan for the Jews is to contradict the core message of the New Testament. Examine Paul's statement in Galatians:

> "You are all sons of God through faith in Christ Jesus, for all of you who were baptized into Christ have clothed yourselves with Christ. There is neither Jew nor Greek, slave nor free, male nor female, for you are all one in Christ Jesus. If you belong to Christ, then you are Abraham's seed, and heirs according to the promise." (*Gal. 3:26–29*)

2   There is no mention of a special plan for the Jews in the New Testament, separate from God's redemptive plan for the Gentiles. Those who advocate the concept of a unique plan for the Jews, at the present time or in the future, have to depend entirely on Old Testament references to justify their theory. Paul's discussion in Romans, chapters 11 and 12, highlights the spiritual restoration of the Jewish people through faith in Jesus Christ – not through a physical or territorial restoration. Paul's argument is based on his strong belief that the restoration of the Jewish people depends upon their acceptance of Jesus Christ.

3 To have a special plan for the Jews or any other race is to diminish the power and the effect of the salvation that God has provided for all people by the death of Jesus Christ on the cross. The best that God could offer the Jews, he has already provided for them through Jesus Christ. Christ is God's best gift to humanity, including the Jewish people.

4 The eschatological theories that claim a special role for the modern State of Israel in the end times do not make theological sense. Why would God want the Jews to be restored to the land and to build a temple where animal sacrifices would be offered? Has not Jesus given his body as the everlasting sacrifice for sins? Why would any Christian support the rebuilding of a temple where animal sacrifices would be offered? Would God be glorified to see Jews practicing animal sacrifices two thousand years after our Lord, the everlasting Lamb of God gave his life for us on the cross? If such a ritual would not please God, why should any Christian support it or encourage the fringe-element few zealously seeking to implement it? Truly, any supposed Christian theology that is not centered in – and does not harmonize with – the cross of Christ is not worth our time and should not have a place in our hearts.

As I lecture in various venues and explain how the old covenant with all its essential components – the nation, the state, the city, the temple, the priesthood and the sacrifice – have been modified in the new covenant, many ask, "What about God's promises to the Jewish people? Have they expired?" My response is under the next heading.

IS GOD THROUGH WITH THE JEWISH PEOPLE?

With the apostle Paul, I say, "By no means!"

I ask then: Did God reject his people? By no means! I am an Israelite myself, a descendant of Abraham, from the tribe of Benjamin. God did not reject his people, whom he foreknew. (*Romans 11:1–2*)

Paul presents himself as an example of a Jew who is not rejected by God. Throughout the last 2000 years, millions of Jews have experienced the wonderful grace that changed the life of Paul. The gates of God's mercy are wide and ever open to both Jews and Gentiles. In the verse below, Paul highlights the fact that God's desire is to bring both Jews and Gentiles into one kingdom. God does not have one kingdom for the Jews and another for Gentiles. The covenant was modified, but God's passion to gather Jews and Gentiles to his kingdom has not changed.

> As far as the gospel is concerned, they are enemies on your account; but as far as election is concerned, they are loved on account of the patriarchs, for God's gifts and his call are irrevocable. Just as you who were at one time disobedient to God have **now** received mercy as a result of their disobedience, so they too have **now** become disobedient in order that they too may **now** receive mercy as a result of God's mercy to you. For God has bound all men over to disobedience so that he may have mercy on them all. (*Romans 11:28–32*)

The word '**now**' in bold print is significant because Paul uses it to refer to the era of the new covenant in Christ. I understand Paul to be saying: Now that Jesus has redeemed humanity through his death on the cross, Jews can obtain mercy, grace and salvation. Therefore the salvation of the Jews can happen now (i.e. at any time in the present) as they come to the Savior and not in a far-away future through the establishment of a state or through the building of a temple where animal sacrifices may resume.

God's promises to the Jewish people and to all people are spiritual and do not necessitate occupying a piece of land or forcibly subjugating another nation through superior military might, political maneuvering and economic manipulation. The promises can be actualized by a humble return of people, both Jews and Gentiles, to God, accepting God's plan for their restoration and salvation. However, the misinterpretation and misapplication of Scripture – granting divine sanction to the Zionist occupation of Palestine – have contributed significantly to the turmoil in the Middle East and, by extension, to wider global unrest. It has brought great suffering, bloodshed and loss of life to millions, and given fuel to militant groups throughout the world. This manipulation of the Bible has also caused much anguish and frustration to Arab Christians, and it continues to be a stumbling-block preventing millions the world over from responding to Christ and welcoming his message.

The Cross challenged by Israeli Watchtower, Wall, and Fence at the Bethlehem Checkpoint

CHAPTER ELEVEN

UNTANGLING THE WEB

God has a dream for all his children. It is about a day when all people enjoy fundamental security and live free of fear. It is about a day when all people have a hospitable land in which to establish a future. More than anything else, God's dream is about a day when all people are accorded equal dignity because they are human beings. In God's beautiful dream, no other reason is required.

God's dream begins when we begin to know each other differently, as bearers of a common humanity, not as statistics to be counted, problems to be solved, enemies to be vanquished or animals to be caged. God's dream begins the moment one adversary looks another in the eye and sees himself reflected there.
– Archbishop Desmond Tutu, 2007

In her book *A Tangled Web: A Search for Answers to the Question of Palestine*, Ethel Born writes: "We must all seek the truth and interpret it as we understand it concerning the Question of Palestine – a tangled web!"[129] In this chapter I will present a summary of my understanding of this tangled web and will suggest an approach on how to untangle it.

The Arab-Israeli conflict is essentially a clash of aspirations. Unless peace educators, peacemakers and politicians understand this, and seriously study and address the aspirations of each of the contending parties, it is futile for them to try to make a worthy contribution toward bringing lasting peace to this bitter conflict.

For hundreds of years many Jews have held a mystical attachment to their ancient homeland, and since the 19th century some have aspired – and continue to aspire – to create and sustain a secure Jewish state on as much of the land called Israel or Palestine as possible. Meanwhile, Arab Palestinians, whose ancestors have lived in Palestine for many hundreds of years (but have always been controlled by outside powers), likewise aspire to have an independent Palestinian state on part or most of the same land. These conflicting aspirations are often inflamed and complicated by nationalistic goals, by greed, by interference from other nations, and by religious convictions – or the manipulation of people proclaiming religious motives.

Consequently, there are groups within both contending parties to the conflict that believe that the land "belongs" to them by historic right, and that to them alone the land has been given, by divine decree. Hence, the name of God and religion is frequently invoked in such claims. These clashing aspirations, regardless of their basis, will continue to stir up the conflict until a compromise is reached and accepted. Any would-be peacemaker must understand both Jewish and Palestinian aspirations before he or she can help the antagonists come to an acceptable compromise. The focus of the following pages is to examine these conflicting aspirations and to analyze the challenges that stand in the way of a viable compromise. In addition, we will speak of the need for an evenhanded, honest broker in the search for peace.

Expressing the clash of aspirations, David Ben-Gurion stated in 1919:

"There is no solution to this question. No solution! There is a gulf, and nothing can bridge it… We, as a nation, want this country to be ours; the Arabs, as a nation, want this country to be theirs."[130]

In 1937, during the British Mandate over Palestine, The Peel Commission report on Palestine stated:

"An irrepressible conflict has arisen between two national communities within the narrow bounds of one small country. There is no common ground between them. Their national aspirations are incompatible."[131]

In 1919, the Zionists, while most of them still resided in Europe, expressed their aspirations when they submitted to the British a proposed map of their idealized future state. It was a state, according to the map, which they hoped would encompass all of historic Palestine (i.e. British Mandatory Palestine, "from the river to the sea"), plus a part of Trans-Jordan, a part of Syria, and a part of Lebanon. These early Zionists were dreaming of getting hold of *all* of historic Palestine and more, leaving no room for a Palestinian state. *(See Map 1, p. 102)*

In 1936 and 1937, the Palestinians revolted against the British. They likewise wanted a Palestinian state on all of historic Palestine, and they rejected the British partition plan that offered the Jewish immigrants a state on a portion of it. Palestinians felt that the Jewish immigrants, who formed a minority, must not be allowed to take over the country and to form their state on part of an already small country.

The inability of the antagonists to tame their aspirations has plunged the Middle East into six major wars, causing the destruction of many lives and indirectly causing two additional wars in Iraq, plus scores of uprisings and bloody confrontations in the region and other parts of the world.

While one may see no harm with a persecuted people aspiring to have a national homeland, the problem begins when one people's aspirations pose a direct threat to the aspirations and the fundamental rights of another people. Lord Balfour, the author of the Balfour Declaration of 1917, could not ignore the clash of aspirations when, in his now-famous pronouncement, he attempted to address this issue. Note the words in italics (emphasis added) in the second half of the Declaration:

"His Majesty's Government view with favour the establishment in Palestine of a national home for the Jewish people, and will use their best endeavours to facilitate the achievement of this object, *it being clearly understood that nothing shall be done which may prejudice the civil and religious rights of existing non-Jewish communities in Palestine*, or the rights and political status enjoyed by Jews in any other country."[132]

Regrettably, from the time the declaration became public until today, many actions *have* been taken by the Zionists, both before and after they established their state, to "prejudice the civil and religious rights of existing non-Jewish communities in Palestine." One people's dream became – and continues to be – another people's nightmare.

Had the British committed to pursuing an evenhanded policy, one that considered and respected the aspirations of both Jews and Palestinians, perhaps we would not still be discussing the Arab-Israeli conflict ninety years after Balfour made his declaration.

While conflicting human aspirations lie at the root of the Arab-Israeli conflict, other factors have long aggravated and complicated the inherent tensions. Among these exacerbating influences are religion, greed, nationalism and international interference.

RELIGION

The early European Zionists, who founded the Zionist movement and later established the Jewish state in Palestine, were generally secular. They aspired to the establishment of a Jewish state, but not for religious reasons. The early Zionists were not messianic. They even held in contempt the traditional Jewish religious communities that were already living in Palestine. Later, however, some religious Jews began using religious slogans to promote and legitimize the Zionist program, and to broaden its appeal. Thus, today in the Israeli Knesset there are a number of political parties that believe, based on their understanding of their sacred Scriptures, that *all* of Palestine must belong to Jews forever and that Palestinians must be transferred to Jordan or to other Arab countries.

Similarly, the early defenders of a free and independent Palestinian state were Arab nationalists, both Muslims and Christians, who were not motivated by religious convictions. For them it was a nationalistic cause. It was not their religions that were directly threatened by the Zionist dream but rather their land. Palestinian Islamists were relatively late on the scene, and it was only after the signing of the Oslo Agreements in 1993 that they turned to political Islam to find an answer to the conflict. Thus, new Islamist movements were formed whose goal was to usurp the power of the secular nationalists who had failed to deliver. These groups – Hamas, Islamic Jihad and others – united around the concept that Palestine was an Islamic *waqf*, or religious trust, meaning that it was land God had given *only* to Muslims. Thus, in their thinking, Muslims must fight a holy war to expel all non-Muslim powers from Palestine.

While many Israelis and Palestinians have appealed to such religious claims, and although we have witnessed a revival of and an increase in religious fervor in both camps in recent years, it is important to emphasize that, to most Israelis and most Palestinians, this is *not* a religious conflict. Palestinians want an independent state next to a Jewish state, and only a small fraction of their population aspires for an Islamic state on all of historic Palestine. Former U.S. President Jimmy Carter, in his book *Palestine: Peace not Apartheid*, cites certain polls which indicate that most Palestinians are ready to have a Palestinian State on 22% of historic Palestine (pre-1967 West Bank and Gaza), thus accepting the reality of a Jewish State on 78% of historic Palestine.[133]

GREED

For some Israelis and Palestinians, the conflict is not just an expression of innocent human aspirations or religious convictions, but rather a matter of greed. For example, while there are Jews who aspire to live in peace alongside their Palestinian neighbors in Israel/Palestine, there are other Israelis who want, and are willing to fight for, the occupation and annexation to Israel of all of historic Palestine. They do this because they realize it is within their *ability* to do so, and, intoxicated with their power and wealth, they believe that no Palestinian resistance or Arab force is able to stop them. Some members of the Likud party and other extreme nationalists in the Israeli Knesset[127] espouse such views.[134] Thus, the Palestinian people have been under crippling military occupations for many years. As the weaker party in this dispute, they may harbor greed, but only the powerful have the means to *satisfy* their greed. A Palestinian may *claim* that all of Palestine belongs to Palestinians. Israelis, however, are able to translate their own claims into reality – with the roar of tanks and bulldozers.

The love of country and homeland is universal, and Arabs and Jews are as nationalistic as men and women anywhere else in the world. However, unchecked nationalistic feelings have inflamed this conflict and added more knots to the tangled web.

Arab ultra-nationalists have considered Israel a cancer in the heart of the Arab world and believed that there will never be peace in the Middle East until this cancer is entirely removed.

Israeli ultra-nationalists are just as determined not to allow Palestinians to have a state, not even in the West Bank. The West Bank, they argue, must be a buffer zone to protect the tiny Jewish state from future Arab invasions. While many Israelis welcomed Israel's 2005 withdrawal from the Gaza Strip, the ultra-nationalists rejected this unilateral "disengagement" and will surely bitterly oppose any Israeli government that dares to consider further withdrawals from the West Bank or from the Golan Heights.

INTERFERENCE OF OTHER NATIONS

Had the Arabs and Jews been left alone to address their aspirations, the Israeli-Palestinian conflict would have ended long ago. But the interference over the years of the British, the Americans, the Russians, the Communists, the Christian Zionists, American Jews, neighboring Arab states and foreign Islamist groups has been detrimental for both sides. The interfering groups brought with them their own domestic and international geo-political interests and often their eschatological-religious and/or political ideologies. Thus, Israel/Palestine became the arena for much globally-connected political and ideological arm-twisting. Today, of course, it would be impossible for the international community to ignore what is taking place in Israel and Palestine or to turn its back on this conflict. The challenge, then, is to *channel* the international involvement into efforts that would bring about genuine reconciliation and build trust between Israelis and Palestinians – that may help to untangle the web.

An important first step for all involved is to recognize and acknowledge the very real, conflicting aspirations of the two sides. Related to this, and equally vital, is the assurance that neither party will be able to deny, dismiss or eradicate the aspirations of the other. Anticipating an earlier pathway to peace, Barry Rubin wrote:

> "The Arab-Israeli conflict was unsolvable as long as it was set in existential terms – requiring either Israel's destruction or the Palestinian Arabs' exile and political nonexistence. Only when both sides perceived that neither could be eliminated did they become ready for an outcome giving each a national framework, a two-state solution in which Israel and Palestine partition the land and live in peace."[135]

Although the case for a two-state solution has been blowing about on the political landscape for years, the parties have not been able to make the necessary compromises to bring it to fulfillment. While the parties to any conflict may all *claim* their commitment to peace, real peace can only be achieved when those parties are willing to make genuine compromises.

OBSTACLES TO COMPROMISE

There are three huge obstacles to achieving key compromises which would end the conflict:

1. Each side assumes that it has already made great compromises.

Palestinian Claims:
- Palestinians in 1988 recognized the state of Israel, based on a 2-state solution.
- On September 7, 1993, just before the signing of the Oslo Principles of Understanding, Yasser Arafat wrote, on behalf of his people, the following words to Israeli Prime Minister Yitzhak Rabin:
  The PLO recognizes the right of the State of Israel to exist in peace and security.

The PLO accepts United Nations Security Council Resolutions 242 and 338.

The PLO commits itself to the Middle East peace process, and to a peaceful resolution of the conflict between the two sides and declares that all outstanding issues relating to permanent status will be resolved through negotiations.[136]

- Arabs meeting in Beirut, Lebanon in 2002 endorsed in principle a Saudi peace plan which clearly stated that all Arab countries would recognize Israel, once an Israeli government recognizes the right of Palestinians to establish a state in the West Bank and the Gaza Strip.
- A poll conducted by the Hebrew University of Jerusalem in March, 2006 revealed that over 60% of Palestinians favored the recognition of Israel in a framework of a future two-state solution plan.[137]

Israeli Claims:
- Israelis likewise point to compromises Israeli leaders made when they accepted the Oslo Principles of Understanding:

   a. Recognizing the Palestine Liberation Organization (PLO).
   b. Permitting Yasser Arafat and his colleagues to return from Tunisia to the West Bank and Gaza and to establish partial autonomy through the Palestinian Autonomy.
   c. Withdrawing their troops from much of the Gaza Strip and the Jericho areas in 1994.
   d. Later withdrawing from 40% of the West Bank, allowing semi-autonomy to 70% of the Palestinian population.

- Israelis also reflect on what they consider former Israeli Prime Minister Barak's generous offer to Yasser Arafat during the 2000 Camp David peace talks, a proposal to withdraw Israeli troops from over 90% of the West Bank.
- Israelis lift up Ariel Sharon's unilateral pullout of all Israeli settlements from the Gaza Strip as yet another gesture of compromise.

Why, then, in spite of all the above "compromises," are Israelis and Palestinians still at an impasse in untangling the web?

2. It is an unequal conflict.

The second challenge to reaching a compromise is that the stronger party has consistently been able to dictate the terms, the timing, and the extent of its commitment and its compromises, while at the same time dictating what compromises are expected from the adversary.

While both sides have suffered much in this ongoing conflict, and both parties long to end the conflict, the conflict does *not* involve equal antagonists, and never has. The suffering of the Palestinians has been disproportionate to that of their Israeli neighbors, due to the many advantages that Israelis have over their neighbors. The following list explains this disparity between the two warring sides:

- The Israeli per capita Gross National Income (GNI) in 2006 was $18,620 while the per capita GNI of Palestinians was $1,120.[138]
- The State of Israel has the President and Congress of the strongest nation on earth, the United States, firmly on her side.
- The Israeli military establishment and the Israeli army ranks third or fourth in the world. Currently the Palestinians do not have an army.
- Despite the fact that it is one of the richest countries in the Middle East and in the world, Israel receives on the average $5 billion a year (over $13 million every day!) in foreign aid – outright grants, military hardware and munitions, and guaranteed loans – from the government of the United States.
- In the last 60 years the State of Israel has acquired 88% of historic Palestine. (55% was allotted to a Jewish state by the world community under the 1947 UN Partition Plan; at the end of its War of Independence, Israel held – and kept – 78%; annexations, settlement activities, etc. since 1967 integrated another 10%). Thus, today Palestinians have limited authority over just 12% of the land. Yet, using the security of Israeli settlers as an excuse, the Israelis *continue* to expropriate Palestinian land, demolish homes, and create conditions that deny Palestinians the right of movement, even *within* the West Bank.
- Israelis have besieged and imprisoned the Palestinian people from

all sides, both physically and economically. Palestinians cannot move freely, either *within their own territories* or abroad, except under the watchful eyes of the Israelis and with their permission, permission doled out capriciously via a control regime of barriers, checkpoints, permits and ever-changing procedures. Most Palestinians are banned from traveling into lands that Israel has taken from them since 1967.

The above facts explain why it is so difficult to reach a fair compromise. All these advantages –this position of power, which ideally could be the springboard to magnanimous concessions – Israel has instead used to effectively stage-manage and stalemate this historic quarrel, all the while maintaining a stranglehold on the Palestinian people themselves. Israel, having the military advantage, the financial resources and the political backing of the U.S., often does not see the value of engaging the Palestinians in peace talks that offer worthy compromises. Instead, Israel imposes odious, oppressive measures to try to bring the Palestinians to their knees and crush them into surrender and resignation, hoping to dictate a peace settlement that is favorable to Israel and involves minimal compromise on her part.

Failure to implement genuine compromises ultimately results in a slow-down or total collapse of negotiations, and this typically leads to renewed rounds of bloody fighting. This inability of the two sides to reach a compromise due to the disparity of the contending parties simply highlights the desperate need for an honest, evenhanded broker to help untangle the web.

3. There is currently no honest, evenhanded peace broker involved.

When two parties become entangled in a fight where one is very powerful while the other is extremely weak, the fight will not stop until (1) the powerful party quits voluntarily, (2) the weaker party surrenders, or (3) a *third party* or parties engage the antagonists in peace negotiations that would lead to ending the discord. So far, Israel does not seem ready to halt its offensive on Palestinian territories, and Palestinians do not seem ready to surrender. The arena is ready for an evenhanded referee to help forge just solutions based on genuine, mutual compromise.

Although the United States has played the role of the peace broker for decades, it has failed to achieve the desired peace mainly because of its unfaltering and mostly uncritical bias toward the Jewish state. In spite of its obvious failure, the U.S. continues trying to mediate and at the same time refuses to share the leadership role with any other party. It is the moral responsibility of the United States either to play a constructive, evenhanded role in moving the antagonists toward meaningful compromise, *or* to hand over this responsibility to another nation or a group of nations that are willing and ready to approach the conflict with the necessary mix of toughness and impartiality.

The entire world is yearning to see an end to the longstanding Arab-Israeli conflict. And yet, if the U.S. is to ever assume a more balanced, constructive role in hammering out a peaceful solution, it can only come as more and more Americans consciously move beyond media sound-bites to investigate for themselves – and grapple with – the stark realities and moral dimensions of this tragic conflict. We must, in the words of Ethel Born, "seek the truth and interpret it as we understand it."[139]

In concluding this chapter let us examine what Jesus Christ had to say about untangling this web.

CHRIST ON CONFLICT AND CONFLICT RESOLUTION

The life of Jesus Christ and his teachings have inspired many who have engaged in conflict resolution and the pursuit of peace. Peacemakers such as Mahatma Gandhi, Martin Luther King, Jr., Nelson Mandela, Desmond Tutu, Jimmy Carter and millions of others – known and unknown – unreservedly

The Cross challenged by Israeli Watchtower, Wall, and Fence at the Bethlehem Checkpoint

acknowledged the inspiration of Jesus' Sermon on the Mount and his other teachings in their efforts to make peace.

As Christians yearn for peace in the Middle East and elsewhere in the world, there needs to be a fresh look at the teachings of Christ about conflict and its resolution. The following verses from Christ's sermon help us to understand the roots of conflict:

"You have heard that it was said to the people long ago, 'Do not murder, and anyone who murders will be subject to judgment.' But I tell you that anyone who is angry with his brother will be subject to judgment. Again, anyone who says to his brother, 'Raca,' is answerable to the Sanhedrin. But anyone who says, 'You fool!' will be in danger of the fire of hell." *(Matt. 5:21–22)*

Sources of Conflict
Jesus points to three expressions of conflict, namely:

1. Active Expression – illustrated by the word 'murder' in, "Do not murder!"
2. Emotional Expression – demonstrated with the word 'anger' in, "Any one who is angry at his brother or *sister* (for no reason)."
3. Verbal Expression – emphasized with the word 'say' in, "anyone who says to his brother or sister, 'Raca' or says, 'you fool.'"

As the active expression of conflict is usually a consequence of the emotional or verbal expressions of conflict, it will be dealt with last.

Emotional Expression: "Any one who is angry with his brother..."
Jesus teaches that conflict originates with the feelings towards others that are harbored in our hearts. Anger for good reason, or for no good reason, is a major emotion we harbor towards others. It is nurtured by feelings of jealousy, greed, fear, racism, a sense of inferiority, or an air of superiority. Hatred driven by anger may be applied or generalized to all people of a certain ethnicity or nationality and be targeted because of their skin color, their religion or their socio-economic status. Because they are different from us, somehow, we may feel threatened by them. Anti-Semitism is a centuries' old example, and in our current post-9/11 climate an example could be drawn from our suspicion and even fear of Arabs and Muslims. Anger and hatred can propel us into conflict that can result in violence,

bloodshed and the destruction of a people's way of life.

Verbal Expression: "…you fool"

Words are often used powerfully by politicians to inflame the very emotions that people harbor in their hearts and to give justification for acting on those emotions – to maim, kill and destroy. Could the Six Day War have been avoided had the Egyptian President Jamal Abdul Nasser and Egyptian propaganda toned down their inflammatory rhetoric? What are the motives or plans behind U.S. President George W. Bush's use of the highly charged label 'Axis of Evil' to refer to North Korea, Iran and Syria? How might it be playing on people's preconceived prejudices? Does Iran's Ayatollah's pronouncement of the United States as the 'Big Satan' impact the relationship between the U.S. and Iran? The use of such evocative language stirs up the very emotions that produce aggression and conflict and consequently the death and injury of millions.

Active Expression: "Do not murder"

Conflict that has its roots in our hearts and in our words, ultimately leads to aggression. Our harbored emotions of anger and hatred intensify and propagate those very emotions too. Given justification and an outlet, these emotions and insults often lead to abuse, torture, murder, war and the destruction of human life, property and other forms of violence. The answer of Jesus is for adversaries to control their angry hearts and their words before they are tempted to kill and before murder becomes inevitable.

The following verses express Jesus' teachings on resolving conflicts:

"Therefore, if you are offering your gift at the altar and there remember that your brother has something against you. Leave your gift there in front of the altar. First go and be reconciled to your brother; then come and offer your gift. "Settle matters quickly with your adversary who is taking you to court. Do it while you are still with him on the way, or he may hand you over to the judge, and the judge may hand you over to the officer, and you may be thrown into prison. I tell you the truth, you will not get out until you have paid the last penny." *(Matt. 5:23–26)*

In these verses Jesus offers three suggestions to resolve conflicts:

1. Make peace before you pray

It would seem that these recommendations of Jesus for settling our conflicts are too radical for most Christians at any time. Jesus clearly states that reconciliation with an adversary must happen before we come to worship. This does not mean that worship takes a second place to reconciliation but that God does not delight in our worship when we are not reconciled to one another.

Imagine the impact on the world and its people…

- If Christians in the United States did not gather for worship until they had made peace with the people of Iraq, Afghanistan, Syria, and Iran;
- If religious Israeli Jews abstained from attending synagogues until, with Palestinians, they resolve the Arab–Israeli conflict;
- If the Muslims, Christians and Jews of Jerusalem determined not to attend their houses of worship until together they find a peaceful solution to the future of their city;
- If Arab Muslims and Christians went and made peace with their Israeli neighbors before going to their mosques or churches to worship;
- If the leaders of the many Christian denominations postponed their religious duties and engaged in a fast or a hunger strike to focus thought and energy on how peace could be brought to the many trouble spots of our world.

Isn't this what Jesus meant in commanding us to leave our sacrifices on the altar and first go to seek reconciliation with our enemies?

2. Make peace while on the way

Jesus simply commands that we settle conflict with an antagonist as soon as possible and while the conflict is still boiling. The picture that Jesus gives is of two antagonists who are fighting while traveling to the same destination. Jesus is saying while still on the way and before reaching the destination, the two persons or parties should reconcile while the opportunity for peace is in front of them and still viable. This will save heartache and destruction for both sides. If the wound is left open, there is a greater opportunity for it to fester and become life threatening. To settle disputes promptly one must:

- Keep negotiations going with an enemy. Too many leaders and politicians in the Middle East and elsewhere around the world prefer to talk peace with friends but never with enemies. Consequently peace is delayed.

- Keep listening. A good negotiator hears the heart and mind of his antagonist. People in the Arab and Islamic world feel injured and are frustrated because policy makers in the West are not willing to hear or address the issues that are of concern to them.
- Negotiate with humility. Politicians want to show their constituencies that they achieved a bargain for their country. A Christian peacemaker wants to achieve a just peace for both sides not wanting one party to win at the expense of the other.
- Be willing to compromise. The Christian negotiator is willing to compromise and make genuine concessions.

One price tag

- Iraq war: (Sept., 2011) – A report by the Government Acountability Office says the US has spent more than $800 billion on military operations on Iraq so far.
- Over 5,000 US soldiers killed
- Over a million Iraqis killed and millions more are now refugees.

---

3. Make peace before you pay

Jesus continues the illustration of the two antagonists who do not make peace and consequently suffer a less than desirable outcome, with one of them suing the other and one losing every penny he had and being sentenced to prison because the conflict was not resolved expediently. Jesus is saying that conflict is very costly, and the sooner we end the conflict the less costly it is to all. The cost can be counted in life and blood, in finances and property, or in emotional and psychological scars.

Imagine…

- How many lives would have been spared had Arabs and Jews resolved their conflict in 1948?
- How many lives would have been spared if Iraqis and Americans had been able to resolve their problems, before or right after the first Gulf War?

- How many lives would have been spared the agony of banishment, starvation, disease and death if Sudanese had succeeded in creating peace between the Janjaweed militias and the tribes in Darfur?

It is easy to see the mounting cost of conflict because it is evident in many parts of the world. Can we imagine a would-be world where future generations in the Middle East and elsewhere around our globe realize justice, peace and security as all of us implement the teachings of Christ in settling our disputes?

CHAPTER TWELVE

COMMON QUESTIONS ABOUT THE ARAB-ISRAELI CONFLICT

The best defense of peace is not power, but the removal of the causes of war, and international agreements which will put peace on a stronger foundation than the terror of destruction.
-Lester B. Pearson, former Canadian Prime Minister

286

Common
Questions
About the
Arab-Israeli
Conflict

> "There were no such thing as Palestinians... It was not as though there was a Palestinian people in Palestine considering itself as a Palestinian people and we came and threw them out and took their country away from them. They did not exist."
> —Golda Meir, former Israeli PM

Some people claim that Arabs created a Palestinian identity in the era of Israeli independence in order to assert Arab claims to the land of Palestine. Before this "invention," they say, those living between the Mediterranean and the Jordan River were not a distinct people but part of the surrounding Arab populations, or simply migrant workers from neighboring lands. Such accusations have, in themselves, political motivations, seeking to justify Israel's taking the land from its historical inhabitants, expelling those people, and denying them their rights. If there is no such thing as Palestine and a Palestinian people, then there is no reason that the so-called "Palestinians" cannot simply be relocated to Jordan or other Arab countries.

"Palestine" came into being as a political unit in Roman times. Throughout subsequent occupations the name remained, though the political boundaries changed over time. Under the Ottoman Empire – which ruled Palestine for exactly 400 years, until the advent of the British – the land of Palestine was part of a larger region that included present day Jordan, Syria and Lebanon, with Damascus functioning as the administrative capital of the area. The region that became Mandatory Palestine under the British in the 1920s was divided into the three districts of Jerusalem, Acre and Nablus.

The people of Palestine have long had a unique self-identity, distinct from other Arabs. They were proud of their Arab ancestry but considered themselves descendants not only of the Arab conquerors of the 7th century, but also of the many other peoples who had lived in the land, or had come there, from time immemorial down to modern times. In the years preceding the fall of the Ottoman-Turkish Empire, a nationalistic movement emerged among the Arabs which demanded independence from their Ottoman rulers, and many Palestinians participated in this movement for national independence. Certainly not all the people of Palestine felt strongly about this issue, but the nationalists represented the opinion held by the majority of the population.

During the British Mandate, Palestine was a distinct political unit, separated even from other British-administered lands such as Transjordan. Then the end of World War II witnessed a process of de-colonization by which indigenous peoples all over the world, including the Palestinians, demanded independence from their colonial overlords. This was not a new demand on the part of the Palestinians, but rather a continuation of their struggle for independence from imperial rule. Yet as the Europeans pulled out of their various colonies around the globe, the Palestinians unfortunately became the victims of the world's last remaining colonial enterprise – Zionism.

This is not to say that the concept of the Palestinians as a distinct people was not further crystallized in the period of Israeli independence. Among the Arab peoples, the Palestinians suffered a unique tragedy in 1947–49, one which certainly reinforced their identity as a people. But the process and chronology by which Palestinians came together as a people (or might have failed to, for that matter) does not in any way de-legitimize their claim to the land. Social identity always develops over time, and is never static. Take the concept of America, for example. If we were to judge by the length of its historical presence in North America, the concept of the United States as a political and social entity would pale compared to the historical presence of Palestine and the Palestinians. Furthermore, the United States only exists in its current form because of the annihilation of the country's indigenous inhabitants, the Native Americans. America's social identity continues to develop and evolve. Yet if a foreign power forced Americans from their homes, who would doubt their right to return and receive compensation?

The idea that the Palestinians are not a distinct people stems from the desire of some to erase Palestinian claims to their land. It also finds its roots in the kind of racism and ignorance that lumps the Arab peoples into a homogenous mass. Anyone who is familiar with the Arabs knows that they are a very diverse people with a multiplicity of cultural and national traditions. This is as true for the Palestinians as it is for the Jordanians, Syrians or Lebanese. The era of Israeli independence was not the catalyst for the concept of the "Palestinian people" but rather – from the other side – the catalyst for the effort to make them disappear.

288

> Emphasizing the inadmissibility of the acquisition of territory by war...
> —UN Security Council Resolution 242, 1967

The United Nations' partition plan of 1947 was, at best, a naïve but good-faith effort on the part of the world community to resolve a longstanding, intractable dispute between two peoples. At worst, some see it as an undemocratic and ultimately unfair proposal primarily based on Zionist aspirations, embraced in part as an expression of the world's shock and guilt over the horrific tragedy of the Holocaust, and in the end pushed through to General Assembly approval by shameless diplomatic arm-twisting on the part of the United States. In hindsight, it may be true that the plan gave the Palestinians more than they currently have, but, at the time, the Palestinians could not have known what was to befall them. It was inconceivable to the Palestinians that they would agree to a plan that gave the majority of their land to a foreign people who were not willing to share it with them. In 1947 the Jews owned less than 7% of the land of British Mandatory Palestine but were granted control over 54% of it in the UN partition plan. Such an arrangement was, for obvious reasons, out of the question for the Palestinians. The UN partition plan was not intended as a binding document to be forced upon the people of Palestine, but rather a plan to be agreed upon by both parties. The Palestinians decided to reject it, while the Zionists had mixed feelings, some believing that the Jews had not received *enough*.

In the end, some official Jewish bodies did vote to "accept" the partition plan, however in actual practice, the Zionist forces in Palestine, from the very beginning, ignored and violated its key provisions. Almost immediately, they began seizing areas not assigned to the Jewish state (most notably Jerusalem and environs, which were to have been under international control) and, in many places, forcing out the Arab civilian population in order to achieve the overwhelming demographic supremacy and the extra land they were convinced they needed for a viable, secure state. When the hostilities of 1948 were over, the Israelis wound up with some 40% more territory than had been allotted to them and had closed their borders to over 700,000 displaced Palestinians. In short, *no one* "accepted" the Partition Plan that was spelled out and adopted by the United Nations.

3. *The Palestinians and other Arabs want the land that Israel conquered from them returned. But since Israel won the wars with the Arabs, shouldn't she get the spoils?*

> No one shall be arbitrarily deprived of the right to enter his own country.
> —Article 12, International Covenant on Civil and Political Rights

Throughout history, humans have used war to advance their interests, and the 20th century was quite possibly the bloodiest, most violent one that humanity has ever experienced. Given that fact, one must question whether human civilization has taken any significant steps forward. Yet there have always been efforts by some to minimize war and its destructive effects. In spite of, or perhaps because of, the sharp increase in man's ability to kill, the struggle to find peaceful ways to resolve conflict has grown stronger. The idea that "might makes right" has given way significantly, in some circles at least, to concepts of justice, peace, and freedom for all people. Since the mid-20th century, these concepts have been articulated and institutionalized as never before in the form of international law. Despite the obvious challenges of *enforcing* international law, it does offer a foundation upon which mutual respect among nations may be built.

The history of the State of Israel, however, is one of consistent departure from standards widely recognized by the world as the minimum for appropriate behavior by nation-states. Basic international law, for example, clearly prohibits territorial gain by means of warfare, in order to ensure that less powerful nations and peoples are not at the mercy of overwhelming military forces, as they always were in the past. Israel's history is a history of often forceful colonization. Generally, the colonial era is thought of as a relic of the past, but Zionism and its offspring, the State of Israel, in their goals and their methods, undeniably represent a type of colonial enterprise against the indigenous Arabs of Palestine. The wars that Israel has fought have served to advance expansionist purposes, just as its ongoing occupation of the West Bank and the continual building of settlements there daily *consolidates* this expansionism. That Israel has not been held accountable and persists in land grabbing, despite widespread criticism by the world community, does not reflect Israel's right to the land, but only its privileged position in a world dominated by its chief ally, the United States. This virtual immunity granted to one state *undermines* all the lessons supposedly learned from the war-torn 20th century and runs counter to efforts being made by many to ensure the 21st century will somehow be more peaceful and just.

290

Common
Questions
About the
Arab-Israeli
Conflict

4. *Wouldn't the situation of the Palestinian refugees be better if the Arab countries had accepted them more openly and not used them for political means?*

The 750,000 refugees from the War of 1948 fled primarily to countries that border Palestine: Lebanon, Syria, Jordan, and Egypt, and to this day, the majority of the refugees in these countries live in poor conditions in refugee camps. The Palestinian refugee problem has always fallen largely on the shoulders of the Arab countries in which they reside, and the history of the relationship between the refugees and the Arabs of their host countries has sometimes been a dark one. There is no doubt that the Arab governments have, at times, used the Palestinians refugees for political purposes. But it is not fair to blame the Arab countries for their plight. For one thing, the neighboring Arab countries did not have the resources to deal effectively with vast numbers of refugees crossing their borders. Indeed, in the years after 1948 they themselves were poor and still handicapped by their experiences under colonial rule. Yet they opened their borders and allowed the refugees in. Jordan in particular absorbed an enormous number of refugees, even granting them citizenship, and today the *majority* of Jordan's population is of Palestinian origin, a fact little known or appreciated. In these host countries today many of the (non-Palestinian) population of Lebanon, Syria, Jordan, and Egypt remain quite poor, some living in even worse conditions than the Palestinian refugees, yet these Arab countries continue to extend services and protection to their refugee populations.

All this is not to over-dramatize the plight of the refugees or to excuse the sometimes uneven treatment given them by the Arab countries. The point is that it is unreasonable to blame the refugee problem on those who hosted them – or, indeed, on the UN agency charged with their welfare – rather than those who drove them from their homes. Despite many UN resolutions calling for the repatriation of Palestinian refugees to their land,

Israel has never been held accountable in any meaningful way for its actions in expelling them. Using the Arab nations as scapegoats is simply one of Israel's strategies to divert attention from itself and its own culpability as the engineers of the Palestinian refugee situation.

5. *I*SN'T THE RETURN OF THE *P*ALESTINIAN REFUGEES TO THEIR LAND IN WHAT
IS NOW *I*SRAEL PROPER AN IMPOSSIBLE REQUEST?

> And justice will produce lasting peace and security.
> *Isaiah 32:17*

The passage of some sixty years since the expulsion of 750,000 Palestinians from their land, and the overwhelming predominance of Israel's narrative in framing the Arab-Israeli conflict, have resulted in an almost total disregard for the right of the Palestinian refugees to return to their homes. Despite the fact that this right to return is clearly mandated in international law and has been reaffirmed almost every year since 1948, any suggestion of exercising it is immediately proclaimed in public discourse to be impractical, if not impossible.

Israel's self-identity – even after sixty years – is both narrow enough and brittle enough that the issue of the return of Palestinian refugees is automatically equated with the state's destruction. Thus, when the issue is raised at all, it is immediately dismissed. Let there be no mistake: the return of approximately five million Palestinian refugees to Israel , *if* that is what is being proposed, would indeed run counter to the Zionist goal of a Jewish state with an overwhelming Jewish majority and total Jewish control.

But linking the *principle* of a "right of return" with this sort of all-or-nothing, "worst-case" scenario is neither realistic nor is it fair to the Palestinians. The vast majority of Palestinians understand the limitations imposed on them by both time and demographic realities, and they are willing to work toward some reasonable agreement with the Israelis. It is important to realize that, in reality, most of the Palestinian refugees would *not* return to their land in Israel, even if permitted to do so. The original refugees and their descendants have been living in exile for two to three generations, and the great majority have managed to proceed with their lives. Many have long since escaped life in the refugee camps and have begun successful careers. Others have intermarried in the various countries to which they were exiled. For the most part, these people are not going to leave everything they have worked for – whether in Jordan, Syria, Lebanon, the U.S., Canada, Australia, or Latin America – and return to a vacant or ruined piece of land in Israel/Palestine.

What the Palestinians want, more than anything else, is some recognition that they were wronged. However, thus far Israel has refused to acknowledge any accountability, moral or otherwise, for the expulsion of the Palestinians in the wars of 1948 or 1967, much less apologize for the tragedies it inflicted upon the Palestinian people. The predominant Israeli perspective expresses no responsibility for the creation of the refugee problem. One popular Israeli myth blames the Arab countries, which supposedly told the Palestinians to leave their homes until the Jews were defeated, at which time they could return. In fact, the Arab leaders did not call on the Palestinians to leave, but instead urged them to remain where they were, and there is no credible documentation proving otherwise. Most Palestinians fled from their homes because they were either under direct Israeli military pressure to do so, or they were frightened by Israeli atrocities in other Palestinian villages whose residents did not flee quickly enough.

The Palestinians deserve the recognition that they were grievously wronged. If Israel would do so, it would be possible to come to some type of agreement on the refugee problem. This may involve some combination of financial compensation and repatriation of refugees to Israel for the purpose of family reunification. The Israelis are still receiving compensation from Germany for the wrongs done to them and their parents during the Nazi era, a response that is both fair and just. Why, then, should the Palestinians be denied the same sort of justice? The small percentage of Palestinian refugees who continue to hold the legal title (*tabu*) to their lands and are not prepared or willing to take financial compensation, must be allowed to return to their homes and fields. Indeed, this segment of the Palestinian refugee population has a greater "right of return" than the Russian or Ethiopian Jews who never had any physical connection to or ownership of the land, or any stake in it at all other than their Jewish religion.

6. WHY DO PALESTINIANS USE "TERRORISM?"

> Because I do it with one small ship, I am called a terrorist.
> You do it with a whole fleet and are called an emperor.
> —A pirate, in St. Augustine's City of God

292

Common
Questions
About the
Arab-Israeli
Conflict

Terrorism is a phenomenon that is now well known in every corner of the globe. One need only look at the site where the World Trade Center in New York City once stood to understand its dreadful consequences. The killing of thousands of innocent people that took place there is horrific and utterly inexcusable. Indeed, it is impossible to defend such acts wherever and by whomever they are carried out, such as suicide bombings in an Israeli street or restaurant.

Just as terrorism is indefensible and deserves universal condemnation, we must also recognize that it comes in different shapes and forms. It cannot be denied that governments around the world have terrorized their citizens and those of other nationalities. Rarely, though, is the term "terrorist" used to describe the actions of such governments. Terrorism is relegated to the acts of rebel movements, revolutionaries, or weak nations and groups who do not fall in line with the will of the world powers. Among these groups are some extreme organizations whose rhetoric is especially apocalyptic or messianic, yet it is naive to assume, simply because the acts of those perpetrators seem senseless, that such so-called "terrorists" do not often have particular political goals in mind. Of course it is wrong for terrorists to kill innocent people to try to further their aims, but the way they react does not nullify the underlying grievances. In *Obstacles to Peace*, Jeff Halper writes:

> People suffering from oppression have a recognized right to resist. They cannot be expected to abrogate their own human rights, indeed, their very lives, without resistance. We often call upon oppressed people to adopt non-violent tactics (which of course they should do), and here is where the double standard becomes part of the system of oppression. Since only states can go to war and "legitimately" use massive military force, people accept their actions, even if they are critical of them. We seldom demand that oppressive states cease their violent means of repression. We might call for "peace" and we might condemn the excessive use of force, but for some reason states are not expected to adopt non-violent policies. Oppressed non-state peoples, by contrast, can only "resist," and since armed resistance on their part is illegitimate, it is easy for states to frame it as "terrorism." Regardless of how we feel about it, armed resistance to oppression is just as "legitimate" as the use of arms by countries.[140]

294

Common
Questions
About the
Arab-Israeli
Conflict

In all likelihood, the first image that crosses the minds of most Westerners upon hearing the word "Palestinian" is a *kaffiye* (headdress)-covered terrorist. Such an image, though, far from accurately portraying an entire population, rightly applies to only a very tiny yet highly visible minority. Any person desiring to pursue peace and justice must have the insight to go beyond such simplistic and demeaning assumptions about ethnic groups. To brand all Palestinians as terrorists, besides being invalid factually, is on the same level, morally, as any other kind of mindless racial-ethnic stereotyping. In reality, most Palestinians have concerns and aspirations similar to those of any other people: they love their children and hope to create a better future for them, they long for true peace and security, and they are unhappy being in a state of perpetual war. Whenever "Palestinian" and "terrorist" are treated as synonymous terms, a 'reality check' is in order!

Palestinian terrorism, to the extent that it does exist, is not the result of blind hate for Israel or the Jewish people. The Palestinian struggle against Israel, in all its forms, is a direct result of the occupation of their land and the suffering of their people under that occupation. A case in point is the settlement of Har Homa that stands on a hill north of Bethlehem. In spite of the fact that the hill (which the Palestinians call Jabal Abu Ghnaim) is in the occupied West Bank, the Israeli government in 1991 approved the confiscation of the land at that large site. Palestinians objected and the international community condemned the move. Both Israeli and Palestinian peace groups demonstrated peacefully against its construction, but the Israeli government dismissed all of this opposition and proceeded with its plans. The first step in construction was the clearing of thousands of beautiful green trees, a unique feature of the hill. Palestinian anger finally boiled over and a number of Palestinians began to demonstrate against Israel's actions by throwing rocks at Israeli soldiers. In retaliation, the Israelis fired on them with live bullets, killing several Palestinian protestors and injuring hundreds more. Although Palestinians eventually ceased their protests over Har Homa, their anger did not vanish. It is just such regularly recurring incidents that create fertile ground for terrorism.

People often say Israel does not deserve terror in response to its confiscation of Palestinian land and its continued regime of occupation and control imposed on the Palestinian people. "What Israel does," they say, "is not terror." Yet Palestinians cannot help but see Israel's policies as terror. They suffer daily as they watch their land being taken, their ancient trees uprooted, their houses arbitrarily demolished and their freedom of movement denied – in short, their basic human rights and dignity trampled. Former U.S. Secretary of State Madeleine Albright once said in defense of Israel, "Terror is not a valid response to bulldozers." Imagine, though, if these bulldozers were destroying houses in Texas to create a Chinese colony that would be economically and politically run by China. Imagine too that America did not have the great military power it possesses but was virtually helpless to defend against the illegal annexation of its land. How would most American citizens react?

Israeli brutalities against Palestinians and the tacit support of the U.S. and other Western countries for these actions have brought the Palestinian people to utter despair. Consequently, a tiny minority of the Palestinian population perpetrates violent acts against Israeli soldiers and civilians because they perceive no more effective means of resisting the occupation. Those members of the Palestinian community may be wrong, tactically and morally, in choosing such strategies, but they are not exceptionally violent, hateful, shortsighted, or vengeful compared to their counterparts in Israel.

The majority of the West seems to forget that many of the tactics used today by the more extreme members of Palestinian society were first tested and used in Palestine *not* by Arabs but by *Jewish* underground militias during their struggle against British rule, when the Zionists were fighting for power. Many today also forget that some of Israel's former prime ministers –Menachem Begin and Yitzhak Shamir, for example – were leaders in those militias. Chairman Arafat's history of violent tactics pales in comparison to those of Israeli Prime Minister Ariel Sharon. The only difference is that

The settlement of Har Homa, to the east of Bethlehem, built on the confiscated Palestinian hill, Jabal Abu Ghneim.

Sharon's atrocities were committed while wearing a general's uniform and supported by the world's superpower. According to Halper, Israel presents itself as the victim, the hapless little kid in what Netanyahu called "a tough neighborhood of bullies." But this has never been the case. Israel, and the Zionist Yishuv [pre-state Jewish populace] that preceded it, always enjoyed international support denied to the Palestinians, as well as economic and military superiority. Israel is the regional superpower. It is a state recognized by the international community with an economy three times larger than Egypt, Palestine, Jordan, Syria, and Lebanon put together - more than 40 times the size of the Palestinians' ($80-plus billion compared to less than $2 billion). It has a formal military alliance with the world's largest superpower, from which it receives more than $3 billion in annual military assistance. It is the world's fourth largest nuclear power, possessing up to 500 nuclear warheads. And it is an occupying power. The Palestinians, by contrast, have no state, no functioning economy, no army, not even the ability to move freely from village to village within their own areas. This asymmetry of power, combined with Israel's determination to retain control over the entire country, thrusts upon Israel an asymmetry of responsibility.[141]

Let me repeat: There is no moral defense for detonating a bomb in a crowded area, or any other act of violence perpetrated against civilians. The point is that there is a double standard firmly in place that demonizes any Palestinian use of violence while legitimizing it when employed by Israel. It is a double standard that not only distorts the reality of Palestinian resistance to Israeli occupation but obscures the nature of the occupation itself. The result is widespread misunderstanding that finds expression in detrimental, unjust policy decisions on the part of world governments.

7. WHY DO PALESTINIANS CONTINUE TO FIGHT?

> No power on earth can stop an oppressed people determined to win their freedom.
> —Nelson Mandela

Admittedly, the persistence of the Palestinians in their struggle often seems futile. Since the beginning of the second popular uprising in the

296

Common
Questions
About the
Arab-Israeli
Conflict

year 2000, around 4,000 Palestinians have been killed and thousands more injured, some of them disabled for life. The Palestinian population is under perpetual siege, imprisoned in their cities and villages and surrounded by Israeli troops, tanks and Jewish settlements. When Palestinians move from place to place within their own territories they often risk their very lives. Hundreds of youths – held in "administrative detention" with no charges brought against them – are incarcerated and sometimes tortured in Israeli jails. And when some Palestinians respond to the occupation with violence, Israel, in retaliation and out of all proportion to the acts, turns on them and on whole communities with the force of a tornado, destroying homes, olive trees, crops, and lives. It serves no purpose, and it is not our desire, to establish a "hierarchy of suffering," yet it *is* fair to say that the impact of this struggle on the Israeli populace pales in comparison to the economic, social, emotional, and human losses that Palestinians experience *every day*.

Unlike the Israelis, Palestinians have no U.S.-made Apache helicopters, or tanks equipped with the most sophisticated instruments of destruction. They do not possess F-16 fighter jets or any weaponry that in any way matches the overwhelming, lethal Israeli force so often used against them. They also don't have the support of the world's leading economic and military power. Yet they continue to fight. The question is: Why?

For years Israeli leaders have deliberately painted an inaccurate picture by insisting that the late Yasser Arafat and the PLO were inciting Palestinians to fight. Israel, the White House, and the American media all bought into this and criticized Arafat for his alleged unwillingness to stop Palestinian attacks against Israel. The truth is that Arafat and his forces had a track record in the Oslo years of arresting Palestinian activists who threatened to fight the Israelis. Arafat's security forces and police frequently stood between Palestinian stone-throwers and Israeli soldiers to prevent or stop confrontations. Of course, Arafat, and his successor Abu Mazen, did not hold all the cards, and they were up against many forces including vehement internal opposition. In addition, during the heat of the second Intifada much of the Palestinian National Authority's infrastructure was systematically destroyed by Israeli bombing and shelling, weakening the PNA and any chance it might have had of reducing Palestinian fighting and arresting extremists. In effect, the Israeli attacks on the Palestinian infrastructure only served to increase hatred and the willingness to attack Israel.

Some hold that Palestinians are fighting because of religious promises of "Paradise," but this explanation is too simplistic and one-dimensional.

While it is true that a number of Palestinian fighters seemingly believe in and hope for a future Paradise, such aspirations are not the reason they fight. Paradise, even with its promise of virgins and everlasting ecstasy, would provide only marginal hope and incentive for a fighter who has already decided to give up his life for his cause. In fact, according to Islamic belief, a Muslim can be granted the same hope for Paradise by making the religious pilgrimage to Mecca called the Hajj. And, if a promised Paradise were the true motivation leading Palestinians to fight, it stands to reason that Muslim Palestinians who live in Israel (Israeli Arabs) would also engage in such attacks against Israel, yet they don't.

What Palestinians want, and are willing to die for, is the same deep-seated impulse for which countless wars have been fought throughout the centuries: Palestinians are fighting and dying for the dream of freedom. They struggle for full independence on what is now only a small part of their historic homeland, the West Bank and the Gaza Strip.

Anyone who assumes that Palestinians fight to destroy the State of Israel should consider the following questions: Why was Palestinian violence against Israel significantly reduced after the signing of the Oslo peace accords? Why, at the same time, were Israelis beginning to enter Palestinian towns casually and without fear? Why, when there was still a ray of hope regarding the peace talks, did the majority of Palestinians condemn suicide bombings? All of these realities point to a Palestinian population willing and capable of living side by side with Jewish Israel.

What is not well-known about the Israeli–Arab conflict is that Israel has systematically taken steps to prevent the achievement of Palestinian independence. For 60 years the Palestinians are the ones who have been the victims of massive ethnic cleansing, deportations, land confiscation, house demolitions, and many other forms of discrimination, acts which serve to crush their aspirations and deprive them of their dignity. Any people given as little hope and having had such a degree of suffering inflicted upon them as the Palestinians *would* become desperate and callous, as many Palestinians indeed now are.

One may ask: If the Palestinians are fighting for such a noble cause, why do they resort to suicide bombings and other terrorist activities? In any country where people are routinely denied justice, constantly pounded by superior military power, and consistently deprived of their rights in the international arena, some extreme elements will, out of desperation, resort to radical means of resistance to try to achieve their legitimate

298

Common
Questions
About the
Arab-Israeli
Conflict

rights. For example, the most prolific use of suicide bombing by a terror organization in recent years has been by the Sri Lankan-based Tamil Tiger rebels, a Marxist-leaning Hindu group. In Palestine, it is the absence and the denial of justice, day in and day out, that is the foremost inducement for Palestinian radicalism.

It is sad that the United States has, in effect, joined forces with Israel to deny the Palestinians justice. The U.S. is responsible for giving Israel weapons to kill suspected militants and members of their families. These weapons are supposedly designated for use in self-defense, but instead they are routinely employed to carry out internationally-banned political assassinations and attacks on population centers. In addition, by repeatedly using its veto privilege in the UN Security Council, the U.S. has consistently shielded Israel from international action, thus indirectly encouraging Israeli state-sponsored terrorism against the Palestinian population. Says U.S. writer on the Middle East Edward S. Herman:

> Thus, instead of having to leave the Occupied Territories Israel continues to push out the locals by force, uproot their trees, steal their water, beggar them by 'closures' and endless restrictions and it suffers no penalties because it has USA approval, protection and active assistance. The partners also deny Palestinians any right to return to land from which they were expelled, so 140-plus contrary United Nations votes and two Security Council Resolutions (both vetoed by the United States) have no effect.[142]

By closing off all avenues to fairness and equity, the U.S. and Israel have created an atmosphere of desperation that expresses itself in Palestinian radicalism. The two partner governments are thus responsible for creating a situation conducive to terrorism.

Instead of asking why Palestinians continue to fight, the more important questions to ask are: Why does Israel continue to occupy Palestinian land, and why the does the U.S. insist on supporting this illegal and immoral occupation? Only an end to Israeli aggression against Palestinians and a balanced U.S. policy in the Middle East, culminating in a Palestinian state, can put an end to the Palestinians' urge to fight.

300

Common
Questions
About the
Arab-Israeli
Conflict

> Systematic persecution of Christians by the Palestinian Authority cannot be substantiated...What we found instead was an intense desire for harmony among both Christians and Muslims from Galilee to Gaza.
> —Evangelicals for Middle East Understanding (EMEU) report, 1998

Christians and Muslims have been living side-by-side in Palestine ever since the birth of Islam over 1,300 years ago. Palestinians of the two faiths, sharing a common history, culture, and language, have together struggled in times of trouble and also shared times of plenty. Generally, the Christian minority has fared well living with the Muslim majority and under Muslim rule, and Palestine has always been regarded within the larger Middle East as a place of particular tolerance. Despite some tensions throughout the centuries, especially those introduced by the Crusades, colonialism, and radical Islamic invaders, Palestinian Christians and Muslims have succeeded in jointly building a tolerant and mutually respectful Palestinian society.

Thus, most Palestinian Christians are surprised when they hear reports from the West about the persecution of Christians by Muslims in Palestine – and lately these stories of Christian persecution seem to be increasing. However, such information is generally inaccurate. Sometimes these perceptions are based on a false understanding of Islam. But often they are the result of deliberate misinformation spread by the Israeli government and some of its Christian Zionist allies, or even by Palestinian Christians who have personal prejudices against Muslims or hope to profit financially.

These allegations of persecution are *not* coming from the Christian leaders in the West Bank or in Israel who have a first-hand account of the situation. If Christians in Israel/Palestine were being persecuted by Muslims, their leaders would certainly be crying out to their fellow Christians in the West for help. Albeit, in my experience as a pastor and Bible College teacher, and as a former president of the Council of Local Evangelical Churches in the Holy Land, I have not heard one sincere and respected Christian leader complain of Islamic persecution in Palestine!

The sources of many of these reports are offices linked to the Israeli Ministry of Foreign Affairs. The Israeli government has often attempted to incite division within Palestinian society and has not refrained from playing the religious card in doing so. For instance, when former Israeli Prime Minister Netanyahu tried to pass a law making it illegal to evangelize in Israel, his government received criticism from a campaign by evangelicals around the world. In order to divert attention from this criticism, Netanyahu's office released a report claiming that the PNA was persecuting Christians by jailing Muslim converts to Christianity. This report was circulated widely in the U.S. media and churches, with no one ever bothering to verify the facts with the Palestinian Christians. When Palestinian evangelicals heard the report they launched their own investigation, and it revealed that the few prisoners in question were in fact not genuine converts but had been jailed for collaborating with the Israeli security services. This sort of false information spread to the West about the supposed Muslim persecution of Christians is, unfortunately, unquestioningly accepted and propagated by many. The effect, sadly, is sometimes to breed actual divisions within Palestinian society that were not there before at all, such reports becoming, in effect, self-fulfilling prophecies.

To claim that Christian leaders are afraid of the Palestinian National Authority and therefore prefer to keep silent is yet another fallacy. Some Christian leaders have in fact openly criticized the Palestinian National Authority and pointed out some of its shortcomings, and these same leaders would not hesitate to speak up if the Palestinian Authority were persecuting Christians. In reality, the PNA does all it can to diffuse tensions between the two communities. Note, for example, that the PNA always appoints a Christian mayor over Bethlehem, in spite of the fact that 70% of the population of the city is Muslim. And Christians generally hold about 15% of the ministerial posts in the PNA government, even though they make up only 2% of the Palestinian population. Likewise, many of Arafat's top advisors – and even his wife – were Christian.

Since Christians are a tiny minority in Palestine living among a Muslim majority, it is not surprising that they face the kinds of anxieties common to most minorities throughout the world, including tendencies toward exclusivism and paranoia. Despite hundreds of years of fair treatment by Muslims, life has had its share of difficulties for the Christian community, and the occupation only tends to aggravate these anxieties. As a result, a small number of Palestinian Christians have come to believe the anti-Muslim rhetoric.

One instance of this took place during the Al-Aqsa Intifada when Palestinian gunmen were shooting at the Israeli colony of Gilo from positions they had taken up in the Palestinian town of Beit Jala, a town with an unusually high proportion of Christians. The town predictably came under Israeli fire in return, and this led some of the Christian residents to complain that the Muslim shooters were intentionally drawing fire to Christian homes. The reality, however, is that Palestinians shot from towns and cities all over the West Bank and Gaza Strip, whether they were inhabited by Christians or Muslims. And throughout the Occupied Territories, including in Beit Jala itself, Muslim houses were destroyed by Israeli shelling right along with Christian houses. Furthermore, many of the Muslim residents of these towns also became upset when gunmen fired from around their homes.

It is a case where certain Christians, out of their own limited perception of reality and perhaps a degree of religious prejudice, supposed some Muslim conspiracy against them. The result was that their shortsighted and uninformed reaction caused unnecessary division within the Palestinian community. The vast majority of the Palestinians participating in armed resistance to Israeli colonization are in fact Muslim, mainly because the majority of Palestinians are Muslim. A small number of Christians, however, have also joined this violent resistance.

To sum up, relations have generally been good between Palestinian Muslims and Christians. While there is still progress to be made toward an even healthier majority-minority relationship, the two faiths continue to live in relative harmony. They work, play, eat – and struggle through the Israeli occupation – together. Their very survival is bound together as one people. It is quite true that the Christian population in the Holy Land is dwindling, but this decline is due mainly to economic and political factors. The hardships of the occupation and the closures of Palestinian territories have been inflicted on the Christian and Muslim populations alike, but the Muslims' opportunities to emigrate are simply much more restricted. Today, Christians in the West Bank and Gaza suffer economically, socially and psychologically from the consequences of a most brutal and inhumane occupation, but the Muslim population, their neighbors, likewise bear the very same yoke of oppression. Thus, it is not only inaccurate but profoundly unfair for anyone to assign to Muslims responsibility for the suffering of the Palestinian Christian community.

By the Author

The high-spirited televangelist stands before a crowd of thousands. He knows the very words that will bring a thunderous applause from the crowd that packs the stadium. Beside him stands an Israeli official who he is equally anxious to impress. With high evangelistic fervor, he launches a verbal attack on Islam and the founder of the Islamic faith. Then he ends his statement with the highest praise for the State of Israel. His words sound like music to his listeners' ears. He feels good about his rhetoric, and so do his guests and his fired-up audience. However, in this age of advanced communications, the televangelist's remarks also reach the homes of the many Muslims who live with us on this planet, and it should be noted that they do not feel so good about the messages they are getting. In fact, many Muslims – in Indonesia, Palestine, Morocco, and the United States, just to name a few countries – are wondering why Evangelical Christians in America are so zealously bashing their faith. Indeed, this is a question that should concern us as well.

Since September 11, 2001 a wave of anti-Muslim feeling has taken over much of America and is still spreading like wildfire in Evangelical circles in the United States and other countries. Officials of respected Evangelical denominations and presidents of esteemed Christian organizations have joined the new trend. Some are publicly insulting Islam and its founder, while others are attacking the Koran and those who follow in its path.

Christians in general, and Evangelicals in particular, would do well to stop and think about where this crusade may be leading us and how it will impact Christian-Muslim relationships around the world. Evangelicals would also do well to consider carefully whether their public, rhetorical war against Muslims will advance or hinder the cause of Christ throughout the Muslim world. Furthermore, Christians might also consider taking a fresh look at the history of Muslim-Christian interactions throughout the last 14 centuries before waving a banner in the current anti-Muslim war of words.

304

*Common
Questions
About the
Arab-Israeli
Conflict*

During the Middle Ages, Pope Urban II campaigned to unite the various competing armies of Christian Europe in a crusade to liberate Jerusalem and the Holy Land from the Muslims. The Pope blessed the Crusades, and the brave fighters of Europe joined to fight what they perceived to be the enemies of God. The church sanctioned the killing of Muslims and other so-called infidels and heretics. Muslim men, women and children were butchered in great numbers. The Crusaders also killed many Jews and great numbers of non-Latin Christians. But the sword of Islam turned against the invading armies, and most of the Crusaders never returned to see their homelands again, deeming all the while that they were fighting and dying for Christ and His church. After 190 years of unspeakable bloodshed, the Muslims had wrested control of Jerusalem and the rest of the Holy Land from the Western invaders, bringing an end to the Crusades. However, the Crusades created deep wounds in Muslim-Christian relations that have yet to be healed.

Today's rhetoric of hate against Islam clears the path for tomorrow's wars against Islamic nations. When our preachers, teachers, TV evangelists and politicians condition us to hate Muslims, they prepare us for the prospect that it might be necessary to kill Muslims or to accept their slaughter in a war.

Before getting caught up in the spirit of the times and joining the crusade of attacking Muslims, American Christians today need to learn what Middle Eastern and European Christians learned centuries ago. The lesson is simple: Live in peace with your Muslim neighbors and they will live in peace with you; oppress them and they will fight back. Even if we believe or assume that Islam is evil, are we called to "repay evil for evil" or to "overcome evil with good" (Romans 12:17–21)?

I have lived most of my life as a member of a small Christian community within a larger Islamic population. The Church that I now pastor in East Jerusalem is located in a predominantly Muslim neighborhood. I know from first-hand experience and from daily contacts with Muslims that most Muslims do not hate Christians. Moreover, most Muslims have nothing to do with terrorism.

The radical Muslim factions who are involved in militant acts against Israel or its allies are Muslims driven more by political reasons than religious agendas. Palestinians have wanted for years to be rid of the Israeli occupation of what they perceive as their homeland. They appealed to the United Nations and the UN failed them. They appealed to the superpowers and to Arab states who also failed them. Alternately, they sought the help of more than a thousand peace conferences, but the conferences did not stop the confiscation of their land and the denial of their human rights. During their struggle, some Palestinians turned to non-violent resistance and others to violent uprisings (intifada), all to no avail. In their utter frustration with all options, some of them turned to radical Islamic movements. As a last resort the cry became: "Islam is the answer."

Islamic movements such as Hamas and Hezbollah are relatively new in the long history of the Arab-Israeli conflict. Nevertheless, most Muslims do not subscribe to these movements. Moreover, we err greatly if we insist on seeing all Muslims in the light of the bloody crimes of September 11 or in view of the dreadful suicide bombings on the streets of Jerusalem and Tel Aviv.

If we want to find the enemy, we must look within us rather than at Islam and Muslims. The enemies of the United States and the Western world are found mainly within the United States and within the Western world. Greed, pride, hypocrisy, racism, moral corruption, xenophobia and social injustice are our worst enemies. These are the sins that make us hate, humiliate, kill and starve whole nations and pollute our planet. For example, for over half a century Arabs and Muslims have been pleading with the West for a just resolution of the Arab-Israeli conflict. Instead of responding fairly, we allowed domestic pressures and lobby groups to steer our foreign policy into supporting one side of the conflict against the legitimate rights of the other side, with disastrous consequences. Instead of promoting justice, our intervention became a factor in complicating and worsening the situation and hindering the cause of peace. Quite often, the arrogance of governments in the West and their unjust policies in the Middle East are the fuel that inflames Islamic fundamentalists.

One out of every five humans on earth is a follower of the Muslim faith, each of whom Christ calls us to love as we love ourselves. Attacking Islam or hating Muslims will not only hinder

306

Common
Questions
About the
Arab-Israeli
Conflict

the cause of Christ in the world, but it will also endanger the lives of Christians who live as minorities in the Islamic world. Whether we live at peace with our Muslim neighbor or not depends as much on us as on them.

(*Published in The Mennonite*, November 19, 2002)

9. WHAT IS THE ROLE OF THE MEDIA IN THE ARAB-ISRAELI CONFLICT?
(Ben White and Tom Powers)

Most people would agree that the role of the news media is to inform the public about events in the world around them while providing background and analysis, enabling them to make sense of and process the facts and issues presented. However, the true impact of the media is much broader: it shapes our perceptions of those facts and thus our opinions on the issues. Also, in a democratic society, at least in theory, our opinions translate into various expressions of political pressure: the ballot box, direct access to our elected representatives, and a host of lobbying and advocacy activities, all of which in turn influence and shape public policy, i.e. the decisions made by our government.

Few would deny that the United States, as the world's only superpower and Israel's primary ally, is in a uniquely powerful position to effect events in the Middle East, for better or for worse. It is therefore worth exploring, as with all public policy, how the media influences and shapes people's perceptions and opinions regarding the Israeli-Palestinian conflict. Indeed, it is an ongoing challenge to look critically at the messages that are being delivered to us through images and the printed and spoken word, with all their undertones, about events in the Israeli-Palestinian arena.

It is interesting, perhaps encouraging, that the two sides in the conflict both make accusations of media prejudice – often against the very same media organizations and outlets! It is a reminder that no reporting and presentation of news or information can be free from bias, whether real or perceived. Perhaps the best we can strive for is to be more aware of it, more ready to "decode" the messages we receive. We can look at some ways in which media bias sometimes manifests itself, namely: (1) the choice of language and terminology and (2) selective reporting – what is included or omitted – and the related problem of lack of context.

Because language – the written or spoken word – is the primary medium by which stories are told, the words and phrases journalists employ, with the sometimes subtle shades of meaning they carry (even on the level of what things are called) can be important in shaping the audience's perceptions and opinions of the conflict. Even with seemingly innocuous phrases like "the two sides" and "cycle of violence," for example, the media gives the impression of two equal parties locked in equally destructive mutual violence. The power relations on the ground, however, are heavily imbalanced. One "side" has the world's most advanced weapons, supplied by the U.S. and other Western nations, and is subsidized to the tune of $3 billion a year. The other "side" is stateless, without a military, and has half of its population living on less than $2 a day. Thus the "cycle" has always had a disproportionate, devastating impact on one party, the Palestinians.

Another example is the term "Jerusalem neighborhood" which was the standard way of referring in news reports to Gilo, the area between Jerusalem and Bethlehem which came under Palestinian fire in 2001 during the Second Intifada. Palestinians, however, often refer to Gilo as an Israeli "colony" or "settlement," since it is in fact built on land occupied by Israel in 1967, and the same is true of several other outlying "Jerusalem neighborhoods" now annexed, many would say illegally, within the municipal boundaries.

Likewise, we often hear an Israeli army action against towns of the West Bank or Gaza Strip called by the rather bland, neutral term "incursion". Yet to the Palestinian civilian populace who bear the brunt of these "incursions," they are forceful military invasions in densely populated civilian areas. These towns and neighborhoods often incurred significant loss of life and property. Also, Israel is many times said to be "retaliating" against Palestinian violence, but how often is it stated the other way round? Palestinians are seldom said to be "retaliating," which suggests some provocation from the Israeli side. Instead the Palestinians are portrayed as starting yet another "cycle of violence" without any rational cause. Again, the journalists' very choice of words almost always carries with it a certain bias toward one side or another.

It should be obvious that no news story can include everything, all the history, background and connections of a particular issue. Every particular journalistic offering has to be "about" something, has to have some focus. Therefore the decisions which the creators of media make – the reporters, writers, producers, editors – about the content of a piece, what to include and what to omit, always introduces a sort of inevitable bias. Thus, a proper perspective of this issue probably calls for us to take a long view, that is, the output of a particular news organization or outlet over time: If, over time, there is not some balanced exposure of various viewpoints and the impact of the conflict on both sides, then a charge of selective reporting and bias may be warranted.

With that perspective, some media observers have detected – on balance – elements of bias in how the Israeli-Palestinian conflict is reported. Glaringly absent from much coverage, for example, is any serious attempt to convey what daily life is like for the Palestinian people: curfews, sieges, beatings, imprisonment without charge, torture, and a vexing regime of roadblocks, checkpoints, and permits (almost entirely internal to the territories).

The reporting of casualty figures introduces problems as well. This is due in part to the nature of the deadly incidents: Occasional, high-profile – and undeniably horrific – suicide bombings against Israelis, *versus* regular and widely-scattered IDF/security actions against Palestinians. In terms of numbers, the latter are far more deadly, a reality often lost in the process of reporting. Just as an example, in the single month of February 2003, a total of eight Israelis were killed compared to 79 Palestinians. However, the daily deaths of a handful of Palestinians, day in and day out, are seldom able to command the headlines in the Western media.

Finally, the media has sometimes been guilty (again, on balance) of presenting events without adequate context, especially the historical context. For example, the now 41-year-old Israeli occupation of the Palestinian territories, the backdrop to many day-to-day news events, is now rarely mentioned. The same is true, perhaps more so, of the expulsion of hundreds of thousands of Palestinians in 1948, the towering injustice that has always overshadowed the conflict. Often likewise glossed over is the constant irritant of the Israeli settlements – and their constant expansion (the settlement population almost doubled in the seven years of the Oslo "peace process"). As the background to the ongoing conflict, many such fundamental issues have all too often been passed over. However in order to claim the banner of fair and insightful reporting the media must illuminate the historical backdrop and seek out and report the linkages to today's events.

Israel has at its disposal, most notably in America, a powerful, efficient and well-organized support lobby, a force which encompasses both Zionist Jews and the growing and vocal Christian Zionist movement. These groups mobilize to put pressure on politicians and journalists at every level, to the extent that criticism of Israel can mean losing your job, cancelled campaign contributions, or being voted out of public office (or, indeed, never elected in the first place). A particularly effective and thus frequently-used weapon in the lobby's arsenal is the accusation of anti-Semitism, a charge likely to be leveled at anyone voicing any sort of criticism, however reasoned and measured, of the State of Israel and its policies and actions.

Such pressure cannot be lost on the larger world of media, that is, media as an institution, as a purveyor of popular culture – and as big business. Some have argued that for-profit media enterprises by their nature suffer from a built-in conflict of interest, a structural fault related to their reliance on advertisers, corporate ownership and increasing monopolization. The result is that major corporate news organizations can become reluctant to highlight the negative aspects of their government's foreign policy, as it will often touch upon the interests of its owners and corporate sponsors. And when unpalatable facts do emerge and must be reported on, they are presented as aberrations of an otherwise ethically "good" policy, rather than reflecting fundamental flaws in the guiding principles.

Finally, a case-study may help answer the question of the media's proper role in the Israeli-Palestinian conflict. The journalistic offering under consideration is a documentary by John Pilger entitled "Palestine is Still the Issue" which was broadcast on British television in 2002. Following its screening there were, predictably, a large number of complaints, along with calls of support. But one highly-placed official publicly condemned the program as "a tragedy for Israel as far as accuracy is concerned," and the case was thus referred to an independent television watchdog. Pilger himself knew very well why there was such a strong response: "What was unusual about the documentary," he wrote, "was that it disclosed in detail the daily humiliation and cultural denigration of the Palestinians, including a sequence showing excrement smeared by Israeli soldiers in a room of children's paintings." In the end, the watchdog organization cleared the broadcaster, saying that impartiality did not "require absolute neutrality on every issue or detachment from fundamental democratic principles."

It is time for the Western media to hold to these "fundamental democratic principles" and to evenhandedly expose the injustices experienced by both Israelis and Palestinians. And we, as the daily consumers of "media", must develop critical eyes and ears, always holding our sources of information accountable for their coverage of this conflict.

> If you want peace, you must work for justice.
> —Pope John Paul VI

Most Palestinians have a clear vision of a workable peace between themselves and their Jewish neighbors. While they feel that a great injustice was done to their people when the State of Israel was created – the often forcible displacement of the bulk of their population, confiscation of their land, and the destruction of hundreds of their villages – they know that the clock cannot be turned back. They wish for their plight to be acknowledged, but also know they cannot seek absolute justice and must settle instead for relative and sometimes symbolic justice, solutions that take account of the present and longstanding realities.

As such, the majority of Palestinians feel that a just peace could be obtained if Israel would allow them a state in those areas occupied in 1967, that is, the West Bank and Gaza. In return, Palestinians would abandon their claim to the rest of historic Palestine (78%), which became the state of Israel in 1948. This two-state solution would allow Israel to legitimately exist side-by-side with the state of Palestine. Of course, this would mean that the Jewish settlements in the Occupied Territories, all of which were erected illegally, would have to be evacuated. A just and humane adjunct to this evacuation would be to leave the thousands of housing units and other buildings intact and available to absorb returning Palestinian refugees. Many observers, including many Israelis, have long felt that these settlements are not only illegal and unjust, but constitute a constant source of tension and friction and render any lasting solution impractical and unworkable.

The Palestinians are willing to erect a future Palestinian state without a standing army and thus, without weapons. Not only would this meet the security concerns of the Jewish state, but it would relieve Palestinians of the burden of military spending and enable them to focus on rebuilding their shattered economy and society.

Any workable peace agreement must deal with the issue of the Palestinian refugees. There are two main considerations that must be addressed when dealing with this issue: (1) the compensation and/or repatriation of the refugees and (2) the security and demographic concerns of Israelis. Palestinians feel entitled to an acknowledgement of their right – in principle

– to return to their homeland from which they fled amid the upheaval of war or, as often as not, from which they were forcefully expelled. If Jews around the globe can claim the "right of return" to "Eretz Israel" after 2,000 years, surely Palestinians can claim the right to return to the homes from which they were driven within the living memory of this generation. Realistically, however, this right of return would never be exercised by most Palestinians, as only a fraction of the refugees would ever opt to return to Israel. But those Palestinian refugees who do not return would be entitled to compensation, enabling them to settle wherever they choose, including in the new state of Palestine.

Jerusalem, the focus of uniquely sensitive and complex issues, should be dealt with entirely separately. Though Israel captured the eastern parts of Jerusalem (including the Old City) in 1967, many of those neighborhoods, most still overwhelmingly Arab in complexion, form an integral part of the Occupied Territories. Therefore they should be part of the new state of Palestine, under Arab sovereignty. Jerusalem holds such importance for both Israelis and Palestinians – historically, spiritually and emotionally – and for people of all three monotheistic faiths, that perhaps it should not remain under the exclusive sovereignty of any single state but be shared in a manner that ensures its accessibility for everyone, including the wider international community of Jews, Muslims and Christians. As a capital for both Israel and Palestine, Jerusalem could enjoy a unique, shared status that would benefit not only both peoples but all the peoples of the earth!

This Palestinian vision of peace, I believe, is endorsed by a majority of Palestinians. It is a vision that developed slowly and painfully over time, though there are still those who hold out for more, claiming all of Palestine for the Arabs, or arguing for a bi-national Jewish-Arab state in all of Palestine/Israel. I truly believe, however, that the vision outlined here, the so-called "two-state solution," constitutes a reasonable compromise, one that would be supported by an overwhelming majority of Palestinians. Most important, it is an arrangement that should enable future generations of Palestinians and Israelis to live in peace and security.

Some immediately argue that Palestinian terrorism would impede and derail this Palestinian vision of peace, and thus they dismiss it out-of-hand. However, once a fair peace settlement is agreed upon and implemented between the two parties, there will be no justification, and indeed no motivation, for militancy and violence from the Palestinian side. It is the belief of most Palestinians that terrorism, whether generated by Palestinians or by Israelis, is a direct result of the unresolved conflict.

312

*Common
Questions
About the
Arab-Israeli
Conflict*

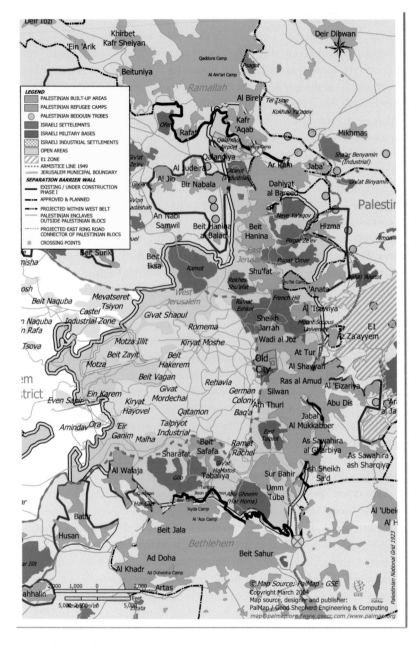

Divided Jerusalem: Israeli efforts to make the city exclusively Jewish has contributed to its disunity.

People unfamiliar with day-to-day realities in the West Bank and Gaza Strip may wonder why the Palestinian people voted for a militant Islamic faction to lead their government. On January 26, 2006, Palestinians went to the polls and in a free and fair election they gave the militant Islamic party Hamas 76 of the 132 parliamentary seats. Some interpreted these results as a clear indication that Palestinians were not ready to live in peace with their Israeli neighbors. Others saw the election of Hamas as proof that Palestinians wanted a government run by strict Islamic law (Shari'a).

However in a poll of Palestinians conducted by pollster Khalil Shakaki in April 2006, 75% of the respondents said they wanted their new government to conduct peace talks with Israel. Another poll by the Ramallah-based Near East Consulting Institute found similarly that 84% of those surveyed in the Palestinian Territories want a peace agreement with Israel, while 86% want the moderate Palestinian Authority president Mahmud Abbas to remain in his post. In other polls, Palestinians expressed clearly that voting for Hamas did *not* reflect a desire to turn Palestine into a strict Islamic state, run according to the dictates of Islamic law.

Mark Perry, a Middle East conflict resolution expert, was interviewed regarding the issue of Hamas's victory and said the following:

"There's a lot of disinformation circulating. We heard that Hamas would impose Islamic rule, but so far that hasn't happened. We heard that Hamas would write Islamic rule into the law of Gaza, and I don't think that will happen either. I don't think there are broad social consequences from Hamas's victory. Nine of the 15 members of Hamas's Shura Council have Ph.D.s in the sciences. They are sophisticated people and not rejectionists of the enlightenment. There are hardliners within Hamas who would push for an Islamic state, but they are relatively few in number, and they're street captains—not in the leadership. Hamas has been strong in Gaza, but there's no Islamic state there—no enforced social programs, no religious police, and a relatively free press. Is Gaza more conservative than the West Bank? Yes, but that's part of a process that's been going on for the past 40 years. It's not because of the recent fighting. You just don't see support for an Islamic state on the ground. This is not Tehran in 1979."
http://harpers.org/archive/2007/06/hbc-90000294

Why then did the Palestinians vote Hamas into their government?

314

Common
Questions
About the
Arab-Israeli
Conflict

a. *To protest against the corruption of many of their leaders of the ruling Fatah Party:* Many Fatah Party leaders (PLO) were tainted by accusations of corruption, and the ruling Fatah chief and Palestinian President Mahmoud Abbas were unable, in the short period, to clean up the government's reputation. Palestinians concluded that the only way to clean up their government was to vote into power the only alternative party that could challenge Fatah, namely, Hamas.

b. *To protest Israel's humiliation of the moderate Palestinians:* For years the Palestinian National Authority, headed first by Yasser Arafat and later by Mahmoud Abbas, had extended a hand of reconciliation to the Israeli leadership, however the Israelis consistently not only shunned Palestinian calls for a just peace but continued taking actions that both angered the Palestinian populace and brought popular scorn on the Fatah government. Every effort of Palestinian moderates to talk reason with Israeli leaders failed. The Israelis had a set agenda and they determined that they did not need the moderate Palestinian leadership obstructing it. Their agenda of completing their settlement project in the West Bank and judaizing East Jerusalem, though disguised from many in the West, was visible to Palestinians. This agenda caused Israeli governments to drag their feet and stall in every round of peace negotiations.

c. *To protest against American policy in Israel/Palestine:* The United States, for several reasons, both domestic and international, was unable to do what was necessary to promote a just and lasting solution to the conflict. The failure of the international community, headed by the U.S., to create a political horizon for Palestinians created a vacuum that was filled by militant Islamist factions. This scenario has been repeated in other Middle Eastern countries. Meanwhile, the U.S. gave lip service to Palestinian moderates, which made those moderates look like they were supporting the status quo and collaborating with its guardians. On Election Day, the Palestinians decided to send a message to the Americans.

d. *To support Hamas' humanitarian work:* Hamas gained popularity by engaging in humanitarian work throughout the Gaza Strip and some parts of the West Bank – providing food for the hungry and other services for the poverty-stricken people. Palestinians decided to vote for the hand that fed them, instead of voting for the hand accused of siphoning off their national treasury.

After Hamas was fairly and democratically elected, the United States refused to cooperate with, talk to, or financially support the new government. The U.S. sent a message to the world that democracy is permitted only when the elected party adopts an agenda that does not conflict with the interests of the U.S. or the Israeli government. The U.S. and Israel decided to bankrupt Hamas in order to bring the government to its knees. Israeli leaders also began rounding up and incarcerating the democratically elected Hamas officials. The irony about all of this is that the United States had previously exerted pressure on Israel to allow Hamas to participate in the elections.

With the U.S. supporting the Fatah Party, and grassroots and international Islamic movements around the world financing Hamas, the stage was set for a Palestinian civil war. Once again, Palestine became a battlefield for international antagonists as each side began arming its members to assure a victory. Fortunately for most Palestinian civilians, a full-fledged civil war did not breakout. But the few battles that did take place in Gaza resulted in the loss of over fifty Palestinian lives, both fighters and civilians. In the end, Hamas claimed victory by taking full control of the Gaza Strip, while Fatah retreated to the West Bank.

Hamas will not be able to bankroll Gaza on its own for very long and Islamists will not be able to continue pouring in millions of dollars just to sustain an entity they know will gradually be cut off from the international community. The best solution for Hamas' leaders is to reconcile with the Palestinian President, and call for new elections. Hamas leaders will eventually realize that neither the international community nor the Palestinians themselves will accept a long-term Hamas-led government in Palestine.

12. WHAT CAN WE DO TO WORK FOR PEACE BETWEEN PALESTINIANS AND ISRAELIS?

The Western world bears much of the responsibility for the plight of the Palestinian people. The horrible history of anti-Semitism, culminating in the tragedy of the Holocaust, was the creation of the West. In attempting to solve the "Jewish question" by establishing a Jewish state in Palestine, the West only created another problem, the "Palestinian question." Furthermore,

Israel's occupation of Palestinian land continues to find legitimacy in the Western world, particularly in the United States. This is a responsibility the West inescapably bears, whether it acknowledges it or not. But rather than wallow in guilt or helplessness, the West must look to the future with determination and find ways to contribute to peace. The following are general suggestions:

a. *Educate yourself.* To a large extent the battle between the Israelis and Palestinians is a battle of information and perceptions, as both sides attempt to win the support of the international community. The various players in the conflict have vastly different understandings of the conflict's history, as well as of current events: thus it requires real effort to wade through the mass of information available, particularly when one wants to find a genuine Palestinian perspective. The contacts listed in Appendix IV of this book will be a beginning.

b. *Educate others.* This can take many forms. It is important, at every opportunity, to challenge the one-sided story presented to people in the West, especially in the United States. When hearing false stereotypes or myths concerning the conflict or those involved, one should not let such comments pass unchallenged, without confronting the falsehoods for what they are. Educating children in the contexts of family, church and school is critical. One may also take the initiative to educate the public at large, through such means as making presentations at church, writing letters to the editors of local or national newspapers, writing to members of Congress and other government leaders, or forming local advocacy groups for cooperative efforts with other concerned individuals.

c. *Christians can work for change within the Church.* The denominational structures of the Church are often underestimated with regard to their power to impact broad global issues. Several denominations have in fact already made strong statements of support for the Palestinians, but a great deal more could be done. The Church provides a ready-made institutional framework through which large numbers of people can be educated and mobilized, and if their influence can be brought to bear upon governments, especially the American government, politicians might think twice before giving virtually unconditional support to Israel.

Furthermore, much theological re-tooling is called for, new perspectives that take into account *both* the Palestinian and the Jewish experiences of the past 100 years. Some theologians since the Holocaust have already put significant effort into rethinking the skewed Christian theology that contributed to, or sometimes warmly embraced, the kind of anti-Semitism that allowed an Auschwitz or Treblinka to happen. This work should continue, weeding out the remaining vestiges of anti-Semitism from the Christian mind and heart. But at the same time, and with no less urgency, any theology that tries to marginalize the Palestinian people or justify their humiliation needs to be strongly challenged. In the theological realm, as in the political, many who have sought to correct historic Western wrongs against the Jews have sadly come down in support of other equally reprehensible wrongs, those committed against the Palestinians, including Palestinian Christians. Christ stands on the side of Jesus, so must the church.

d. *Join those already working on Middle East issues.* There are many advocacy and human rights groups across Europe and North America working on Middle East issues. Contact one or several of them and find out how to become involved in supporting their work.

e. *Embrace nonviolent public protest.* One way of voicing concerns to the government, while simultaneously educating the public, is to organize and/or participate in vigils, marches, rallies or other peaceful forms of public protest. Organizing these types of highly-visible events takes work, but if well-planned they can be very fruitful and effective in drawing attention to the issues of justice central to the Palestinian-Israeli problem.

f. *Help through financial contributions.* Any financial contributions channeled to Palestinians in order to ease their economic and social difficulties should be done responsibly. This requires that such help be given in a spirit of solidarity and partnership, with the aim of doing justice, and not as "charity" which is experienced by the recipient as patronizing and ultimately demeaning. With this in mind, there are many effective and worthwhile avenues for sharing one's financial resources with Palestinian people, without creating an unhealthy dependence on charity.

g.. Lift up the situation in intercessory prayer. Our faith in a loving, merciful and just God should spur us to intercede fervently on behalf of all the peoples of Israel and Palestine, until the hostilities end and peace is restored to the land.

POSTSCRIPT

Perhaps the most striking fact about the years 2008-2012 or since *Palestinian Memories* was first published is that nothing major has happened to move the Israelis and the Palestinians closer to peace. The main obstacles to peace that I listed in the first edition continue to disallow Israelis and Palestinians from reaching an agreement that would end hostilities: no breakthroughs (see page 161-163), no serious negotiations (see pp 235-240), no end to building Jewish settlements in East Jerusalem and in the West Bank (pp161), no end to the siege of Gaza (see pp 136-140), no halt in building the segregation wall (pp 213-215), and no change in Israeli efforts to Judaize Arab East Jerusalem (pp 311-312).

Internationally, there has been no change in the US's unconditional support for the State of Israel and its policies towards the Palestinians (pp 223-230). In spite of the fact that a new US president gave hope to Americans, Arabs, and the entire world that he would be the man to bring about change, regrettably, he resumed politics as usual. In a speech in Cairo in June 2009, President Obama committed to "personally pursue" the establishment of a Palestinian state "with all patience that the task requires." He added, "Israelis must acknowledge that just as Israel's right to exist cannot be denied, neither can Palestine's." Obama must have underestimated the strength of the pro-Israel and Christian Zionist lobbies (see chapter eight: pp 223-230). His administration's fight to block the Palestinian bid for statehood at the UN is sufficient evidence that all his hopes for solving the Israeli-Palestinian conflict shattered as they collided with the forces of these two lobbies. Moreover, Obama demonstrated to the world that a US president who is seeking to be reelected for a second term will not be able to bring the Arab-Israeli conflict to a satisfactory conclusion.

Regardless, unpredicted and unimagined change happened in the Arab world as massive popular political revolutions, dubbed "the Arab Spring," shook the region. This revolution has already resulted in great changes in the region and will have an impact on the future of the church in Palestine and the rest of the Middle East. This political and social earthquake, which is still ongoing, began by forcing the Tunisian dictator, Ben Ali Zain El Abideen, to resign and to flee the country.

The political tsunami quickly reached Egypt and caused the downfall of President Hosni Mubarak. The revolution is still going on in Egypt as young revolutionaries want to get rid of all of the symbols of the old regime.

In Libya, Muamar Gaddafi underestimated the resolve of the opposition and the international community to oust him and end his autocratic regime.

He literally fought the rebels to the last drop of his blood, but with the help of NATO, his dictatorship crumbled. The rebels and NATO won; Gaddafi was killed. In the end, his sons and close supporters either died or were thrown in prison.

In Yemen, the Arab Spring drove millions of Yemenis to demonstrate in most large cities for many months against the regime of the strongman and dictator, Abdullah Saleh. Like Gaddafi, he decided to crush the non-violent rebellion through any means necessary. But the Yemeni opposition made it difficult for him, as most of the rebels insisted on pursuing the path of non-violent resistance and refused to be dragged into civil war. In one rare attack on his palace by a rival faction, President Saleh was injured and had to leave the country for medical treatment. In 2012, under great domestic and international pressure, he resigned and left the country. The road to democracy for Yemen remains long and perilous.

In Bahrain, the rebellion against the regime is still going on after one year of demonstrations. The fact that the rebels belong to the majority Shiite population and are fighting against a Sunni-controlled government gives a sectarian face to the rebellion. Saudi Arabia, fearing Iranian intervention on behalf of the Shiite majority, sent tanks and troops to protect the Sunni kingdom.

As I write, deadly confrontations are taking place in Syria between government troops who are loyal to President Bashar Al Assad and popular opposition to his regime. Assad decided to fight back and ordered his troops and secret police to kill, injure, imprison, and torture the rebels. So far, over six thousand Syrians have been killed. Despite the brutal crackdown, and despite the fact that the Arab states and the international community have been unable to stop the carnage, the rebellion goes on. Assad has butchered so many of his people that it would be next to impossible to see a role for him in the future political landscape of Syria.

The Arab Spring is causing radical political changes in the region and is having an impact beyond the Middle East and North Africa. Dictators and manipulative leaders worldwide are terrified of the possibility that their marginalized masses will emulate the Arab Spring. Presidents, kings, and sheiks are becoming aware that they can't do business as usual. Absolute monarchies are being replaced by constitutional monarchies and constitutions are being revised and reformed to meet the thirst of the masses for democracy. For the first time in the Arab World, the men at the helm are realizing that they can be dragged to courts by their own people and forced to give an account for their political corruption and abuse of power.

The impact of the Arab Spring on the Arab-Israeli conflict and the future of the Christian communities is still not certain; however, Israel is wary that some of her allies in the Middle East and North Africa are fast disappearing. Israel lost a strong ally in Egyptian President Mubarak. King Abdullah of Jordan will not be able to continue to accommodate US and Israeli interests in Jordan as a result of the objections of his people. With the renewed power of the Muslim Brotherhood in Egypt, diplomacy between Egypt and Israel will not be the same. The Muslim Brotherhood has always aspired to end the Israeli occupation of the West Bank and put an end to the choking economic blockade of the Gaza Strip. The Egyptian masses will no longer bow to US pressure or close their eyes to Israeli aggression in the Gaza Strip and in the West Bank.

The focus of the world on the Arab Spring has distracted attention from the core challenge in the Middle East, namely, the Palestinian-Israeli conflict. However, as soon as the dust settles, Israel may find itself surrounded by Arab masses that are fed up with her intransigence. In the near future, these masses could be governed by leaders who may listen to their people rather than continue to be stooges of Israeli and US demands. Assuming that Israel desires to live in peace with her neighbors, she must come down from her place of superiority and start a genuine dialogue with Palestinians that will bring about true reconciliation.

Some of Israel's chauvinistic policies caused her to lose an important Middle Eastern ally even before the Arab Spring began. The rising political and economic power of Turkey, a country with a majority Muslim population, was destined to clash with Israel over her policies in the West Bank and the Gaza Strip. First, Turkey was incensed over Israel's brutal attacks on the Gaza Strip. The assault began on December 27th, 2009. According to Israeli sources, the attacks were in response to rockets that resistance groups in Gaza launched against southern Israel. One Israeli was killed by these rockets. The Israeli response was heavy and according to international human rights sources, 1,470 Gazans were killed, many of them civilians, including women and children. The bombing caused the destruction of entire residential areas, and in some cases the residents were trapped and killed under the ruins of their homes. Over 4,000 homes were destroyed by the bombing. Out of the thirteen Israeli casualties during the same time, four of them were killed by "friendly" (Israeli) fire and three of them were civilians.

The excessive use of force outraged the Arab and Muslim world. Turkey was the most vocal in expressing disgust with the Israeli leadership. The relationship between Israel and Turkey continued to slide after the attack.

The turning point took place on May 31st, 2010, when Israeli commandos raided a flotilla that was carrying food and medical supplies to Gaza with the intended purpose of breaking the Israeli blockade. The commandos descended on the largest ship of the flotilla, the Mavi Marmara, and killed nine people, most of whom were Turks. Turkey demanded an open apology from Israel. Israeli leaders expressed regret for the loss of life but refused to admit wrong doing or apologize. Instead they blamed the peace activists for attacking the Israeli commandoes with rods and water hoses to prevent them from landing. The Turks insist that normal relationship with Israel will not be resumed until an official apology is given.

The preoccupation of the Arab countries with the Arab Spring, the inability of the US administration to influence the Israelis to negotiate with good faith, and never-ending Israeli settlement construction in the West Bank continued to frustrate the Palestinian leadership in Ramallah. Palestinian President Mahmoud Abbas decided to take his case to the UN to seek recognition of statehood for Palestine. In a dramatic speech at the UN, Abbas presented his bid for statehood amidst cheers from most members of the international body. In response, both Israel and the US decided to inflict punitive measures against Palestine for seeking a free and independent state. They gave the same objection that they give to any move towards peace: peace and Palestinian statehood must be the result of direct negotiations between the two parties. They ignore the fact that direct negotiations have been taking place on and off over 20 years with no results. (For more on this please read the article below).

Israel has always bragged that it is the only democracy in the Middle East. Often, US members of Congress based US support for the State of Israel on the claim that it is the only democracy in the region. Many Israeli thinkers are concerned that Israel is fast sliding away from true democracy in order to accommodate itself to the dreams, goals and political aspirations of a burgeoning right-wing population. The irony is that as many Israelis are turning their backs on democracy, millions in the Arab world, including Palestinians, are passionately embracing it.

The Effect of the Arab Spring on the Christian Communities in the Middle East and North Africa

Whenever there is turmoil in a majority Muslim country, minorities, including Christians, are affected in a negative way. In Libya, for example, before the revolution, 1.2 million Christians, most of them foreign workers, lived in the country. A million of these had to flee the country or risk being killed or imprisoned. During the Egyptian uprising, thousands of Christians fled to the West. Now Christians are fleeing Syria. The reason Christians leave is mainly because they become an easy target for radical and fundamental Islamist groups who seize the chaotic conditions and the breakdown of law and order to kill and persecute Christians. The bombing and burning of churches and the assaulting and killing of Christians, both in Iraq and in Egypt, are clear illustrations of the savagery of some radical groups. Often, leaders of failed regimes ignite these attacks on Christian communities to send a message to Western Christians that without the protection of the regime, Christians would be in danger. The irony is that some of the cruelest dictators in the Middle East and North Africa were committed to protecting the Christian communities to gain the favor of Western countries. This has placed the Christian communities in a dilemma. In Syria, for example, Christians are concerned over the fall of the Bashar Al Assad regime for fear of the unknown government that would replace him.

Christians in the region are concerned about the rise of the Muslim Brotherhood and their dominance in governments that have been liberated from dictatorships. While Christians along with their Muslim compatriots have suffered under tyrannical dictatorships, they wonder whether life would be better under regimes that are run by the Muslim Brotherhood and Salafi (radical fundamentalist Muslims) parties.

In spite of all the political and psychological obstacles that Palestinians are still facing, both Muslims and Christians have not given up on seeking a just resolution to the conflict. Palestinian church leaders and theologians recently came up with the Kairos Palestine Document, which expresses their aspirations to reconcile with Israelis through non-violent means (www.kairospalestine.ps).

Bethlehem Bible College has held conferences in March 2010 and March 2012 on the theology of the Land, under the title "Christ at the Checkpoint" (www.christatthecheckpoint.com). These conferences express the Palestinian cry to Western Christians, especially Evangelicals, to draw near to the conflict and attempt to understand it through the eyes of the Prince of Peace.

Western Christians Should Support
a Palestinian Statehood

Late last week Palestinian President Mahmoud Abbas spoke at the United Nations to request an official recognition of Palestine as an independent state with full statehood status at the UN.

The majority of Christians and church leaders in the West Bank and the Gaza Strip support the Palestinian bid to seek full statehood at the United Nations. This position is not driven by anti-Israeli or anti-American sentiments but rather by the fact that most Arab Christians believe that without a resolution of the Arab-Israeli conflict they have no future in the Middle East, and without Palestinian statehood, there will be no end to the conflict.

The political turmoil in Palestine and the neighboring countries has prompted many Christians to abandon their homelands and seek refuge in Western countries. This trend will continue until the political chaos that springs up from the Arab-Israeli conflict ends.

Consequently, Western Christians who are concerned for the future of the Church in the Palestinian territories and the rest of the Middle East need to support the Palestinian drive for statehood.

Palestinians, like most people, are seeking a free, independent and peaceful state on 22 percent of historic Palestine and have already recognized Israel's sovereignty on 78 percent of the land. Palestinians have shown willingness to swap land with the State of Israel in order to make accommodations for what Israelis call 'new facts on the ground.' In addition, Palestinians are willing to consider the Israeli demand that a future Palestinian state would be demilitarized and allow for measures that create secure borders for the State of Israel.

Furthermore, as the Middle East and North Africa experience tremendous political awakenings, peace with the Palestinians is the top guarantee to peace and security for the State of Israel. A genuine peace treaty will bring as much peace to the Israelis as to the Palestinians and to many countries of the world including the United States.

Those who pray for "the peace of Jerusalem" need, at the same time, to support the immediate creation of a Palestinian state.

Christians tarnish their testimony in the world when they continue to endorse or be passive about the lingering injustice in Palestine.

The Israeli government refused to halt the building of Jewish settlements in the West Bank and East Jerusalem in order for negotiations to resume. Even when the American administration requested a two months' freeze on settlement construction to allow for negotiations, the Israeli government wouldn't cooperate. Now, Israelis are accusing Palestinians of refusing to return to negotiations.

How can one negotiate with a friend on dividing a cake when, all the while, the friend is eating the cake?

It is not that Palestinians are against negotiations, but rather, they are exhausted by two decades of fruitless and painful wrangling with Israeli leaders. It is our Christian duty to become aware of what is going on in political circles and on the ground and then to take a stand with the truth. Christians are not called to be morally passive and politically indifferent but rather to be active in promoting solutions that will bring about reconciliation and an end to the suffering of both Israelis and Palestinians.

Some Christians hesitate supporting the Palestinian bid for statehood for fear that it may result in creating a militant Islamic state. Fortunately, the current move for statehood is driven by the most secular, progressive and non-violent branch of the PLO. For this reason, Hamas, the Islamist movement in Palestine is not in agreement with the move.

The danger is this: If the Palestinian Authority fails to deliver to Palestinians an independent Palestinian state due to US and Israeli political maneuverings, in the near future, the secular Palestinian government will surely fall and only Hamas will be left to lead the Palestinian struggle for independence. This does not bode well for Israelis, Palestinians, future peace talks, or for the Christian communities in the Middle East.

By Alex Awad
September 26, 2011
Published by, **Sojourners** (Electronic Page)

APPENDIX I

GLOSSARY OF TERMS FOR THE ARAB-ISRAELI CONFLICT

The following list is not meant to be exhaustive, but rather sufficient for a general understanding of the conflict. It must be said that many of these terms and their definitions inevitably carry political connotations, thus the reader may well find other definitions for the same words in other sources that have a different perspective on the conflict than that of the author.

The American Israel Public Affairs Committee (AIPAC) – AIPAC is the foremost pro-Israel lobby group in the U.S. Started in the 1950s, the organization claims to have 65,000 members across the nation. Their website makes the organization's modus operandi clear: "Through more than 2,000 meetings with members of Congress – at home and in Washington – AIPAC activists help pass more than 100 pro-Israel legislative initiatives a year."

Anti-Semitism – Hatred of Jews and/or other Semitic people. Although Arabs are, ethnically speaking, Semites, the term "anti-Semitism" is rarely used to refer to hostility toward Arabs.

Arab – A person who speaks the Arabic language and identifies him- or herself with Arab culture.

Arab Christian – An Arab who believes in Jesus as the Messiah. Arab Christians consider themselves descendants of the early Church. There are approximately 25 million Arab Christians around the world, 15 million of whom live in the Middle East and North Africa. Of all the Arab countries, Egypt has the largest Christian population, while Lebanon has the most Christians as a percentage of its total population. In Palestine, Arab Christians comprise less than 2% of the population, numbering between 180,000 and 200,000; the percentage is roughly the same within Israel proper.

Arab Muslim – An Arab who believes in Allah (God), that Muhammad was God's final prophet, and in the Qur'an (Holy Book) as God's final revelation. While most Arabs are Muslim, only 20% of all Muslims are Arabs.

Bypass road – Roads built in the West Bank and Gaza Strip by the Israeli government intended to link Israeli colonies to each other and to Israel proper. They are called "bypass roads" precisely because they bypass Palestinian communities whose residents are generally barred from using them. These roads are under Israeli control, and their construction necessitates the forceful takeover of Palestinian land by Israel. This is all done on behalf of Israeli settlers, for the purpose of establishing Jewish neighborhoods and colonies in the occupied West Bank and East Jerusalem.

Confiscation – The process of bringing under Israeli control properties or other assets in the West Bank, including East Jerusalem (and in the Gaza Strip until 2005). The State of Israel embarked on this policy following the War of 1967 and continues to confiscate Palestinian land to this day. The words "seizure" and "expropriation" carry essentially the same meaning, with the latter implying an action given the cloak of legitimacy by some aspect of Israeli law.

East Jerusalem – According to the 1947 UN Partition Plan, Jerusalem and its environs (including Bethlehem) was supposed to be an internationalized city under the UN's trusteeship. But in 1948 Israel conquered the western half of Jerusalem and it became a divided city. Then, during the Six-Day War of 1967, Israel conquered and occupied the eastern half of Jerusalem. (The Israeli terminology for this action is that they "reunified" the city.) On June 28, 1967 Israel unilaterally expanded the borders of East Jerusalem from an area of 6.5 km^2 (the boundaries as designated by Jordan) to 70.5 km^2. This area is part of what is sometimes called "Greater Jerusalem" and includes land from many West Bank villages while avoiding densely populated Palestinian areas. Today, when people speak of East Jerusalem, they sometimes mean that part of the city that was under Jordanian jurisdiction from 1948–1967 (6.5 km^2), while at other times they mean the portion of expanded East Jerusalem annexed since 1967 (70.5 km^2).

Fatah – Founded by Yasser Arafat and others in 1959, it then advocated armed struggle to liberate all of Palestine by Palestinians, while remaining independent of all Arab governments. The movement, the largest and strongest PLO faction, was headed by Arafat from its conception until his death in 2004. Fatah advocates a democratic, secular, multi-religious Palestinian state. Mahmoud Abbas is the current leader of Fatah.

Gaza Strip – The territory on the Mediterranean southwest of Israel proper. The Gaza Strip was defended by Egypt in the 1948 war and conquered by the Israelis in the 1967 war. It is home to approximately 1.4 million Palestinians.

Green Line or 1949 Armistice Line – The Green Line refers to the boundary between Israel proper and the West Bank. The line was agreed upon by the Arab countries and Israel after the 1948 war and is still recognized as Israel's border by the international community.

Hamas – One of largest and most active militant Islamist resistance movements. Besides using radical and violent means to fight against the occupation and for the liberation of Palestine, Hamas is heavily engaged in humanitarian and educational services to the poor of the West Bank and the Gaza Strip.

International Committee of the Red Cross (ICRC) – The ICRC, along with national societies from 178 countries and their International Federation, form the International Red Cross and Red Crescent Movement. The Red Cross was founded in 1863 and today is an international humanitarian agency dedicated in times of war to alleviating the suffering of wounded soldiers, civilians, and prisoners of war. It also provides assistance in response to natural disasters.

Intifada – An Arabic word that literally means "to shake off," it is used to express the Palestinian revolt or rebellion against Israeli occupation.

Israel Defense Forces (IDF) – Founded in 1948, the armed forces of the IDF encompass Israel's land, sea and air defenses. Most Israelis, both men and women, begin their compulsory military service at the age of 18 and serve at least three years. Men must stay in the reserves until they are 55, serving up to 45 days a year active duty. Arabs and the ultra-orthodox Jews are exempt. A number of retired senior officers have gone on to become important political figures.

Israel Proper – That territory defined by the international borders and armistice lines of the Jewish state after the 1948 war.

Israeli Arabs – Palestinians who are citizens of the State of Israel. These are Arabs who were not forced out of Israel proper during the wars of 1948 and 1967 (although some had been internally displaced), and their descendants have remained in Israel proper and retained Israeli citizenship.

Israeli – A citizen of the State of Israel.

Jew – A person born of a Jewish mother or who converted to the Jewish faith. It is worth noting that in recent years, in order to facilitate family reunification (particularly large-scale Russian immigration), Israel's "law of return" has been extended to any person who has at least one grandparent on either side who meets this definition. The whole issue of "who's a Jew," especially regarding the validity (or not) of non-Orthodox conversions, is a perennial one in Israeli society.

Jihad – An Arabic word that means "struggle." Jihad is sometimes interpreted as "holy war," but in fact it means *any* struggle against evil, either in society or within an individual. In Islam, the "inner Jihad," the struggle against one's own evil, is said to be the most important struggle.

Labor Party – The Israel Labor Party was formed in 1968 when three labor parties merged. Labor's traditionally socialist and Zionist policies have included encouraging Jewish immigration and advocating a largely state-managed economy. The Labor Party, traditionally, has been keen to stress the importance of negotiations in reaching peace with the Arabs over the Occupied Territories.

Likud Party – Likud was founded in 1973 out of an alliance of right-wing parties. It has fought to hold onto the Occupied Territories and it maintains a hawkish stance on matters of national security. On the economic front, it supports privatization and other neo-liberal economic policies.

Messianic Jew – A Jew who accepts Yeshua (Jesus) as his/her Messiah while continuing to maintain a Jewish identity and observe Jewish customs and traditions.

Occupied Territories – The land seized and occupied by Israel in the 1967 Six-Day War. They include East Jerusalem (annexed by Israel and included within Jerusalem's municipal boundaries), the West Bank, the Gaza Strip (until the 2005 withdrawal), and the Golan Heights. UN Resolution 242 calls for Israel to withdraw from these territories.

Operation Defensive Shield – Israeli military re-invasion of West Bank cities that had been previously granted limited autonomy under the Oslo Accords in March/April 2002. The operation subjected most of the population to prolonged curfews, left the Palestinian National Authority infrastructure in ruins, and caused widespread damage to public and private property.

Oslo Accords – The series of peace talks that began with secret negotiations in Norway between PLO members and Israeli officials and led to the signing of the Declaration of Principles in September 1993. Implementation followed in 1994, and further negotiations included the Taba Agreement (Oslo II) in 1995. The Oslo agreements divided the West Bank into three zones: Areas A, B and C. In Area A (17.2% of the West Bank as of October 2000), the PNA had sole jurisdiction and security control, with Israel retaining authority over movement into and out of these areas. In Area B (23.8%), the PNA was given civil authority and responsibility for public order, while Israel maintained a security presence and "overriding security responsibility." The remaining 59% of the West Bank, Area C, remained under total Israeli occupation. The West Bank (and the Gaza Strip, until 2005) remains occupied territory under International Law.

Palestine – The Romans first applied the name Palestine to the area between the Mediterranean Sea and the Jordan River, soon after crushing the Second Jewish Revolt in 135 AD. Though the official borders changed somewhat according to the various outside ruling powers, this sliver of land continued, over the centuries, to be called Palestine. Today, the word carries strong political connotations. Generally, Palestine refers to the 27,090 km^2 political entity that was designated by the British Mandate which took possession of the region from the Ottoman Empire during the First World War. In 1988, the Palestinian National Assembly (Parliament in exile) adopted the "two-state solution" as a settlement to the Palestinian-Israeli conflict, with the purpose of establishing the State of Palestine in the West Bank and Gaza Strip.

Palestinian Arab – An Arab native to historic Palestine, and his/her descendants. This definition thus includes Palestinians both inside and outside the Green Line. For many Israeli Arabs, however, especially younger generations removed from the events of 1948, the use or non-use of the label "Palestinian" is a question of individual self-identification.

Palestinian (National) Authority (PNA or PA) – The elected governmental officials of the Palestinian people since the Oslo Accords in 1993. Yasser Arafat was the President of the PNA from his election in 1996 until his death in 2004; Mahmoud Abbas has served as president since 2005.

Palestinian National Council (PNC) – The legislative and decision-making body of the PLO founded in 1964, it serves as a quasi-parliament in exile, representing Palestinians worldwide.

Palestinian Liberation Army (PLA) – The PLO's military branch. When originally formed in 1964, it consisted of three brigades, headed by Yasser Arafat. After the Oslo Accords, some of its members were absorbed into the PNA security apparatus.

Palestine Liberation Organization (PLO) – Founded in 1964 by 422 Palestinian national figures. The PLO was taken over by Yasser Arafat's Fatah movement in 1969, becoming an umbrella organization for many Palestinian factions and establishing a number of bodies for civil society. The UN acknowledged the PLO in 1974 as the representative of the Palestinian people, and in 1988 the PLO recognized Israel's right to exist, at the same time declaring Palestinian independence.

Phalangist – A member of a Lebanese military organization, Phalanges Libanaises. Defending the Maronite Church politically and militarily in Lebanon since 1958, the far right group was an anti-Palestinian ally of Israel during the invasion of Lebanon. With the complicity of their powerful backers, the group carried out the infamous massacre at the Sabra and Shatilla refugee camps.

Pogrom – An act of organized violence or killing against a minority group, sometimes officially sanctioned or encouraged. Pogroms are articularly associated with the Jewish communities of Eastern Europe and Russia in the 19th and early 20th centuries, when there were frequent violent outbursts of anti-Semitism.

Settlement – Built-up areas in the West Bank (and formerly the Gaza Strip) where Jewish-Israeli communities have been planted, mostly with the permission, direct assistance, and military protection of the Israeli government. Although often referred to as "settlements," the word "colony" more accurately reflects the reality - the Israelis residing in the West Bank are living on someone else's land.

Tanzim – A subsidiary of Fatah in the Occupied Palestinian Territories that operates as a loose collection of militias for enforcing order. It was seen as the leading force in directing the Al-Aqsa Intifada.

Terrorism – The FBI defines terrorism as "the unlawful use of force or violence against persons or property to intimidate or coerce a Government, the civilian population, or any segment thereof, in furtherance of political or social objectives." The U.S. Department of Defense defines terrorism as, "the calculated use of violence or the threat of violence to inculcate fear intended to coerce or to intimidate governments or societies in the pursuit of goals that are generally political, religious, or ideological." The EU defined terrorism in December 2002 as "offenses intentionally committed by an individual or a group against one or more countries, their institutions or people, with the aim of intimidating them and seriously altering or destroying the political, economic, or social structures of a country."

United Nations Relief and Works Agency for Palestine Refugees in the Near East (UNRWA) – UNRWA was established in December 1949 to assist the Palestinian refugees displaced during the War of 1948. Since beginning operations in 1950 it has been responsible for providing vital health and education services to Palestinian refugees living both in the Occupied Territories and in neighboring Arab countries.

West Bank – The territory west of the Jordan River defended by the Kingdom of Jordan in the 1948 war, defined by the so-called "Green Line," and conquered by the Israelis in the 1967 war. Jordan officially gave up its claims to the area in 1988. The West Bank is home to approximately 2.4 million Palestinians.

Withdrawal – Withdrawal refers to the pulling out of military forces from portions of the West Bank and/or Gaza Strip. The Israeli's prefer to call such action "redeployment," implying that the troops are merely relocating their positions and may move back at any time, without transfer of sovereignty.

Zionism – The nationalistic philosophy that developed among Jews in Europe in the mid-to-late 19th century, it aspires to create and sustain a homeland for the Jewish people. Anti-Semitism in Europe, which ultimately culminated in the Holocaust, motivated many Jews to settle in Palestine as part of the Zionist program.

APPENDIX II

KEY BIOGRAPHIES

Mahmoud Abbas – Abbas (or Abu Mazen) was born in Safad in 1935 and left as a refugee for Syria in 1948. He was a founding member of Fatah and became a leading Palestinian figure devoted to the search for a peaceful solution to the Palestinian-Israeli conflict. Abbas coordinated the negotiation process during the Madrid conference and headed the Palestinian negotiating team for the Oslo talks. He signed both the 1993 Declaration of Principles and 1995 Interim Accords on behalf of the PLO. He drafted, together with his Israeli counterpart Yossi Beilin, the controversial "Framework for the Conclusion of a Final Status Agreement Between Israel and the PLO" (better known as Abu-Mazen-Beilin Plan) in October 1995. After pressure from the U.S. and Israel for an 'untainted' negotiating partner, he was nominated as Prime Minister by Arafat in March 2003 and was appointed chairman of the PLO after the death of Arafat in November 2004. In January 2005 he was elected as president of the PA.

Yasser Arafat – Arafat was born in 1929 in Cairo. He grew up mainly in Cairo and, for a brief period, in Jerusalem. He was a co-founder of the first Fatah cell in 1957, and a founder of the Fatah party in 1959. Arafat addressed the UN General Assembly in New York in 1974 as leader of the Palestine Liberation Organization. He proclaimed the independent Palestinian State in 1988 and had secret negotiations with Israel from 1992 onwards, leading to the signing of the Declaration of Principles (peace accord) between PLO and Israel on September 13, 1993. When Arafat returned to Palestine in 1994, he set up the PNA and was appointed as President and Minister of Interior. More recently, Arafat was increasingly sidelined in negotiations by Israeli Prime Minister Ariel Sharon and U.S. President George W. Bush. During Operation Defensive Shield in 2002, Israeli forces entered Ramallah and destroyed nearly all of Arafat's headquarters, and thereafter Arafat was confined to his compound by the Israeli military. Arafat died in November 2004 in Paris.

Ehud Barak – Barak was born in 1942, joined the Israel Defense Forces in 1959, and fought in the wars of 1967, 1973, and 1982. In the course of his military career became the most decorated soldier in the history of the IDF, achieved the rank of Lieutenant General, and in 1991 assumed the post of Chief of the General Staff. In 1999, Barak was elected Prime Minister of Israel, and his relatively brief tenure saw the IDF's complete withdrawal from Lebanon, the failed Camp David peace talks, and the start of the Al-Aqsa Intifada in September 2000. Barak was defeated by Ariel Sharon in the 2001 elections.

Marwan Barghouti – Barghouti was born in 1959. He was deported to Jordan by Israel in May 1987 for his organizational role in the first Intifada. Over the years he has spent six years in Israeli prisons, where he learned to speak fluent Hebrew. When he returned from exile to the West Bank in April 1994, he went on to win an independent seat in Ramallah's municipal council in the January 1996 elections. Barghouti became a major local leader in the Al-Aqsa Intifada until his arrest by Israeli forces in April 2002. In 2004 he stood trial in Israel, a legal process he refused to recognize, and was sentenced to five consecutive life sentences in prison.

Menachem Begin – Begin was born in Poland in 1913. Taking a leading role in the Irgun, a group of pre-state underground Jewish militants, Begin masterminded an increase in violent activity, including the bombing of the King David Hotel in Jerusalem on July 22, 1946. The Irgun organization was incorporated into the IDF in 1948. Begin dominated the right-wing political opposition during the first three decades of independent Israel, providing the foundations for the formation of the Likud party. Begin became Prime Minister in 1977 for six and a half years. His most famous achievement was the signing of the peace treaty with Egypt's President Sadat in 1979. In 1981 Begin ordered the Israel Air Force to destroy the nuclear reactor in Osirak near Baghdad, Iraq, an act that was internationally condemned. In 1982 he launched "Operation Peace for Galilee", an invasion of southern Lebanon. He resigned from his post in September 1983 and died in March 1992.

David Ben-Gurion – Ben-Gurion was a Zionist leader and Israel's first and longest-serving Prime Minister. Born in Poland in 1886, he led both the Histadrut, or General Federation of Labor, and the Jewish Agency, the pre-state government-in-waiting, before becoming Israel's first Prime Minister in 1948. In the first five years of his tenure he oversaw an immigration policy under which the country's population nearly doubled. In 1953 Ben-Gurion resigned from the government for two years before again becoming Prime Minister in 1955. In 1963 he resigned once more, and finally retired from public life in 1970 at the age of 84. Ben-Gurion died in 1973.

Moshe Dayan – Dayan served in the IDF as Chief of Staff between 1953 and 1958. In 1959 he was elected to the Knesset, and on the eve of the Six-Day War in 1967 was appointed as Minister of Defense. Between 1977 and 1979 Dayan served as Minister of Foreign Affairs.

Theodore Herzl – Herzl was born in Budapest, Hungary, on May 2, 1860. He soon moved to Paris, where he witnessed the rise of anti-Semitism and became convinced that the only solution to the Jewish problem was an exodus of Jews to a national home. Herzl published a pamphlet, *The Jewish State*, in 1896, and succeeded in convening the first Zionist Congress in 1897. This Congress established the World Zionist Organization to help create the economic foundation for the proposed Jewish state. Herzl died in 1904.

Benjamin Netanyahu – Netanyahu was born in Tel Aviv in 1949. In 1984 he was appointed Israel's ambassador to the United Nations, a position he held for four years. In 1988 he became Deputy Minister of Foreign Affairs for the Likud Party, and in 1996 defeated the incumbent Labor Party candidate Shimon Peres to become the ninth Prime Minister of the State of Israel. Netanyahu served as Prime Minister until 1999 and went on to serve as Minister of Foreign Affairs from November 2002 until February 2003, when he was appointed Minister of Finance.

Shimon Peres – Peres was born in Byelorussia in 1923. He had held a number of military and civilian governmental positions leading up to his first term as Prime Minister from 1984 to 1986. Peres conducted the negotiations that led to the signing of the Declaration of Principles with the PLO in September 1993, which won him the 1994 Nobel Peace Prize along with Rabin and Arafat. Peres' second term as Prime Minister was for seven months following the assassination of Rabin in 1995. In March 2001 he was appointed Minister of Foreign Affairs and Deputy Prime Minister in the National Unity government headed by Ariel Sharon, serving until October 2002 when he resigned together with the other Labor ministers. In recent years Peres left the Labor party to join the new centrist Kadima party of Ariel Sharon. In May 2006 Shimon Peres was appointed Vice Prime Minister and Minister for the Development of the Negev and Galilee.

Yitzhak Rabin – Rabin was born in Jerusalem in 1922 and during the British Mandate was a member of the pre-state Zionist defense force, the Haganah. He began his military career with the IDF in 1948, which culminated in his appointment as Chief of the General Staff in 1962. After the familiar shift from military to politics, Rabin became Prime Minister in 1974. Rabin resigned prior to the 1977 elections, but returned as the country's leader in 1992. His second term as Prime Minister saw him conclude the Oslo Agreements with the Palestinians and the Treaty of Peace with Jordan. In 1995, Rabin was assassinated in Tel Aviv by a right-wing Jewish extremist.

Ariel (Arik) Sharon – Sharon was born in 1928. He served in the IDF for more than 25 years, during which time he fought in every one of Israel's major wars. In 1953, Sharon founded and led the "101" special commando unit which carried out the infamous Qibya massacre in Jordan in 1953 where IDF troops blew up 45 houses and killed 69 Palestinian civilians in a so-called "reprisal raid". In 1956 Sharon was appointed commander of a paratroop brigade which fought in the Sinai Campaign, and he later participated in the 1967 Six-Day War as commander of an armored division. Sharon retired from the IDF with the rank of Major General, but was recalled to active military service to participate in the October 1973 Yom Kippur War, again as a commander of an armored division. Sharon was appointed Defense Minister in 1981, serving in this post during Israel's 1982 invasion of Lebanon. During this invasion the Lebanese militia, under the supervision of the Israeli army, killed over 800 Palestinians living in the Lebanese refugee camps of Sabra and Shatilla. An Israeli inquiry found Sharon responsible for the massacre, however Sharon later returned to government and served in a number of departments, becoming instrumental in expanding Israeli settlements. His visit to the al-Haram ash-Sharif on September 28, 2000 sparked the Al Aqsa Intifada. On February 6, 2001, Sharon was elected Prime Minister and went on to win re-election in January 2003, having overseen the re-occupation of Palestinian cities and one of the bloodiest periods in his nation's history. Ariel Sharon conceived and carried out Israel's unilateral withdrawal from Gaza in August 2005, and in November he formed a new centrist party, Kadima ("Forward"). On January 4, 2006 he suffered a serious stroke and fell into a coma; as of the time of writing he has been moved into long-term care.

Chaim Weizmann – Weizmann was born in Motol, Russia in 1874. Trained as a scientist in Germany and Switzerland, he later spent several years in England where, as a Zionist leader he was instrumental in the issuing of the 1917 Balfour Declaration. In the 1920s and 30s, now in Palestine, he spent two terms as president of the World Zionist Organization and also headed the Jewish Agency. Weizmann played key roles in moving the UN toward passage of the 1947 Partition Plan and in securing U.S. recognition of the new State of Israel. He was chosen to serve as the first President of Israel, a role he filled until his death in 1952.

Sheikh Ahmad Yassin – Yassin was a Palestinian religious leader who was born in 1937. A refugee in Gaza since 1948, he was completely paralyzed following an accident in his youth. Yassin was the founder of the Islamic Center in Gaza in 1973, and later was hailed as the creator, spiritual leader and key figure of Hamas, the Islamic Resistance Movement in the Occupied Territories. Yassin believed that Palestine belonged to Islam and advocated an Islamic state in all of Palestine. Yassin was assassinated by Israeli forces in Gaza in March 2004.

APPENDIX III

DOCUMENTS OF INTERNATIONAL LAW RELEVANT TO THE ARAB-ISRAELI CONFLICT (EXCERPTS)

342

Documents
of
International
Law Relevant
to the
Arab-Israeli
Conflict
(Excerpts)

- Universal Declaration of Human Rights of 1948
- UN General Assembly Resolution 194 of December 11, 1948
- Fourth Geneva Convention Relative to the Protection of Civilian Persons in Time of War of 1949
- Protocol Additional to the Geneva Conventions of August 12, 1949 'Protocol 1'
- International Covenant on Civil and Political Rights of 1966
- International Covenant on Economic, Social and Cultural Rights of 1966
- UN Security Council Resolution 242 of November 22, 1967
- UN Security Council Resolution 267 of July 3, 1969
- UN Security Council Resolution 338 of October 22, 1973
- UN Security Council Resolution 465 of March 1, 1980
- UN Security Council Resolution 681 of December 20, 1990
- UN Security Council draft Resolutions vetoed by USA pertaining to Israeli settlements and land confiscation.
- UN Security Council draft Resolutions vetoed by USA pertaining to implementation of Fourth Geneva Convention.

UNIVERSAL DECLARATION OF HUMAN RIGHTS OF 1948

Article 17: No one shall be arbitrarily deprived of his property.

UN GENERAL ASSEMBLY RESOLUTION 194 OF DECEMBER 11, 1948

Paragraph 11: Resolves that the refugees wishing to return to their homes and live at peace with their neighbors should be permitted to do so at the earliest practicable date, and that compensation should be paid for the property of those choosing not to return and for loss of or damage to property.

FOURTH GENEVA CONVENTION RELATIVE TO THE PROTECTION OF CIVILIAN PERSONS IN TIME OF WAR OF 1949

Article 27: Protected persons… shall at all times be humanely treated, and shall be protected especially against all acts of violence.

Article 31: No physical or moral coercion shall be exercised against protected persons, in particular to obtain information from them or from third parties.

Article 33: No protected person may be punished for an offence he or she has not personally committed. Collective penalties and likewise all measures of intimidation or of terrorism are prohibited.

Article 47: Protected persons who are in (the) occupied territory shall not be deprived, in any case or in any manner whatsoever, of the benefits of the present Convention by any change introduced, as the result of the occupation of a territory, into the institutions or government of the said territory.

Article 49: Individual or mass forcible transfers, as well as deportations of protected persons from occupied territory to the territory of the Occupying Power or to that of any other country occupied or not, are prohibited, regardless of their motive. . . The Occupying Power shall not deport or transfer parts of its own civilian population into the territory it occupies.

Article 50: The Occupying Power shall, with the cooperation of the national and local authorities, facilitate the proper working of all institutions devoted to the care and education of children.

Article 53: Any destruction by the Occupying Power of real or personal property belonging individually or collectively to private persons, or to the state, or to other public authorities, or to social or cooperative organizations, is prohibited.

Article 56: To the fullest extent of the means available to it, the Occupying Power has the duty of ensuring and maintaining… the medical and hospital establishments and services, public health and hygiene in the occupied territory… Medical personnel of all categories shall be allowed to carry out their duties.

Article 58: The Occupying Power shall permit ministers of religion to give spiritual assistance to the members of their religious communities.

Article 71: Accused persons who are prosecuted by the Occupying Power shall be promptly informed in writing, in a language which they understand, of the particulars of the charges preferred against them, and shall be brought to trial as rapidly as possible.

Article 146: High Contracting Parties undertake to enact any legislation necessary to provide effective penal sanctions for persons committing, or ordering to be committed, any of the grave breaches of the present Convention as defined in the following Article.

Article 147: Grave breaches… shall be those involving any of the following acts, if committed against persons or property protected by the present Convention: willful killing, torture or inhuman treatment, including biological experiments, willfully causing great suffering or serious injury to body or health, unlawful deportation or transfer or unlawful confinement of a protected person, compelling a protected person to serve in the forces of a hostile Power, or willfully depriving a protected person of the rights of fair and regular trial prescribed in the present Convention, taking of hostages and extensive destruction and appropriation of property, not justified by military necessity and carried out unlawfully and wantonly.

Article 148: No High Contracting Party shall be allowed to absolve itself or any other High Contracting Party of any liability incurred by itself or by another High Contracting Party in respect of breaches referred to in the preceding Article.

Both Israel and the U.S. are High Contracting Parties to the Fourth Geneva Convention.

PROTOCOL ADDITIONAL TO THE GENEVA CONVENTIONS OF 12 AUGUST 1949 'PROTOCOL 1'

Article 79: Journalists engaged in dangerous professional missions in areas of armed conflict shall be considered as civilians.

INTERNATIONAL COVENANT ON CIVIL AND POLITICAL RIGHTS OF 1966

Article 12: 1) Everyone lawfully within the territory of a State shall, within that territory, have the right to liberty of movement and freedom to choose his residence. 2) Everyone shall be free to leave any country, including his own.

Article 19: Everyone shall have the right to freedom of expression; this right shall include freedom to seek, receive and impart information and ideas of all kinds, regardless of frontiers, either orally, in writing, or (in) print, in the form of art, or through any other media of his choice.

INTERNATIONAL COVENANT ON ECONOMIC, SOCIAL AND CULTURAL RIGHTS OF 1966

Article 1: 1) All peoples have the right of self-determination. By virtue of this right they freely determine their political status and freely pursue their economic, social and cultural development. 2) All Peoples may, for their own ends, freely dispose of their natural wealth and resources without prejudice to any obligations arising out of international economic co-operation, based upon the principle of mutual benefit and international law. In no case may a people be deprived of its own means of subsistence.

Article 6: The States Parties to the present Covenant recognize the right to work, which includes the right of everyone to the opportunity to gain his living by work which he freely chooses or accepts, and will take appropriate steps to safeguard this right.

Article12: The States Parties to the present Covenant recognize the right of everyone to the enjoyment of the highest attainable standard of physical and mental health.

346

_____

Documents
of
International
Law Relevant
to the
Arab-Israeli
Conflict
(Excerpts)

Article 13: The States Parties to the present Covenant recognize the right of everyone to education. They agree that education shall be directed to the full development of the human personality and the sense of its dignity, and shall strengthen the respect for human rights and fundamental freedoms.

UN SECURITY COUNCIL RESOLUTION 242 OF NOVEMBER 22, 1967

_____

Emphasizing the inadmissibility of the acquisition of territory by war and the need to work for a just and lasting peace in which every State in the area can live in security.

1. Affirms that the fulfillment of Charter principles requires the establishment of a just and lasting peace in the Middle East which should include the application of both the following principles: (i) Withdrawal of Israeli armed forces from territories occupied in the recent conflict; (ii) Termination of all claims or states of belligerency and respect for and acknowledgement of the sovereignty, territorial integrity and political independence of every State in the area and their right to live in peace within secure and recognized boundaries free from threats or acts of force. . .

2. Affirms further the necessity. . . For achieving a just settlement of the refugee problem.

UN SECURITY COUNCIL RESOLUTION 267 OF JULY 3, 1969

_____

The Security Council... reaffirming the established principle that acquisition of territory by military conquest is inadmissible... censures in the strongest terms all measures taken to change the status of the city of Jerusalem; confirms that all legislative and administrative measures and actions taken by Israel which purport to alter the status of Jerusalem, including expropriation of land and properties thereon, are invalid and cannot change that status.

UN SECURITY COUNCIL RESOLUTION 338 OF OCTOBER 22, 1973

2. Calls upon the parties concerned to start immediately after the cease-fire the implementation of Security Council resolution 242 (1967) in all of its parts;

3. Decides that, immediately and concurrently with the cease-fire, negotiations shall start between the parties concerned under appropriate auspices aimed at establishing a just and durable peace in the Middle East.

UN SECURITY COUNCIL RESOLUTION 465 OF MARCH 1, 1980

Affirming once more that the Fourth Geneva Convention relative to the Protection of Civilian Persons in Time of War, of August 12, 1949, is applicable to the Arab territories occupied by Israel since 1967, including Jerusalem,

Deploring the decision of the Government of Israel officially (to) support Israeli settlements in Palestinian and other Arab territories occupied since 1967,

Taking into account the need to consider measures for the impartial protection of private and public land, property, and water resources,

Bearing in mind the specific status of Jerusalem and, in particular, the need for protection and preservation of the unique spiritual and religious dimension of the Holy Places in the city,

Drawing attention to the grave consequences which the settlement(s) policy is bound to have on any attempt to reach a comprehensive, just and lasting peace in the Middle East,

Strongly deplores the continuation and persistence of Israel in pursuing those policies and practices and calls upon the Government and people of Israel to rescind those measures, to dismantle the existing settlements and in particular to cease, on an urgent basis, the establishment, construction and planning of settlements in the Arab territories occupied since 1967, including Jerusalem.

Calls upon all States not to provide Israel with any assistance to be used specifically in connection with settlements in the Occupied Territories...

348

Documents
of
International
Law Relevant
to the
Arab-Israeli
Conflict
(Excerpts)

UN SECURITY COUNCIL RESOLUTION 681 OF DECEMBER 20, 1990

Gravely concerned at the dangerous deterioration of the situation in all the Palestinian territories occupied by Israel since 1967, including Jerusalem, and at the violence and rising tension in Israel...

5. Calls upon the High Contracting Parties to the Fourth Geneva Convention of 1949 to ensure respect by Israel, the occupying Power, for its obligations under the (Fourth Geneva) Convention . . .

UN Security Council draft resolutions directly condemning illegal Israeli settlements and confiscation of Palestinian land which were vetoed by the United States:

- *S/12022 March 24, 1976*
  Vote: 14 in favor, 1 veto (U.S.)

- *S/15895 August 1, 1983*
  Vote: 13 in favor, 1 veto (U.S.), 1 abstention

- *S/17769 January 29, 1986*
  Vote: 13 in favor, 1 veto (U.S.), 1 abstention

- *S/1995/394 May 17, 1995*
  Vote: 14 in favor, 1 veto (U.S.)

- *S/1997/199 March 7, 1997*
  Vote: 14 in favor, 1 veto (U.S.)

- *S/1997/241 March 21, 1997*
  Vote: 13 in favor, 1 veto (U.S.), 1 abstention

- *S/2001/270 27 March 2001*
  Vote: 9 in favor, 1 veto (U.S.), 4 abstentions

UN Security Council draft resolutions insisting that Israel comply with the Fourth Geneva Convention relative to the Protection of Civilian Persons in Time of War of August 12, 1949 (under which such settlements are illegal) vetoed by the United States:

- *S/14943 of April 1, 1982*
  Vote: 13 in favor, 1 veto (U.S.), 1 abstention

- *S/14985 of April 20, 1982*
  Vote: 14 in favor, 1 veto (U.S.)

- *S/15895 August 1, 1983*
  Vote: 13 in favor, 1 veto (U.S.), 1 abstention

- *S/17459 September 12, 1985*
  Vote: 10 in favor, 1 veto (U.S.), 4 abstentions

- *S/17769 of January 29, 1986*
  Vote: 13 in favor, 1 veto (U.S.), 1 abstention

- *S/19466 January 29, 1988*
  Vote: 14 in favor, 1 veto (U.S.)

- *S/19780 of April 14, 1988*
  Vote: 14 in favor, 1 veto (U.S.)

- *S/20463 of February 17, 1989*
  Vote: 14 in favor, 1 veto (U.S.)

- *S/20677 of June 9, 1989*
  Veto: 14 in favor, 1 veto (U.S.)

- *S/20945 of November 6, 1989*
  Veto: 14 in favor, 1 veto (U.S.)

- *S/1997/199 March 7, 1997*
  Vote: 14 in favor, 1 veto (U.S.)

- *S/2001/270 March 27, 2001*
  Vote: 9 in favor, 1 veto (U.S.), 4 abstentions

APPENDIX IV

FULL TEXTS OF KEY PEACE PROPOSALS

- Israel-PLO recognition
- Camp David
- Taba
- Tenet Cease-fire plan
- Saudi Peace Initiative
- Road Map

Letter from Yasser Arafat to Prime Minister Rabin:

September 9, 1993

Yitzhak Rabin
Prime Minister of Israel

Mr. Prime Minister,

The signing of the Declaration of Principles marks a new era in the history of the Middle East. In firm conviction thereof, I would like to confirm the following PLO commitments:

The PLO recognizes the right of the State of Israel to exist in peace and security.

The PLO accepts United Nations Security Council Resolutions 242 and 338.

The PLO commits itself to the Middle East peace process, and to a peaceful resolution of the conflict between the two sides and declares that all outstanding issues relating to permanent status will be resolved through negotiations.

The PLO considers that the signing of the Declaration of Principles constitutes a historic event, inaugurating a new epoch of peaceful coexistence, free from violence and all other acts which endanger peace and stability. Accordingly, the PLO renounces the use of terrorism and other acts of violence and will assume responsibility over all PLO elements and personnel in order to assure their compliance, prevent violations and discipline violators.

In view of the promise of a new era and the signing of the Declaration of Principles and based on Palestinian acceptance of Security Council Resolutions 242 and 338, the PLO affirms that those articles of the Palestinian Covenant which deny Israel's right to exist, and the provisions of the Covenant which are inconsistent with the commitments of this letter are now inoperative and no longer valid. Consequently, the PLO undertakes to submit to the Palestinian National Council for formal approval the necessary changes in regard to the Palestinian Covenant.

Sincerely,

Yasser Arafat
Chairman
The Palestine Liberation Organization

Letter from Prime Minister Rabin to Yasser Arafat:

September 9, 1993

Yasser Arafat
Chairman
The Palestinian Liberation Organization

Mr. Chairman,

In response to your letter of September 9, 1993, I wish to confirm to you that, in light of the PLO commitments included in your letter, the Government of Israel has decided to recognize the PLO as the representative of the Palestinian people and commence negotiations with the PLO within the Middle East peace process.

Yitzhak Rabin
Prime Minister of Israel

Trilateral Statement on the Middle East Peace Summit at Camp David
July 25, 2000   353

President William J. Clinton
Israeli Prime Minister Ehud Barak
Palestinian Authority Chairman Yasser Arafat

Between July 11 and 24, under the auspices of President Clinton, Prime Minister Barak and Chairman Arafat met at Camp David in an effort to reach an agreement on permanent status. While they were not able to bridge the gaps and reach an agreement, their negotiations were unprecedented in both scope and detail. Building on the progress achieved at Camp David, the two leaders agreed on the following principles to guide their negotiations:
1. The two sides agreed that the aim of their negotiations is to put an end to decades of conflict and achieve a just and lasting peace.
2. The two sides commit themselves to continue their efforts to conclude an agreement on all permanent status issues as soon as possible.
3. Both sides agree that negotiations based on UN Security Council Resolutions 242 and 338 are the only way to achieve such an agreement and they undertake to create an environment for negotiations free from pressure, intimidation and threats of violence.
4. The two sides understand the importance of avoiding unilateral actions that prejudge the outcome of negotiations and that their differences will be resolved only by good faith negotiations.
5. Both sides agree that the United States remains a vital partner in the search for peace and will continue to consult closely with President Clinton and Secretary Albright in the period ahead.

Israeli-Palestinian Joint Statement

27 January 2001

The following is the official text of the joint statement released at the close of the Taba talks by Israeli and Palestinian negotiators as published in the Jerusalem Post (Jan 28, 2001):

"The Israeli and Palestinian delegations conducted during the last six days serious, deep and practical talks with the aim of reaching a permanent and stable agreement between the two parties.

"The Taba talks were unprecedented in their positive atmosphere and expression of mutual willingness to meet the national, security and existential needs of each side.

"Given the circumstances and time constraints, it proved impossible to reach understandings on all issues, despite the substantial progress that was achieved in each of the issues discussed.

"The sides declare that they have never been closer to reaching an agreement and it is thus our shared belief that the remaining gaps could be bridged with the resumption of negotiations following the Israeli elections.

"The two sides take upon themselves to return to normalcy and to establish [a] security situation on the ground through the observation of their mutual commitments in the spirit of the Sharm e-Sheikh memorandum.

"The negotiation teams discussed four main themes: refugees, security, borders and Jerusalem, with a goal to reach a permanent agreement that will bring an end to the conflict between them and provide peace to both people.

"The two sides took into account the ideas suggested by President Clinton together with their respective qualifications and reservations.

"On all these issues there was substantial progress in the understanding of the other side's positions and in some of them the two sides grew closer.

"As stated above, the political timetable prevented reaching an agreement on all the issues.

"However, in light of the significant progress in narrowing the differences between the sides, the two sides are convinced that in a short period of time and given an intensive effort and the acknowledgment of the essential and urgent nature of reaching an agreement, it will be possible to bridge the differences remaining and attain a permanent settlement of peace between them.

"In this respect, the two sides are confident that they can begin and move forward in this process at the earliest practical opportunity.

"The Taba talks conclude an extensive phase in the Israeli-Palestinian permanent status negotiations with a sense of having succeeded in rebuilding trust between the sides and with the notion that they were never closer in reaching an agreement between them than today.

"We leave Taba in a spirit of hope and mutual achievement, acknowledging that the foundations have been laid both in reestablishing mutual confidence and in having progressed in a substantive engagement on all core issues.

"The two sides express their gratitude to President Hosni Mubarak for hosting and facilitating these talks.

"They also express their thanks to the European Union for its role in supporting the talks."

TENET CEASE FIRE PLAN

Source: Israel Ministry of Foreign Affairs

Full Texts of Key Peace Proposals

The security organizations of the Government of Israel (GOI) and of the Palestinian Authority (PA) reaffirm their commitment to the security agreements forged at Sharm al-Sheikh in October 2000 embedded in the Mitchell Report of April 2001.

The operational premise of the workplan is that the two sides are committed to a mutual, comprehensive cease-fire, applying to all violent activities, in accordance with the public declaration of both leaders. In addition, the joint security committee referenced in this workplan will resolve issues that may arise during the implementation of this workplan.

The security organizations of the GOI and PA agree to initiate the following specific, concrete, and realistic security steps immediately to reestablish security cooperation and the situation on the ground as they existed prior to 28 September.

1. The GOI and the PA will immediately resume security cooperation.

A senior-level meeting of Israeli, Palestinian, and U.S. security officials will be held immediately and will reconvene at least once a week, with mandatory participation by designated senior officials.

Israeli-Palestinian DCOs will be reinvigorated. They will carry out their daily activities, to the maximum extent possible, according to the standards established prior to 28 September 2000. As soon as the security situation permits, barriers to effective cooperation – which include the erection of walls between the Israeli and Palestinian sides – will be eliminated and joint Israeli-Palestinian patrols will be reinitiated.

U.S.-supplied video conferencing systems will be provided to senior-level Israeli and Palestinian officials to facilitate frequent dialogue and security cooperation.

2. Both sides will take immediate measures to enforce strict adherence to the declared cease-fire and to stabilize the security environment.

Specific procedures will be developed by the senior-level security committee to ensure the secure movement of GOI and PA security personnel traveling in areas outside their respective control, in accordance with existing agreements.

Israel will not conduct attacks of any kind against the Palestinian Authority Ra'is facilities: the headquarters of Palestinian security, intelligence, and police organization; or prisons in the West Bank and Gaza.

The PA will move immediately to apprehend, question, and incarcerate terrorists in the West Bank and Gaza and will provide the security committee the names of those arrested as soon as they are apprehended, as well as readout of actions taken.

Israel will release all Palestinians arrested in security sweeps who have no association with terrorist activities.

In keeping with its unilateral cease-fire declaration, the PA will stop any Palestinian security officials from inciting, aiding, abetting, or conducting attacks against Israeli targets, including settlers.

In keeping with Israel's unilateral cease-fire declaration, Israeli forces will not conduct "proactive" security operations in areas under the control of the PA or attack against innocent civilian targets.

The GOI will re-institute military police investigations into Palestinian deaths resulting from IDF actions in the West Bank and Gaza in incidents not involving terrorism.

3. Palestinian and Israeli security officials will use the security committee to provide each other, as well as designated U.S. officials, terrorist threat information, including information on known or suspected terrorist operation in − or moving to − areas under the other's control.

Legitimate terrorist and threat information will be acted upon immediately, with follow-up actions and results reported to the security committee.

The PA will undertake preemptive operations against terrorists, terrorist safehouses, arms depots, and mortar factories. The PA will provide regular progress reports of these actions to the security committee.

Israeli authorities will take action against Israeli citizens inciting, carrying out, or planning to carry out violence against Palestinians, with progress reports on these activities provided to the security committee.

4. The PA and GOI will move aggressively to prevent individuals and groups from using areas under their respective control to carry out acts of violence. In addition, both sides will take steps to ensure that areas under their control will not be used to launch attacks against the other side nor be used as refuge after attacks are staged.

The security committee will identify key flash points, and each side will inform the other of the names of senior security personnel responsible for each flash point.

Joint Standard Operating Procedures (SOP's) will be developed for each flash point. These SOP's will address how the two sides handle and respond to security incidents; the mechanisms for emergency contact; and the procedures to deescalate security crises.

Palestinian and Israeli security officials will identify and agree to the practical measures needed to enforce "no demonstration zones" and "buffer zones" around flash points to reduce opportunities for confrontation. Both sides will adopt all necessary measures to prevent riots and to control demonstration, particularly in flash point areas.

Palestinian and Israeli security officials will make a concerted effort to locate and confiscate illegal weapons, including mortars, rockets, and explosives, in areas under their respective control In addition, intensive efforts will be made to prevent smuggling and illegal production of weapons. Each side will inform the security committee of the status and success of these efforts.

The Israeli Defense Forces (IDF) will adopt additional non-lethal measures to deal with Palestinian crowds and demonstrators, and more generally, seek to minimize the danger to lives and property of Palestinian civilians in responding to violence.

5. The GOI and the PA, through the auspices of the senior-level security committee, will forge – within one week of the commencement of security committee meetings and resumption of security cooperation – an agreed-upon schedule to implement the complete redeployment of IDF forces to positions held before 28 September 2000.

Demonstrable on-the-ground redeployment will be initiated within the first 48 hours of this one-week period and will continue while the schedule is being forged.

6. Within one week of the commencement of security committee meetings and resumption of security cooperation, a specific timeline will be developed for the lifting of internal closures as well as for the reopening of internal roads, the Allenby Bridge, Gaza Airport, Port of Gaza, and border crossings. Security checkpoints will be minimized according to legitimate security requirements and following consultation between the two sides.

Demonstrable on-the-ground actions on the lifting of the closures will be initiated within the first 48 hours of this one-week period and will continue while the timeline is being developed.

The parties pledge that even if untoward events occur, security cooperation will continue through the joint security committee.

SAUDI PEACE INITIATIVE

March 28, 2002

Following is an official translation of the full text of a Saudi-inspired peace plan adopted by an Arab summit in Beirut on Thursday:

The Arab Peace Initiative

The Council of Arab States at the Summit Level at its 14th Ordinary Session, reaffirming the resolution taken in June 1996 at the Cairo Extra-Ordinary Arab Summit that a just and comprehensive peace in the Middle East is the strategic option of the Arab countries, to be achieved in accordance with international legality, and which would require a comparable commitment on the part of the Israeli government.

Having listened to the statement made by his royal highness Prince Abdullah bin Abdul Aziz, crown prince of the Kingdom of Saudi Arabia, in which his highness presented his initiative calling for full Israeli withdrawal from all the Arab territories occupied since June 1967, in implementation of Security Council Resolutions 242 and 338, reaffirmed by the Madrid Conference of 1991 and the land-for-peace principle, and Israel's acceptance of an independent Palestinian state with East Jerusalem as its capital, in return for the establishment of normal relations in the context of a comprehensive peace with Israel.

Emanating from the conviction of the Arab countries that a military solution to the conflict will not achieve peace or provide security for the parties, the council:

1. Requests Israel to reconsider its policies and declare that a just peace is its strategic option as well.
2. Further calls upon Israel to affirm:
    a. Full Israeli withdrawal from all the territories occupied since 1967, including the Syrian Golan Heights, to the June 4, 1967 lines as well as the remaining occupied Lebanese territories in the south of Lebanon.
    b. Achievement of a just solution to the Palestinian refugee problem to be agreed upon in accordance with UN General Assembly Resolution 194.
    c. The acceptance of the establishment of a sovereign independent Palestinian state on the Palestinian territories occupied since June 4, 1967 in the West Bank and Gaza Strip, with East Jerusalem as its capital.
3. Consequently, the Arab countries affirm the following:
    a. Consider the Arab-Israeli conflict ended, and enter into a peace agreement with Israel, and provide security for all the states of the region.
    b. Establish normal relations with Israel in the context of this comprehensive peace.
4. Assures the rejection of all forms of Palestinian patriation which conflict with the special circumstances of the Arab host countries.
5. Calls upon the government of Israel and all Israelis to accept this initiative in order to safeguard the prospects for peace and stop the further shedding of blood, enabling the Arab countries and Israel to live in peace and good neighbourliness and provide future generations with security, stability and prosperity .
6. Invites the international community and all countries and organisations to support this initiative.
7. Requests the chairman of the summit to form a special committee composed of some of its concerned member states and the secretary general of the League of Arab States to pursue the necessary contacts to gain support for this initiative at all levels, particularly from the United Nations, the Security Council, the United States of America, the Russian Federation, the Muslim states and the European Union.

The following is a performance-based and goal driven roadmap, with clear phases, timelines, target dates, and benchmarks aiming at progress through reciprocal steps by the two parties in the political, security, economic, humanitarian, and institution-building fields, under the auspices of the Quartet.

The destination is a final and comprehensive settlement of the Israel-Palestinian conflict by 2005, as presented in President Bush's speech of 24 June, and welcomed by the EU, Russia, and the UN in the 16 July and 17 September Quartet Ministerial statements.

A two state solution to the Israeli-Palestinian conflict will only be achieved through an end to violence and terrorism, when the Palestinian people have a leadership acting decisively against terror and willing and able to build a practicing democracy based on tolerance and liberty, and through Israeli's readiness to do what is necessary for a democratic Palestinian state to be established, and a clear, unambiguous acceptance by both parties of the goal of a negotiated settlement as described below.

The Quartet will assist and facilitate implementation of the plan, starting in Phase I, including direct discussions between the parties as required. The plan establishes a realistic timeline for implementation. However, as a performance-based plan, progress will require and depend upon the good faith efforts of the parties, and their compliance with each of the obligations outlined below. Should the parties perform their obligations rapidly, progress within and through the phases may come sooner than indicated in the plan. Non-compliance with obligations will impede progress.

A settlement, negotiated between the parties, will result in the emergence of an independent, democratic, and viable Palestinian state living side by side in peace and security with Israel and its other neighbors. The settlement will resolve the Israel-Palestinian conflict, and end the occupation that began in 1967, based on the foundations of the Madrid Conference, the principle of land for peace, UNSCRs 242, 338 and 1397, agreements previously reached by the parties, and the initiative of Saudi Crown Prince Abdullah – endorsed by the Beirut Arab League Summit – calling for acceptance of Israel as a neighbor living in peace and security, in the context of a comprehensive settlement. This initiative is a vital element of international efforts to promote a comprehensive peace on all tracks, including the Syrian-Israeli and Lebanese-Israeli tracks.

The Quartet will meet regularly at senior levels to evaluate the parties' performance on implementation of the plan. In each phase, the parties are expected to perform their obligations in parallel, unless otherwise indicated.

Phase I:

Ending Terror and Violence, Normalizing Palestinian Life, and Building Palestinian Institutions

Present to May 2003

In Phase I. the Palestinians immediately undertake an unconditional cessation of violence according to the steps outlined below; such action should be accompanied by supportive measures undertaken by Israel. Palestinians and Israelis resume security cooperation based on the Tenet work plan to end violence, terrorism, and incitement through restructured and effective Palestinian security services. Palestinians undertake comprehensive political reform in preparation for statehood, including drafting a Palestinian constitution, and free, fair and open elections upon the basis of those measures. Israel takes all necessary steps to help normalize Palestinian life. Israel withdraws from Palestinian areas occupied from September 28, 2000 and the two sides restore the status quo that existed at that time, as security performance and cooperation progress. Israel also freezes all settlement activity, consistent with the Mitchell report.

At the outset of Phase I:

Palestinian leadership issues unequivocal statement reiterating Israel's right to exist in peace and security and calling for an immediate and unconditional ceasefire to end armed activity and all acts of violence against Israelis anywhere. All official Palestinian institutions end incitement against Israel.

Israeli leadership issues unequivocal statement affirming its commitments to the two-state vision of an independent, viable, sovereign Palestinian state living in peace and security alongside Israel, as expressed by President Bush, and calling for an immediate end to violence against Palestinians everywhere. All official Israeli institutions end incitement against Palestinians.

Security

Palestinians declare an unequivocal end to violence and terrorism and undertake visible efforts on the ground to arrest, disrupt, and restrain individuals and groups conducting and planning violent attacks on Israelis anywhere.

Rebuilt and refocused Palestinian Authority security apparatus begins sustained, targeted, and effective operations aimed at confronting all those engaged in terror and dismantlement of terrorist capabilities and infrastructure. This includes commencing confiscation of illegal weapons and consolidation of security authority, free of association with terror and corruption.

GOI takes no actions undermining trust, including deportations, attacks on civilians; confiscation and/or demolition of Palestinian homes and property, as a punitive measure or to facilitate Israeli construction; destruction of Palestinian institutions and infrastructure; and other measures specified in the Tenet Work Plan.

Relying on existing mechanisms and on-the ground resources, Quartet representatives begin informal monitoring and consult with the parties on establishment of a formal monitoring mechanism and its implementation.

Implementation, as previously agreed, of U.S. rebuilding, training and resumed security cooperation plan in collaboration with outside oversight board (U.S. – Egypt – Jordan). Quartet support for efforts to achieve a lasting, comprehensive cease-fire.

All Palestinian security organizations are consolidated into three services reporting to an empowered Interior Minister.

Restructured/retrained Palestinian security forces and IDF counterparts progressively resume security cooperation and other undertakings in implementation of the Tenet work plan, including regular senior-level meetings, with the participation of U.S. security officials.

Arab states cut off public and private funding and all other forms of support for groups supporting and engaging in violence and terror.

All donors providing budgetary support for the Palestinians channel these funds through the Palestinian Ministry of Finance's Single Treasury Account.

As comprehensive security performance moves forward, IDF withdraws progressively from areas occupied since September 28, 2000 and the two sides restore the status quo that existed prior to September 28, 2000. Palestinian security forces redeploy to areas vacated by IDF.

Palestinian Institution-building

Immediate action on credible process to produce draft constitution for Palestinian statehood. As rapidly as possible, constitutional committee circulates draft Palestinian constitution, based on strong parliamentary democracy and cabinet with empowered prime minister, for public comment/debate. Constitutional committee proposes draft document for submission after elections for approval by appropriate Palestinian institutions.

Appointment of interim prime minister or cabinet with empowered executive authority/decision-making body.

GOI fully facilitates travel of Palestinian officials for PLC and Cabinet sessions, internationally supervised security retraining, electoral and other reform activity, and other supportive measures related to the reform efforts.

Continued appointment of Palestinian ministers empowered to undertake fundamental reform. Completion of further steps to achieve genuine separation of powers, including any necessary Palestinian legal reforms for this purpose.

Establishment of independent Palestinian election commission. PLC reviews and revises elections law.

Palestinian performance on judicial, administrative, and economic benchmarks, as established by the International Task Force on Palestinian Reform.

As early as possible, and based upon the above measures and in the context of open debate and transparent candidate selection/electoral campaign based on a free, multiparty process, Palestinians hold free, open, and fair elections.

GOI facilitates Task Force election assistance, registration of voters, movement of candidates and voting officials. Support for NGOs involved in the election process.

GOI reopens Palestinian Chamber of Commerce and other closed Palestinian institutions in East Jerusalem based on a commitment that these institutions operate strictly in accordance with prior agreements between the parties.

Humanitarian Response

Israel takes measures to improve the humanitarian situation. Israel and Palestinians implement in full all recommendations of the Bertini report to improve humanitarian conditions, lifting curfews, and easing restrictions on movement of persons and goods, and allowing full, safe, and unfettered access of international and humanitarian personnel.

AHLC reviews the humanitarian situation and prospects for economic development in the West Bank and Gaza and launches a major donor assistance effort, including to the reform effort.

GOI and PA continue revenue clearance process and transfer of funds, including areas, in accordance with agreed, transparent monitoring mechanism.

Civil Society

Continued donor support, including increased funding through PVOs/NGOs, for people to people programs, private sector development and civil society initiatives.

Settlements

GOI immediately dismantles settlement outposts erected since March 2001.

Consistent with the Mitchell Report, GOI freezes all settlement activity (including natural growth of settlements).

Phase II. Transition

June 2003–December 2003

In the second phase, efforts are focused on the option of creating an independent Palestinian state with provisional borders and attributes of sovereignty, based on the new constitution, as a way station to a permanent status settlement. As has been noted, this goal can be achieved when the Palestinian people have a leadership acting decisively against terror, willing and able to build a practicing democracy based on tolerance and liberty. With such a leadership, reformed civil institutions and security structures, the Palestinians will have the active support of the Quartet and the broader international community in establishing an independent, viable, state.

Progress into Phase II will be based upon the consensus judgment of the Quartet of whether conditions are appropriate to proceed, taking into account performance of both parties. Furthering and sustaining efforts to normalize Palestinian lives and build Palestinian institutions, Phase II starts after Palestinian elections and ends with possible creation of an independent Palestinian state with provisional borders in 2003. Its primary goals are continued comprehensive security performance and effective security cooperation, continued normalization of Palestinian life and institution-building, further building on and sustaining of the goals outlined in Phase I, ratification of a democratic Palestinian constitution, formal establishment of office of prime minister, consolidation of political reform, and the creation of a Palestinian state with provisional borders.

International Conference: Convened by the Quartet, in consultation with the parties, immediately after the successful conclusion of Palestinian elections, to support Palestinian economic recovery and launch a process, leading to establishment of an independent Palestinian state with provisional borders.

Such a meeting would be inclusive, based on the goal of a comprehensive Middle East peace (including between Israel and Syria, and Israel and Lebanon), and based on the principles described in the preamble to this document.

Arab states restore pre-intifada links to Israel (trade offices, etc.).

Revival of multilateral engagement on issues including regional water resources, environment, economic development, refugees, and arms control issues.

New constitution for democratic, independent Palestinian state is finalized and approved by appropriate Palestinian institutions. Further elections, if required, should follow approval of the new constitution.

Empowered reform cabinet with office of prime minister formally established, consistent with draft constitution.

Continued comprehensive security performance, including effective security cooperation on the bases laid out in Phase I.

Creation of an independent Palestinian state with provisional borders through a process of Israeli-Palestinian engagement. Launched by the international conference. As part of this process, implementation of prior agreements, to enhance maximum territorial contiguity, including further action on settlements in conjunction with establishment of a Palestinian state with provisional borders.

Enhanced international role in monitoring transition, with the active, sustained, and operational support of the Quartet.

Quartet members promote international recognition of Palestinian state, including possible UN membership.

Phase III:
Permanent Status Agreement and end of the Israeli-Palestinian Conflict
2004–2005
Progress into Phase III, based on consensus judgment of Quartet, and taking into account actions of both parties and Quartet monitoring. Phase III objectives are consolidation of reform and stabilization of Palestinian institutions, sustained, effective Palestinian security performance, and Israeli-Palestinian negotiations aimed at a permanent status agreement in 2005.

Second International Conference: Convened by Quartet, in consultation with the parties, at beginning of 2004 to endorse agreement reached on an independent Palestinian state with provisional borders and formally to launch a process with the active, sustained, and operational support of the Quartet, leading to a final, permanent status resolution in 2005, including on borders, Jerusalem, refugees, settlements; and, to support progress toward a comprehensive Middle East settlement between Israel and Lebanon and Israel and Syria, to be achieved as soon as possible.

Continued comprehensive, effective progress on the reform agenda laid out by the Task Force in preparation for final status agreement.

Continued sustained and effective security performance, and sustained, effective security cooperation on the basis laid out in Phase I.

International efforts to facilitate reform and stabilize Palestinian institutions and the Palestinian economy, in preparation for final status agreement.

Parties reach final and comprehensive permanent status agreement that ends the Israel-Palestinian conflict in 2005, through a settlement negotiated between the parties based on UNSCR 242, 338, and 1397, that ends the occupation that began in 1967, and includes an agreed, just, fair, and realistic solution to the refugee issue, and a negotiated resolution of the status of Jerusalem that takes into account the political and religious concerns of both sides, and protects the religious interests of Jews, Christians, and Muslims worldwide, and fulfills the vision of two states, Israel and sovereign, independent, democratic and viable Palestine, living side-by-side in peace and security.

Arab state acceptance of full normal relations with Israel and security

Joint Understanding Read by President Bush at Annapolis Conference
Memorial Hall and include the names of Bush, Abbas and Olmert
United States Naval Academy
Annapolis, Maryland

PRESIDENT BUSH: *The representatives of the government of the state of Israel and the Palestinian Liberation Organization, represented respective by Prime Minister Ehud Olmert, and President Mahmoud Abbas in his capacity as Chairman of the PLO Executive Committee and President of the Palestinian Authority, have convened in Annapolis, Maryland, under the auspices of President George W. Bush of the United States of America, and with the support of the participants of this international conference, having concluded the following joint understanding.*

We express our determination to bring an end to bloodshed, suffering and decades of conflict between our peoples; to usher in a new era of peace, based on freedom, security, justice, dignity, respect and mutual recognition; to propagate a culture of peace and nonviolence; to confront terrorism and incitement, whether committed by Palestinians or Israelis. In furtherance of the goal of two states, Israel and Palestine, living side by side in peace and security, we agree to immediately launch good-faith bilateral negotiations in order to conclude a peace treaty, resolving all outstanding issues, including all core issues without exception, as specified in previous agreements.

We agree to engage in vigorous, ongoing and continuous negotiations, and shall make every effort to conclude an agreement before the end of 2008. For this purpose, a steering committee, led jointly by the head of the delegation of each party, will meet continuously, as agreed. The steering committee will develop a joint work plan and establish and oversee the work of negotiations teams to address all issues, to be headed by one lead representative from each party. The first session of the steering committee will be held on 12 December 2007.

President Abbas and Prime Minister Olmert will continue to meet on a bi-weekly basis to follow up the negotiations in order to offer all necessary assistance for their advancement.

The parties also commit to immediately implement their respective obligations under the performance-based road map to a permanent two-state solution to the Israel-Palestinian conflict, issued by the Quartet on 30 April 2003 -- this is called the road map -- and agree to form an American, Palestinian and Israeli mechanism, led by the United States, to follow up on the implementation of the road map.

The parties further commit to continue the implementation of the ongoing obligations of the road map until they reach a peace treaty. The United States will monitor and judge the fulfillment of the commitment of both sides of the road map. Unless otherwise agreed by the parties, implementation of the future peace treaty will be subject to the implementation of the road map, as judged by the United States.
November 27, 2007

APPENDIX V

RESOURCES FOR FURTHER INFORMATION AND
INVOLVEMENT

Al Haq
www.alhaq.org

Alternative Information Center
www.alternativenews.org

Americans for Middle East Understanding (AMEU)
www.ameu.org

Applied Research Institute
www.arij.org

BADIL
www.badil.org

Bethlehem Bible College/The Shepherd Society
www.bethlehembiblecollege.edu

B'tselem
www.btselem.org

Christian Peacemaker Teams
www.prairienet.org/cpt

Churches for Middle East Peace
www.cmep.org

Council for Palestinian Restitution and Repatriation
www.rightofreturn.org/frames.html

The Electronic Intifada
www.electronicintifada.net

Evangelicals for Middle East Understanding (EMEU)
www.emeu.org

Foundation for Middle East Peace
www.fmep.org
The Gaza Community Mental Health Programme (GCMHP)
www.gcmhp.net

Gush Shalom
www.gush-shalom.org

Ha'aretz newspaper
www.haaretz.com

Health, Development, Information and Policy Institute (HDIP)
www.hdip.org

Holy Land Trust
www.holylandtrust.org

372
Resources for
Further
Information
and
Involvement

Institute for Palestine Studies
www.ipsjps.org

INTERPAL
www.interpal.org

Israel/Palestine Center for Research and Information
www.ipcri.org

The Israeli Committee Against House Demolitions (ICAHD)
www.icahd.org

The Jerusalem Fund for Education/The Palestine Center
www.palestinecenter.org

Jewish Unity for a Just Peace
www.junity.org

Jewish Voice for Peace
www.jewishvoiceforpeace.org

Jews United Against Zionism
www.netureikarta.org
LAW
www.lawsociety.org

Middle East International
www.meionline.com

Middle East Policy Council
www.mepc.org

Musalaha
www.musalaha.org

Not in My Name
www.nimn.org

The Palestine Children's Relief Fund
www.wolfnet.com/~pcrf

Palestine Chronicle
www.palestinechronicle.com

Palestinian Human Rights Monitoring Group
www.lebnet.com/phrmg

Palestine Monitor
www.palestinemonitor.org

Palestine Red Crescent Society
www.palestinercs.org

Palestinian Academic Society for the Studies of International Affairs
www.passia.org

Palestinian Center for Human Rights (PCHR)
www.pchrgaza.org

Palestinian Hydrology Group (PHG)
www.phg.org
The Palestinian Initiative for the Promotion of Global Dialogue & Democracy
www.miftah.org

The Palestinian Environmental Non-Governmental Organizations Network (PENGON)
www.pengon.org

PalMap
www.palmap.org

Peace Now
www.peacenow.org.il

Stop the Wall Campaign
www.stopthewall.org

Union of Health Work Committees
www.gaza-health.org

The United Nations Office for the Coordination of Humanitarian Affairs (UNOCHA)
www.reliefweb.int/hic-opt/

The United Nations Relief and Works Agency for Palestine Refugees (UNRWA)
www.unrwa.org

BIBLIOGRAPHY

Abdul Hadi, Mahdi, 'Awakening Sleeping Horses And What Lies Ahead', Palestinian Academic Society for the Study of International Affairs, (PASSIA), October 2000

A Survey of Palestine, Jerusalem: British Government Printer, 1945–1946

Ball, George W. and Douglas B., *The Passionate Attachment*, New York: W.W. Norton, 1992

Born, Ethel, *A Tangled Web: A Search for Answers to the Question of Palestine*, Women's Division, General Board of Global Ministries, The United Methodist Church, 1989

Burge, Gary M., *Whose Land? Whose Promise? What Christians are not being told about Israel and the Palestinians*, Cleveland: The Pilgrim Press, 2003

Carter, Jimmy, *Palestine: Peace Not Apartheid*, Simon & Schuster, 2006

Cassidy, Sheila, 'Assault and Massacre', *Remembering Deir Yassin: The Future of Israel and Palestine* ed. Daniel McGowan and Marc H. Ellis, New York: Olive Branch Press, 1998

Chapman, Colin, *Whose Promised Land? The Continuing Crisis Over Israel and the Palestinians*, A Lion Publishing plc, Oxford, England, 2002

Chomsky, Noam, *Fateful Triangle: The United States, Israel, and the Palestinians*, Cambridge: South End Press, 1999

Cockburn, Andrew and Leslie, *Dangerous Liaison: The Inside Story of the U.S.-Israeli Covert Relationship*, Harper Collins, 1992

Farsoun, Samih and Zacharia, Christina, *Palestine and the Palestinians*, Harper Collins, 1997

Flapan, Simha, *The Birth of Israel: Myths and Realities*, Pantheon Books, 1988

Friedman, Thomas, *From Beirut to Jerusalem*, London: Harpers Collins, 1993

Gee, John R., *Unequal Conflict: The Palestinians and Israel*, New York: Olive Branch Press, 1998

Halper, Jeff, *Obstacles to Peace*, Jerusalem: PalMap of GSE, 2004

Khalidi, Rashid, *Palestinian Identity: The Construction of Modern National Consciousness*, New York: Columbia University Press, 1997

Khalidi, Walid, *Before their Diaspora: A Photographic History of the Palestinians 1876–1948*, DC: Institute for Palestine Studies, 1991

Lane-Poole, Stanley, *Saladin and the Fall of the Kingdom of Jerusalem*, Beirut: Khayats, 1964

Lapidoth, Ruth and Hirsh, Moshe, *The Arab-Israeli Conflict and its Resolution: Selected Documents*, Dordrecht: Martinus Nijhoff Publishers, 1992

Mansfield, Peter, *The Arabs*, London: Penguin, 1992

Morris, Benny, *1948 and After, Israel and the Palestinians*, Oxford: Clarendon Press, 1994
Reinhart, Tanya, *Israel/Palestine: How to end the war of 1948*, New York: Seven Stories Press, 2002

Sachar, Howard, *A History of Israel: From the Rise of Zionism to Our Time*, New York: Knopf, 1985

Said, Edward, *The Question of Palestine*. New York: Times Books, 1979

Said, Edward, 'Zionism from the Standpoint of Its Victims', *The Edward Said Reader*, New York: Vintage Books, 2000

Segev, Tom, *One Palestine, Complete: Jews and Arabs Under the British Mandate*, Owl Books, 2001

Sizer, Stephen, *Christian Zionism: A Roadmap to Armageddon?*, InterVarsity Press, 2005

Vester, Bertha Spafford, *Our Jerusalem, An American Family in the Holy City 1881–1949*, Ariel Publishing House, Jerusalem, 1988

END NOTES

PART ONE

[1] Kuttab, George, My Family & Palestine – My Beloved Homeland, Philadelphia, 2003; pp 7–8

[2]

أَلَمْ يَجِدْكَ يَتِيماً فَآوَى – وَوَجَدَكَ ضَالاًّ فَهَدَى –

وَوَجَدَكَ عَآئِلاً فَأَغْنَى – فَأَمَّا الْيَتِيمَ فَلاَ تَقْهَرْ – وَأَمَّا السَّآئِلَ فَلاَ تَنْهَرْ – وَأَمَّا بِنِعْمَةِ رَبِّكَ فَحَدِّثْ

And He found you poor and made you rich. Therefore, treat not the orphan with oppression.
And repulse not the one who asks. And proclaim the grace of your Lord."
The Holy Quran - Surat Ad-Duha (Chapter 93:8)

[3] Spafford-Vester, Bertha, Our Jerusalem; An American Family in the Holy City, Jerusalem: Ariel Publishing House, 1988, pp 51–52

[4] On Friday, April 9, 1948 the Jewish terrorist groups Irgun and Lehi attacked the Palestinian village of Deir Yassin on Jerusalem's western outskirts, killing an estimated 100 villagers, mostly women, children and the elderly.

[5] Andrew, Janssen, Light Force: The Only Hope for the Middle East, Hodder & Stoughton, London, 2004. pp 102-105.

CHAPTER ONE

[6] Lane-Poole, S., Saladin and the Fall of the Kingdom of Jerusalem, Beirut: Khayats, 1964, p. 234

[7] Mansfield, P., The Arabs, London: Penguin, 1992, p. 39

[8] Sacher, H., A History of Israel: From the Rise of Zionism to Our Time, New York: Knopf, 1985, p. 41

[9] Ibid., pp. 36-41

[10] Ibid., p. 42

[11] Ibid., p. 44

[12] Ibid., p. 42

[13] Lapidoth, R and Hirsh, M., The Arab-Israeli Conflict and its Resolution: Selected Documents, Dordrecht: Martinus Nijhoff Publishers, 1992, p. 1

[14] Khalidi, R., Palestinian Identity, New York: Columbia, 1997, p. 19

[15] Segev, T., One Palestine Complete: Jews and Arabs under the British Mandate, London: Owl Books, p.

[16] Said, E., 'Zionism from the Standpoint of Its Victims', The Edward Said Reader, New York: Vintage Books, 2000, p.128

[17] Smith, C. D., Palestine and the Arab-Israeli Conflict, New York: St. Martin's Press, 1988, p. 36

[18] Ibid., p. 55

[19] Sizer, S., Christian Zionism, Leicester, 2004. pg 64

[20] Ibid., p. 65

[21] The Question of Palestine, New York: United Nations, 1979, pp. 4-5

[22] Khalidi, W., Before their Diaspora: A Photographic History of the P alestinians 1976-1948, Washington DC, Institute of Palestinian Studies, 1991, p.189

[23] A Survey of Palestine, Jerusalem: British Government Printer, 1945–1946.

[24] The Question of Palestine, pp. 14-15

[25] Smith, Palestine and the Arab-Israeli Conflict, p. 100

[26] Ibid, p.114

[27] Ibid, p.120

[28] United States Holocaust Museum, http://www.ushmm.org/wlc/article. php?lang=en&ModuleId=10005417

[29] Ball, G. W. and. Ball, D. B., The Passionate Attachment, New York: W.W. Norton, 1992, p. 85

[30] A Survey of Palestine, 1945-1946.

[31] Chapman, C, Whose Promised Land? Glasgow: Lion Publishing, 2002, p.25.

CHAPTER TWO

[32] The Question of Palestine, p. 20.

[33] Cassidy, S., 'Assault and Massacre', Remembering Deir Yassin: The Future of Israel and Palestine eds. McGowan, D. and Ellis, M. H., New York: Olive Branch Press, 1998.

[34] Farsoun, S. and Zacharia, C., Palestine and the Palestinians, Harper-Collins, 1997, p. 116

[35] Flapan, S., The Birth of Israel: Myths and Realities, Pantheon Books,

1988, p.232

36 Arakie, M., The Broken Sword of Justice: America, Israel and the Palestine tragedy, Quartet Books, London, 1973, p 82

37 Morris, B., 1948 and After, Israel and the Palestinians, Oxford: Clarendon Press, pp.1-48

38 Gee, J. R., Unequal Conflict, New York: Olive Branch Press, 1998, p.57

39 Sizer, Christian Zionism, p. 86

40 Halper, J., Obstacles to Peace, Jerusalem: PalMap of GSE, 2004, p.62

41 Cockburn, A. and L., Dangerous Liaisons: The Inside Story of the Covert U.S.-Israeli Relationship, Oxford: Lion Publishing, pp. 153-154

42 Moshe Dayan, Ha'olam, Hazeh, 8 July 1968

43 Cockburn, Dangerous Liaisons, pp. 174-175

44 Smith, Palestine and the Arab-Israeli Conflict, pp. 242, 268

45 Friedman, T., From Beirut to Jerusalem, London: Harpers Collins, 1993, pp. 156-166

CHAPTER THREE

46 Smith, Palestine and the Arab-Israeli Conflict, p. 248

47 B'tselem, http://www.btselem.org

48 Halper, Obstacles to Peace, p.16

49 'Report on the water conditions in the Occupied Palestinian Territories', The Water Commission for the Study of Water Conditions in the Third Round of Talks of the Multilateral Negotiations on the Water Issue, 1993, http://www.arij.org/pub/corissues/

50 Halper, Obstacles to Peace, p.19

51 Reinhart, T., Israel/Palestine: How to end the war of 1948, New York: Seven Stories Press, 2002, pp.223-4

52 Halper, Obstacles to Peace, p.13

53 Ibid, p.13

54 Ibid, p.37

55 B'tselem, http://www.btselem.org/English/Publications/Summaries/200205_Land_Grab.asp

56 B'tselem, http://www.btselem.org/English/Publications/ummaries/200408_Forbidden_Roads.asp

57 Halper, Obstacles to Peace, p.19

[58] B'tselem, www.btselem.org

[59] B'tselem, www.btselem.org

[60] Halper, Obstacles to Peace, p.31

[61] Kifner, J., New York Times, December 16 1987.

[62] Black, C. L. Jr., 'Let Us Rethink Our 'Special Relationship' With Israel', JCOME, 1989, pp. 21-22, http://www.middleeast.org/black

[63] Gee, Unequal Conflict, p.114

[64] Burge, G. M., Whose Land? Whose Promise? Ohio: The Pilgrim Press, 2003, p.47

[65] B'tselem, http://www.btselem.org/English/Deportation/Statistics.asp

[66] Kifner, J., New York Times, January 23 1988.

CHAPTER FOUR

[67] 1993 Declaration of Principles, Article V.3, http://www.fmep.org/documents/Oslo_Accords.html

[68] 'Recapitulating the Redeployments: The Israel-PLO 'Interim Agreements", Geoffrey Aronson, http://www.palestinecenter.org/cpap/pubs/20000427ib.html

[69] Halper, Obstacles to Peace, pp. 1, 13-14

[70] Ibid. p.30

[71] Ibid. p.30

[72] Abdul Hadi, M., 'Awakening Sleeping Horses and What Lies Ahead…', Palestinian Academic Society for the Study of International Affairs, (PASSIA), October 2000, http://www.passia.org/publications/infor mation_papers/awakening.html

[73] 'Camp David – The Reality of the Myth', The Council for Arab-British Understanding, http://www.caabu.org/press/factsheets/camp-david.html

[74] Abdul Hadi, 'Awakening Sleeping Horses', October 2000.

CHAPTER FIVE

[75] Zanger, M., 'Spinning a War', http://www.tompaine.com/Archive/

scontent/4444.html

[76] "Erased In A Moment: Suicide Bombing Attacks Against Israeli Civilians', Human Rights Watch, October 2002, http://www.hrw. org/reports/2002/isrl-pa/ISRAELPA1002-03.htm

[77] CNN Late Edition, October 15 2000, http://cnnstudentnews.cnn. com/TRANSCRIPTS/0010/15/le.00.html

[78] Abdul Hadi, 'Awakening Sleeping Horses', October 2000

[79] Foundation for Middle East Peace (FMEP) Special Report, Vol. 11, No. 5 http://www.fmep.org/reports/vol11/no5/index.html

[80] 'At a glance: Occupied Palestinian Territory', United Nations Children's Fund (UNICEF), http://www.unicef.org/infobycountry/ opt.html

[81] Israel Defense Forces statistics, http://www1.idf.il/SIP_STORAGE/ DOVER/files/7/21827.doc

[82] 'At a glance: Occupied Palestinian Territory', United Nations Children's Fund (UNICEF), http://www.unicef.org/infobycountry/ opt.html

CHAPTER SIX

[83] B'tselem, http://www.btselem.org/english/freedom_of_movement/ curfew.asp

[84] PASSIA Diary 2003, p.317.

[85] Ibid, p.318.

[86] Ibid, p.318.

[87] Indymedia Newswire, http://newswire.indymedia.org/en/news wire/2004/05/803265.shtml

Authors note: In the immediate aftermath of Operation Defensive Shield, many Palestinians were overwhelmed by the scale of destruc tion visited upon their cities, and such quotations reflect their expe rience rather than being, at every point, statements of known fact. An Amnesty International report concluded that over 130 Palestinians had been killed in Nablus and Jenin during the Operation, and that the Israeli occupation forces were guilty of a number of war crimes. (http://web.amnesty.org/library/Index/engMDE151432002?OpenDo cument&of=COUNTRIES\ISRAEL/OCCUPIED +TERRITORIES)

[88] Kafala, T., 'Rebuilding the Palestinian Authority', May 10 2002, http://news.bbc.co.uk/1/hi/world/middle_east/1979358.stm

[89] Halper, Obstacles to Peace, p.16.

[90] CIA World Factbook, http://www.cia.gov/cia/publications/factbook/print/we.html

[91] Halper, Obstacles to Peace, p.18.

[92] 'West Bank and Gaza Update', World Bank Group, April–June 2003, http://lnweb18.worldbank.org/mna/mena.nsf/Attachments/Update+May+2003+English/$File/may+lay-en-Blue03.pdf

[93] PASSIA Diary 2003, p322.

[94] Halper, Obstacles to Peace, p.18.

[95] Ibid, p.15

[96] Complete essays are on http://www.najah.edu/english/reports/report11.htm

[97] The Health, Development, Information and Policy Institute (HDIP), http://www.hdip.org/fact%20sheets/fact%20sheetpage.htm

[98] 'Palestinian Children: Beyond the Statistics', The Palestinian Initiative for the Promotion of Global Dialogue and Democracy (MIFTAH), http://www.miftah.org/Display.cfm?DocId=3929&CategoryId=11

[99] PASSIA Diary 2003, p. 323

[100] The Palestine Monitor, Intifada Statistics, http://www.palestinemonitor.org/factsheet/Palestinian_intifada_fact_sheet.htm

[101] The Gaza Community Mental Health Program (GCMHP), http://www.gcmhp.net/File_files/ReportApril142k4.html

[102] Halper, Obstacles to Peace, p.19

[103] 'Conclusions and Recommendations of the Committee against Torture: Israel. 23/11/2001. CAT/C/XXVII/Concl.5', Office of the High Commissioner for Human Rights, http://www.unhchr.ch/tbs/doc.nsf/(Symbol)/60df85db0169438ac1256b110052aac5?Opendocument

[104] HDIP, http://www.hdip.org/new_web/factsheet_intifada.htm

[105] 'Rafah Humanitarian Needs Assessment', The United Nations Relief and Works Agency for Palestinian Refugees (UNRWA), p.18, http://

www.un.org/unrwa/news/unrwa_ocha_report.pdf

[106] The Palestine Monitor, Intifada Statistics, http://www.palestinemoni
tor.org/factsheet/Palestinian_intifada_fact_sheet.htm

[107] 'Palestine Facts and Info', PASSIA, http://www.passia.org/index_
pfacts.htm

[108] Palestinian Prisoners Society, 'Palestinian Prisoners inside Israeli Occu
pation's Jails', http://www.ppsmo.org/e-website/Press04/E-009-
04.htm

[109] www.stopthewall.com

CHAPTER EIGHT

[110] Arakie, M., The Broken Sword of Justice: America, Israel and the Pales
tine tragedy, London: Quartet Books, 1973. pp 14-15

[111] Strategy Page, http://www.strategypage.com/dls/articles/2004617.asp

[112] Curtiss, R., 'U.S. Aid to Israel: The Subject No One Men
tions', The Link, October 1997, http://www.ameu.org/page.
asp?iid=97&aid=134&pg=13

[113] Black, 'Let us Rethink Our Special Relationship' p.15

[114] Mark, C., 'Israel: U.S. Foreign Assistance', Congressional Research Re
port, 2002, http://www.adc.org/IB85066.pdf

[115] Abourezk, J., 'The hidden cost of free congressional trips to Israel',
Christian Science Monitor, 26 January 2007, http://www.csmonitor.
com

[116] Ball and Ball, The Passionate Attachment, pp.306-307.

[117] Ibid, p.309.

CHAPTER NINE

[118] Black, 'Let us Rethink Our Special Relationship' p. 17

[119] Keinon, H., 'Sharon rejects EU bid to start Mitchell plan now', The
Jerusalem Post, November 19 2001, http://home.planetinternet.be/
~sintlod6/spotlight/fed_reg/michel/michel_midden_oosten_
15112001/israel/jerusalem_post_19112001_1.htm

[120] 'U.S. Church Leaders, Citing Risks, Fault President Bush for Con

cessions to PM Sharon', April 15 2004, http://www.bethlehemmedia.
net/press16.htm

[121] 'Sharon Declares Road Map Dead; Bush to Reassure Jordan', UN
Wire, April 28 2004, http://www.unwire.org/UN
Wire/20040428/449_23258.asp
[122] 'Moderates launch Middle East plan', 1 December 2003, http://news.
bbc.co.uk/1/hi/world/middle_east/3252530.stm
[123] Shavit, A., "The Big Freeze," Haaretz, October 8, 2004

CHAPTER TEN

[124] The '700 club' CBN, 2002, 2005
[125] Campolo, T., 20 Hot Potatoes that Christians are Afraid to Touch, W.
Publishing Group, 1988, p 231
[126] Sizer; Christian Zionism, pg 251.
[127] Is Reagan Planning for Nuclear Armageddon? www.rumormillnews.
com/ARMAGEDDON%20THEOLOGY.htm
[128] "Beliefs, observances and values among Israeli Jews, 2000" – conducted
by the Guttman Center of the Israeli Democracy Institute.
http://www.avi-chai.org/Static/Binaries/Publications/EnglishGutt
man_0.pdf

CHAPTER ELEVEN

[129] Born, E., A Tangled Web: A Search for Answers to the Question of Pal
estine (Women's Division, General Board of Global Ministries, The
United Methodist Church, 1989), p. 76
[130] David Ben-Gurion (June 1919), as quoted in Time magazine (24 July
2006)
[131] The Peel Commission Report, 1937

[132] UN Information System on the Question of Palestine (UNISPAL): http://unispal.un.org/unispal.nsf/0/e210ca73e38d9e1d052565fa00705 c61?OpenDocument

[133] Carter, J., Palestine: Peace Not Apartheid, Simon and Schuster, p.211

[134] Israel Baytenu ("Israel is our home") is a party in the Israeli Knesset that promotes the forced transfer of Palestinian citizens of Israel to a Palestinian state.

[135] Rubin, B., 'The Arab-Israeli Conflict Is Over,' Middle East Quarterly, September 1996.

[136] Exchange of Letters between Rabin and Arafat, Sept. 9, 1993: http://www.mideastweb.org/osloletters.htm

[137] Israeli-Palestinian Public Opinion Polls, http://truman.huji.ac.il/polls.asp

[138] Source: World Bank.

[139] Born, E., A Tangled Web, p. 76

CHAPTER TWELVE

[140] Halper, Obstacles to Peace, p. 80

[141] Ibid. pp. 8-9

[142] Herman, E. S., Israel's Approved Ethnic Cleansing, Part II: Fog Watch, 2006

INDEX

389